Houses on Country Roads

ALSO BY IAN THOMPSON

Four Corners Country (with photographs by Dick Arentz)

The Durango & Silverton Narrow-Gauge Railroad

The Towers of Hovenweep

The Escalante Community

A Historical Guide to the San Juan Skyway

Treasures of the Past: The Ancient Villages of Mesa Verde
(Video Cassette)

Ian Thompson's
Houses on Country Roads
*Essays on the Places, Seasons, and Peoples of
the Four Corners Country*

Foreword by
Russell Martin

THE HERALD PRESS
Durango   Colorado

© 1995 by *The Durango Herald*

All rights reserved, including the right to reproduce this book or portions thereof in any form, store in a retrieval system, or transmit in any form or by any means, electronical, mechanical, photocopy, recording, or otherwise, without permission in writing from the publisher, except by a reviewer who may quote brief passages in a review.

ISBN 1-887805-00-1 15.95

Library of Congress Catalog Card Number: 95-80217

BOOK DESIGN AND TYPOGRAPHY
Roy Paul

COVER PHOTOGRAPH
Bill Proud

Originally published as the "Four Corners Almanac" in *The Durango Herald*, 1985–1995.

FIRST EDITION

To my sons

Geoffrey and Jonathan

Foreword

"THE SEASONS PASS WITH PREDICTABLE RHYTHM," Ian Thompson writes.

"There are seasons of drought and seasons of flood. There are seasons of flowers and seasons of snow. There is always the changing light." For half a century he has observed these subtle rhythms, the slow dance of one season into another that is at once prosaic and profound, and Ian Thompson is as deft at chronicling the cyclical sweep of time on a particular piece of earth as anyone I know.

A fifth-generation Coloradan, the singular landscape to which he is linked with both body and soul is the Four Corners Country—a phrase that seems to belong to him by now, one that roughly describes the San Juan River Basin where the states of Colorado, New Mexico, Arizona, and Utah converge at a single point. At the wide and unwieldy center of this remarkable western place is the valley called Montezuma, a broad and up-tilted and canyon-ringed dish that was the heart of the flourishing Pueblo culture from about A.D. 1 to 1300, a valley where a few of us still live today.

In 1985 the man most of us know as "Sandy" briefly came home to this valley where he had grown up to try to get his midlife bearings back. He had been only a stone's throw away by western standards, yet the day-to-day distinctions between life in the small Colorado city of Durango and the land away to the west that my great-grandfather had simply referred to as "space" were, well, substantial. As a kind of therapy, perhaps, and as a means of sending missives of reassurance back to the many people in Durango who cared enormously about him—and who worried about him a bit—he began to write a column for the Sunday edition of *The*

Durango Herald, a weekly stock-taking of the weather, the slow ebb of seasons, and the ways in which people lived on this alternately difficult and welcoming land, the ways in which they had lived here a thousand years before. It was a kind of clear-eyed and careful almanac that Sandy began to keep, and a decade later he still finds himself in the Montezuma Valley and continues to fill his "Four Corners Almanac" with a relentless—and now much-anticipated—precision.

No stranger to the tedium and the occasional transcendent surprise of the writing trade, Sandy has been associated with the *Herald*, either as a columnist or an editor, since 1970. He edited *The Silverton Standard* as well back in earlier days and did research and writing for the Western Interstate Commission for Higher Education, and his 1986 book, *Four Corners Country*—accompanied by Dick Arentz's exquisite black-and-white photographs—has become a regional classic. Along the way, he also found time to serve as a Durango city council member, mayor, and as a board member of the Colorado Endowment for the Humanities. Once anchored again in Montezuma County, he served for six years as executive director of Crow Canyon Archaeological Center, years during which the center ascended to its prominence in that field as well as to ongoing national renown. Two books and a video interpreting the prehistoric Pueblo culture followed in the 1990s, and he is currently at work on a long-term project that seeks to introduce contemporary Indian perspectives into the science of archaeology as it is currently practiced throughout the Four Corners region.

But foremost among his many endeavors, Ian Thompson is someone who turns careful and honest observation into reflective, even meditative, reportage. A reserved and always unimposing fellow whose resolve is nonetheless often palpable, it isn't surprising that Sandy's writing is similarly spare and elegantly simple. Like the land and people he observes, he sees little use for pretense, for finding "deep" meanings in things, when an evening's amber light on slickrock or a raven's flight seem to possess meaning enough in themselves.

Read as a continuum, the essays in this collection become as rhythmic as the seasons themselves, as subtly vibrant and variable as the terrain that is his home. He jokes that not much that's heart-stopping happened during the decade he describes here—and it's true that we probably won't see a movie version of this book—yet you will find the fascination of a scientist herein, the descriptive powers of a poet, the anglings toward truth of a man both inherently alert yet necessarily wary. These meditations on place—the region Ian Thompson knows so intimately yet discovers each week anew—are a pleasure, an artwork, a gift, an almanac of the heart.

Russell Martin

Introduction

ONLY WEEKS BEFORE I WROTE the first of these columns in January 1985, I moved from a busy neighborhood in the center of Durango, Colorado, into an isolated farmhouse on a lonely country road fifty miles to the west. It was not far from where I lived for a time when I was a high school student in Dolores. This time I returned there alone, far from my teenaged sons and my Durango friends. That move was a step in a difficult transition in my life. My marriage was ending. I had just served four years as a city councilman and a term as mayor during a turbulent era in Durango politics. I was still deeply involved in a variety of community activities. I expected to return to Durango in a few weeks. That was not to be. The first essay included in this collection, an essay published on February 24, 1985, is a reference to that transition. I mention it here because it provides a context for the decade that followed, an explanation of how I came to be where I am. My move from Durango was the first step in an unplanned, uncharted odyssey that continues today.

I have written more than five hundred of these essays since January, 1985. Only 161 of them are included in this collection. In the process of selecting those included here, I re-read all of the essays. This review of a decade of my life makes me realize that the healing began long before I was aware that it had. Many of these essays are about solitude in nature. Solitude, surrounded by wildness and beauty, is a source of healing. Reviewing these essays reminded me, as well, that I was never alone for long. The names of old friends begin reappearing in these essays, and the names of new friends appear for the first time, to be repeated as the years progress. I am fortunate, indeed, to have such friends—and many more whose names are not in the essays included here.

Many of these essays are about the Pueblo people who lived here centuries ago and about their houses, which can still be found on the mesas and in the canyons of the Four Corners Country. Their voices can still be heard on the wind; their achievements can still be seen in clay and stone. Their living descendants have taught me a great deal in the last decade.

Once the essays included here were selected, I faced the question of whether to go back and update their content. Less than a year after I began writing these essays, I became executive director of the Crow Canyon Archaeological Center near Cortez. I was immediately plunged into issues surrounding archaeological research. Although I knew something at the time about the archaeology of the Four Corners Country, I knew absolutely nothing about how this kind of research was conducted. I've learned a lot about the subject since and, thus, was able to recognize errors in some of my earlier essays about the "Anasazi" who lived here centuries ago. I decided not to correct the errors, but to let them remain in place. I'm an observer of archaeological research, not an authority on the subject. This volume is intended more as meditation than as science. I have long since stopped using the term "Anasazi" to describe the Pueblo peoples that once occupied the San Juan River Basin. I now use the term "Puebloans" because that is preferred by the living peoples whose ancestors inhabited this place. But I left the term in the early essays where it originally appeared. Jennifer Usher did correct my grammar, punctuation, and spelling errors. I could not have done that myself.

These essays are a continuation of a long association with *The Durango Herald*. I began writing guest editorials in 1969, became associate editor in 1970, and returned to writing guest editorials in 1974. I wish to thank Morley Ballantine, executive editor; Richard Ballantine, publisher; and the late Arthur Ballantine for allowing me the freedom to write what I chose and as I wished. I hope to write many more of these essays in the "Four Corners Almanac" in the years to come.

I am grateful to Ed and Jo Berger who lent me a house on a country road, a place to begin again. Friends who have given of their time to help me compile this volume include Anne Putnam,

Roberta Leicester, Roy Paul, Shirley Dennison, Russell Martin, Ruth Slickman, Jim and Betty Biggins, and my late mother, Amy Thompson.

Ian Thompson
Cortez, Colorado—1995

February 24, 1985

COUNTRY ROADS HERE INVITE EVENING WALKS. East first, toward the La Plata Mountains glowing in the low sun, then north up the plateau toward vast, snowy fields and the rim of the Dolores Canyon. A small wood, gloomy in its own growing shadow, borders Dawson Creek where east meets north. I turn up the road, hurry past the darkening grove to the dazzling fields that lie ahead, and enter suddenly into the warm sunlight. The snow-covered fields sweep away from the road toward gentle ridges. Only winding ditches fringed by red willows break the flow of drifted snow. I turn west. Warm days and cold nights have glazed a mirror on the snow. A path of reflected light, lavender and gold upon that molten crust, leads from me to the setting sun. My end of that path walks with me with each step I take. I stop and look into that westward trail of brilliance.

I recall the following lines:

> As every blossom fades and all youth sinks
> into old age, so every life's design.
> Each flower of wisdom, every good, attains
> its prime and cannot last forever.
> At each life's call the heart must be prepared
> to take its leave and commence afresh,
> courageously and with no hint of grief
> submit itself to other, newer ties.
> A magic dwells in each beginning and
> protecting us it tells us how to live.

The words are those of Herman Hesse, from his *Magister Ludi*, and are the epigram in the book *A Magic Dwells: A Poetic and Psychological Study of the Navajo Emergence Myth* by Dr. Sheila Moon.

> At each life's call the heart must be prepared
> to take its leave and commence afresh,
> courageously and with no hint of grief.

That is a terrible demand of Hesse's . . . "with no hint of grief." Is it possible? I do not know.

I look down that shimmering path leading into the heart of the setting sun and am tempted to set my feet upon it, to follow that path to its destination. But, then, the sun is gone, the path of light is gone, and the drifted snow gives back only the chill blue of the sky above.

As I turn homeward Mesa Verde catches the last crimson light. An owl calls from the dark wood at the corner. A magic dwells in that pure sound, and I recall the conclusion of Sheila Moon's book:

> . . . we each have many aspects—the above, the below, the dark, the light, substance, spirit—which reflect the divine as well as the human. Unless we are concerned with them, the cyclic rhythm of our selfhood cannot be.
>
> We have sought to be more than human—that is our greatness—but we have insisted on our own definitions of how—that is our littleness.
>
> If we can learn, as the Navajo Emergence Myth shows, the simple and hard lesson of emergence, of going into the darker places to follow the restless longing upward, of letting no small thing stay forgotten and unhonored, then we shall be whole.

Above me the emerging stars move at the same pace as I—following, leading, or staying even, I do not know. Again, from down in the grove, the owl calls. A magic dwells there, "A magic dwells in each beginning . . ."

April 14, 1985

ON PASSOVER EVENING A FEW DAYS AGO my son and I went to the home of some nearby friends. Our route took us along country roads between greening pastures to their home in a juniper forest on a canyon rim. We had been invited to join them for Passover Seder.

We were greeted by our friends, their infant son, and our hostess's parents from Denver. Her father is a silver-haired man of imposing height and laughing eyes. Her mother is a vivacious, articulate woman, a journalist by training, whose informed views of the world can turn any conversation into an in-depth seminar on the evening news.

An air of relaxed togetherness marked the gathering. We watched through the great east windows of the house as the last sun faded on the snowy La Platas and the first lights flashed on in the Montezuma Valley. We gathered then at the Seder table. We men donned black yarmulkes and took our place at plates hidden beneath matzo covers.

Each of us was given the Haggadah, the book containing "what is said" at the Passover Seder. In the center of the table were the unlit Passover candles, glasses of salt water, an empty wine cup for the prophet Elijah, and the Passover plate containing spring greens, a roasted egg, a chicken neck, bitter herbs, and charoset—a paste of almonds, apples, and raisins seasoned with honey and sweet wine.

The mother explained to us that Passover Seder is an ancient Jewish tradition celebrating the beginning of the Exodus, led by Moses, from Egypt into freedom.

Seder is observed now, she explained, not only in the memory of the Exodus but with concern for all the multitudes of human beings who live under grinding oppression now. A sense of that, of the billions of suffering and oppressed human beings on this planet today, swept through that quiet room. There was a sense, too, that each of us in that room was on our private journey and that such traditions as the one we were observing renewed us on our way.

The mother lit the candles. The father began reading from the Haggadah. He then designated, to each of us in our turn, passages to read. The words, in modern English interspersed with brief passages of Hebrew, are profoundly poetic. Our hostess, trained in languages, read her Hebrew passages with such graceful power that even the baby at her elbow stopped his crying to listen. Some of the passages, such as the Ten Commandments, we read in unison.

We broke the third matzo, the greens were dipped in salt water and eaten, the roasted egg and chicken neck held up for all to see, the bitter herbs consumed, and the charoset passed around. Dishes of sliced egg in salt water were passed around.

Then the feast began: Gefilte fish, matzo balls in chicken broth, asparagus, roast chicken, and honey cake. The feast ended. The father said, "We have eaten our Passover meal as free men. Let us give thanks to the source of all life and freedom." In unison we did. Elijah's wine cup was filled and the door opened to allow him in.

Our hostess and I reflected on the fact that in the nineteenth century my great-grandfather, a Quaker, and her great-grandfather, a Jew, had ranches in the same all-but-forgotten place in Colorado, a place of rock and sage. We wondered if they had, a century or so ago, sat down to Passover Seder together. Given who those men were, they probably had. Time does come back around to itself.

May 12, 1985

THIS VAST EARTH CIRCLE IN WHICH I LIVE has been transformed since I arrived here a brief five months ago. Then the snow lay two feet deep on the fields sweeping toward every horizon. The sun moved dimly in the far southern sky. The clouds were the flat grey monochromes of winter.

The raggedness of the La Plata Mountains to the east was muffled by deep snows. The gentler Abajos and Ute Mountain stood white against the sky. The sheer bluffs of Mesa Verde, impervious to snow, lent the only color to the south.

On the morning of the winter solstice, my first week here, the sun rose over Mancos Hill to the south of the La Platas. This week it rises over Greyrock Peak to the north of those mountains. I've watched its northward progression—the summer-ward march of the dawn—with fascination. It has been easily marked along the rank of peaks and ridges marking the eastern edge of this world.

The northern march of the sunsets is more difficult to define from my home. The land from here swells upward in vast, smooth waves receding into the westward distances. This week from a friend's home atop the highest of those western ridges before the land gently tilts toward the San Juan River, we watched the sun set into the Bear's Ears on Elk Ridge in Utah. During my first week here we'd watched it sink into Monument Valley, far to the south of the Bear's Ears. In March it vanished behind the rounded peak of Navajo Mountain. By June it will set behind the ramparts of the

Abajos themselves.

The earth here has responded to the sun's return. The snow has retreated to the highest ranges. The fields are countless receding shades of green and red. Wild plum thickets along the fence lines—billowing masses of white plum blossoms—mimic the towering cumulus clouds boiling into the evening skies. Teeming pastures are now brushed by the commanding song of the meadowlark and the softer calls of nesting pheasants. Frogs sing from nearby bogs in the dusk. The icy sleep of winter has given way to the lifeburst of spring.

It would be too easy for me to use this earth circle in which I live as a mirror in which to chart the seasons of the world within myself. It would be too easy, as well, to project the world within myself onto this earth circle in an effort to understand the world without. To do so would mean I saw neither clearly.

Yet, since the within and the without are encompassed by a greater whole, there might be a few parallels. Perhaps the seasons of the psyche are longer and deeper than those of this earth circle. But there may be a source of warmth within, which, like the sun without, draws a blanket of frozen sleep over the psyche when in retreat but which, like the sun, returns to the center of the inner world and warms the soul toward summer and life once more.

Perhaps all that is needed is to find the boundaries of the soul in order to chart the retreat and return of that inner sun and to trust that it has returned, warmth and psyche bound together, as surely as are the sun and seasons across this earth circle.

I have begun to think it possible.

June 9, 1985

THE IRREPRESSIBLY CHEERFUL CALL OF THE KINGBIRD now awakens me at first light each morning. It is a sound which makes it impossible to view the dawn as anything but refreshing—a sound much better than the high tech insistence of my alarm clock. The bird is so predictable that there's no need to squint out the window into the pale darkness wondering if it's too early to get up. When the kingbird calls from the spruces outside that open window, it is the precise moment to arise and watch the light come in slow, soft waves across this place once more.

The kingbird's perky call always seems to end when I'm up. The end of his morning chatter signals the onset of a melodious rush of birdsong whose purpose must be to call the sun up from behind the ragged ridges in the east. Meadowlarks, mourning doves, blackbirds, robins, sparrows, magpies, western tanagers, and more join the dawn concerto. Crickets and frogs grow silent as the light grows brighter.

The song of one bird—a musical, medium-pitched staccato—keeps me slightly frustrated each evening. Heard occasionally during the day, the ventriloquil notes fill the dusky bowl of twilight, their location hard to pinpoint. By the time the haunting, friendly call seems to be floating earthward from just above, the sky is too dark to see any form but a fluttering, hovering small bird against the first stars. My son Geoffrey, who doesn't give up when confronted by the challenges of identification, has tentatively decided that the song is that of a small species of kingfisher. It looks like a small kingfisher. We don't know yet. I'm glad he keeps wondering.

Yet another bird had me wondering recently. As I came quietly upon a pond, the bird and I startled one another. The bird flew into the upper reaches of an oak and began scolding in high-pitched bursts. It was an iridescent black with a long tail that had a life of its own. There was an exotic air to the bird. I think it was a boat-tailed grackle—a bird more common to Tucson than to these fields and ponds.

The last of the lilacs are fading in the farmyards here now, their place taken by great mounds of yellow and copper roses and white spirea. Peonies are opening—late—on the lower slopes.

The strawberries are ripening in my garden faster than we can eat them, and my son Jonathan is experimenting with ways to dry them for backpacking food. Thus far he has succeeded so wildly that he eats the results of his experimentation without ever leaving the yard. He takes time out from his bike training to create a whimsical garden in the vast plot that slopes down from the lane here. Getting irrigation water to the garden through a complex maze of smaller ditches, through forests, across lawns, under lanes, and past the strawberries to the newly planted rows requires real concentration.

If he succeeds at his gardening, the plot by autumn will be a jungle of cantaloupes, watermelons, gourds, Indian corn, pumpkins, and other less challenging vegetables.

While he's applying himself so industriously, I remain content to arise, at first light to the cheerful call of the kingbird and to search the skies of dusk for the elusive bird whose song hails the end of day.

July 21, 1985

ONE NIGHT RECENTLY I AWAKENED to the welcome sound of rain pounding on the barn roof next door and dripping from the boughs of evergreens outside my window. Lightning crackled and thunder boomed in the blackness that lay over the fields. I couldn't resist the urge to get up and watch the storm sweep across this vast land. The fresh, cool respite was all too brief. The rain ended before it had done much more than settle the dust on these country roads.

It's been a dry summer. Earlier that night my son and I had watched from the front lawn as a wildfire moved along a ridge in the middle distance, perilously close to great fields of winter wheat, golden ripe and tinder dry, stretching away to the western horizon.

As we watched the smoke drift across the sky, my son commented on the powerlessness of farmers here against the whims of the elements that wield such influence over their lives. These ridges have been farmed, off and on, for the last fifteen hundred years. Evidence is emerging that man's efforts to harness the elements, to influence the whims of nature, are no more successful today than they were seven hundred years ago when the first farmers here were struggling in a futile, last-ditch attempt to maintain their foothold in an ancient homeland. Only the approaches differ.

Then, as they often have in recent months, my son's thoughts turned to the subject of power—and powerlessness—in general. Whenever I listen to my son, I try very hard to recall my own thoughts on the subject when I was his age, seventeen, and living then as now in this place. When he talks about power, he often qualifies, modifies, the term with the phrase "to make a difference." The power to make a difference. It is a phrase with a familiar ring, it is a phrase that voiced itself in my own head at the age of seventeen.

But there the similarity ends. When I first heard that phrase speaking itself to me, it was near the end of the "Silent Fifties." Eisenhower was president. Americans were the most fortunate people on earth—and we knew it. The future was a golden, ever-expanding horizon. To make a difference was my destiny. The why and how—or even if—of the matter, in contrast to my son's thoughts, never once entered my head.

It's an odd state of mind to even try to recall anymore. I'm sure I would never want to relive it. I look around at my once undaunted contemporaries and see many of them who have put the term "to make a difference" out of their heads entirely, who get downright defensive if they even hear the phrase. A few hours of earnest discussion a year and passing a petition now and again is plenty adequate to get them off the hook.

Come to think of it, my son and his contemporaries may be doing it the right way around. To the great frustration of their elders, they're asking the hard questions first. Maybe we should have done the same.

As I listen to my son wondering thoughtfully out loud in my presence, I have come to understand that he isn't asking these questions of me. Neither I, nor anyone else on the face of the earth, can give him the answers. He is, I see, his own man now, and it is my turn to learn from him. Thus far, I thought as the brief rain moved on in the darkness, I have learned that in some of the questions are some of the answers.

July 28, 1985

A VOICE CALLING MY NAME from high above startled me awake. I crawled from my rain-soaked sleeping bag and a few minutes later stood atop a sheer cliff of Wingate Sandstone facing east into the first ashen light of dawn. Weathered prayer feathers, left by a previous visitor to that haunting spot, fluttered damply from a nearby twig. Clouds blotted out all but the brightest stars. Thin mists wove their way among the pines and aspens on the ridges a thousand feet beneath us.

The sun, a fiery crimson orb, rose from the southern flanks of the Abajo Mountains. The mists sparkled a phosphorescent rose. The wet walls of Arch Canyon glistened like iridescent pearl. The sage below and the clearing sky above shone turquoise. A falcon's cry pierced the dawn. A storm-swept night had given way to a light-swept day.

We were atop the highest point of the Bear's Ears, a prominent landmark rising from the southern terminus of Elk Ridge in southeastern Utah. Most of the Four Corners Country can be seen from there, an immensely vast circle in which nature stages awesome dramas.

The evening before we faced westward into the setting sun. To the south was Black Mesa fronted by Monument Valley. We could see Monitor Mesa and Paiute Mesa rising above the glistening waters of Lake Powell. Above that loomed Navajo Mountain.

Below us were the white rims of Natural Bridges National Monument and, beyond them, Jacob's Chair silhouetted against the lavender Henry Mountains, which were in turn silhouetted against the bronze dusk. From behind the Henrys stretched the crests of the Kaiparowits and Aquarius Plateaus beyond the canyons of the Colorado. To the north, the walls of Dark Canyon, topped by the LaSals, faded into night.

Behind us, to the east in late dusk, a towering bank of bronzed cumulus built above the La Plata Mountains a hundred miles away. Lightning flashed within the clouds. Lightning danced in multiple strikes from boiling cloud to shimmering earth.

We watched the approach of the storm from the east, a solid wall of rain and lightning, as it blotted out the country and arrived at nearby Comb Ridge. Then, our vision splotched by the afterimages of lightning, we reluctantly admitted that we were camped atop the highest lightning rod for many miles around. In the pitch blackness we stumbled down a very steep slope a couple of hundred feet. I crammed my sleeping bag against the matted branches of a small bush I hoped would remain rooted through the night and, exhausted by a day of canyon country climbs, fell asleep sure that my discomfort was a small price to pay for safety from the lightning.

I awoke to pounding rain lit by crackling lightning. The poet T. S. Eliot said fear could be found in a handful of dry dust. I found fear in a faceful of stinging rain and the awful sight of lightning streaking across the void below me. My sleeping bag was a dam against the sheet of water pulsing down the slope from above. There was no place to hide, no place to run. I shouted through the din and to my great relief heard my friend's response.

The lightning stopped and I slept until called to view the dawn. As the rising sun turned the newly washed world to crimson, I mentioned an approaching change in my life and the sacrifice it will entail. My friend paraphrased Krishnamurti, saying that life is choice and the only power to make choices is within the self. Considerations of sacrifice have no part in it.

There, in that immense beauty in which self is so minute as to be nothing, I thought of the freedom of the human spirit. No matter where the human spirit resides, no matter the conditions surrounding it, it is free. We create our own illusion of self as victim, as captive. Often we struggle against restraints that don't exist.

September 15, 1985

THERE IS AN AUTUMNAL EDGE to the dawn wind now as it rushes across the wooded canyon rims where I live. The morning light complements the wind with an equinoctial cast of its own. More tangible proof than the wind and light that summer's end is near are the caps of first snow on the peaks in the east—Lone Cone, the Dolores Peaks, Mount Wilson, El Diente, Lizard Head, Greysill, and the La Platas. When first light glissades down that dusting of snow, the peaks loom somber and heavy as unpolished silver against the lemon sky.

Beans are being harvested from vast nearby fields on the rolling plateau to the north where wheat stubble and newly plowed earth, deep red, join to reflect the rising sun.

Slowly, haltingly I learn the new routines of life without electricity, heating, phone, and indoor plumbing. The hour-long round-trip to retrieve mail and phone messages is easier to put off with each passing day.

Life here is decidedly indoor/outdoor. Cooking must be done outside—either on a campfire or on a butane grill provided by Bill and Mickie Thurston of Durango. I use the campfire as much as possible so as to conserve the butane for rainy days. Laundry is done daily in a big pan of cold water and once weekly in hot water at the Laundromat at the end of a long and bumpy road into town. I've learned to shave and brush my teeth in cold water, too, and wonder why I've always thought of hot water as one of life's necessities.

Not having a phone quickly transforms itself from burden to blessing. At first I caught myself listening for the phone to ring or reluctant to wander out of earshot for fear that it might. When recognition of a phoneless state dawns, the feeling of freedom is welcome. I miss my evening chats with my sons in Durango, but they've been out here enough to know the difficulties of getting to a phone in the evening hours.

Writing longhand, by kerosene lamp, rather than at a brightly lit typewriter quickly moves from burden to blessing as well. When I accrue enough of the written word to make it worthwhile, I drive into the Crow Canyon Archaeological Center to type a second draft. There is a certain flowing satisfaction to composing in longhand. More than once I've lost track of time and written far longer than I would if seated at a typewriter or word processor. I've begun to wonder if there is not a connection between creating in longhand and "whole brain" vs. left or right brain activity. Fortunately, there's no one around to ask.

My solitude is occasionally broken by wanderers curious about the massive archaeological site where I live—a site obscured by an ancient stand of junipers and piñon pine—but they are self-sufficient visitors who like, themselves, to explore unaccompanied. If the dusk silence gets too heavy, it is a ten-minute westward walk to a solitary neighbor's house and an evening of philosophical discourse. He has a battery-powered radio—I do not—so he usually knows if the world is still out there or has been blown away catching me unawares.

I'm not a back-to-basics advocate, comfort is too pleasurable. But for the time being—until winter drives me into more developed shelter—I'm finding that the initial disruption of a move into primitive surroundings quickly progresses into an economical routine of wood gathering, wick trimming, water carrying, and silence that cleanses the mind as briskly as shaving in cold water cleanses and refreshes the face.

December 29, 1985

A CRIPPLED RED FOX, probably a trapping victim, makes a daily appearance in the pasture below my home.

The creature, its coat matching the red willow patch farther down the hill, comes at dawn just as the pasture is transformed by the golden fire of sunrise. Despite its mangled hind leg, the animal communicates no self-pity as it goes about its morning routine. The fox limps along the grassy fringe of a ditch sniffing out mice and other small beings seeking out their own breakfast there.

It is a small, slender animal, sleekly alert, but its diminutive size does not diminish its magnificent dignity. It holds out its bushy tail, nearly as large as its body, in a proud curve as it looks here and there in the morning light. The fox seems so unaware of its handicap that even a brief glimpse of it is an inspiring recollection the rest of the day. I leave for work just after the fox turns toward the rising sun and vanishes into the nearby forest.

On the day of winter solstice Bob and BJ Boucher and Stanton and Pat Englehart came here from Durango to observe the earliest sunset of the year. We walked then through the fox's territory to a rocky point overlooking the junction of two small canyons while the sun vanished behind Goodman Point to the west. In the east the snowy La Platas glowed crimson beneath a lavender sky. Twilight that evening lingered for an hour after the sun slipped from view.

On Christmas Eve my sons, here for the holidays, opted not to decorate the traditional indoor tree but to bestow that honor on a yucca on the front lawn. The decor is simple, gold and silver balls hung from the yucca's spikes. No lights. The mirrored spheres reflect the light of the stars and moon in a way that seems the perfect reflection of the spirit of the season. Frozen ponds nearby reflect that same light with the look of burnished pewter.

It may be just my imagination but it seems that the sky lightens a bit earlier each morning over the eastern end of Mesa Verde as viewed from my kitchen window. I look forward to the northward advance of the sun toward the La Platas as evidence that our solstice stroll did some good and the days are growing longer.

It's too soon, though, to want an end to winter. The fields here are saturated from November rains but a deep snowcover would ensure the completion of the seasonal cycle and make the thaws of April more welcome when they come. As it is, the feeling now is more of late March than of late December. The school children I pass on my way to work look as if they share an anticipation of more snow—otherwise their Christmas sleds will greet spring as sparkling new as the day they appeared beneath the tree.

When I arrive at work at Crow Canyon, a spot that seems more secluded than my house, a pair of golden eagles circles above the fields and forests. The eagles join the fox in the images that assure one that man has not been, and is not, alone in this vast circle of earth and sky.

January 12, 1986

EACH DAY IS LONGER NOW but it is the time of year when winter sunsets still linger long over a frozen land. The spectacle is irresistible. The eye is drawn first to the immediate, to the last sunshine on nearby fields, fences, and forest fringes. With the fading of that fire one's eyes follow the last light up the land toward the broken ridges of the Chuskas in New Mexico, the gentle summits of the Abajos in Utah, and the ragged peaks of the La Platas nearby. Each of those snowy landforms reflects the crimson alpenglow of the twilit sky.

Then comes the instant when the spectator is most cognizant of Earth's rapid spin eastward into its own shadow and night. The land fades and the first stars draw the eyes to the sky. In the valleys the lights of distant towns flicker on, determined to resist the deepening darkness. Finally the sky above, distantly chill, and the earth below, humanly defined, sparkle in two part harmony.

From my home I can see the long approach of planes toward a distant airport, their lights flashing insistently against the dark ramparts of Mesa Verde. Often the only sound I hear is that of the evening news, transmitted via satellite, of events around the globe. If I listen carefully, there is a response to those reports from beyond my front door: the muted yip of a coyote or the soft first call of an owl.

It is in that instant when time and light are perfectly balanced in space between day and night. It is the instant most conducive to allowing the mind to break free of the restraints of the immediate, to move beyond its own fixation with this one point in space and time.

We are rapidly approaching not only the end of the century but the end of a millennium as measured by our own units against our own particular cultural reference point in time.

But here, as the lights flicker on against the darkening earth, it is not difficult to imagine another era when this space was occupied by a place and people for whom our own way of marking the passing circles of seasons would have had no meaning whatsoever. It was a time when the human mark against the dusk here would not have been fluorescent light but firelight. Those people did not think in units of centuries and millennia so, therefore, would not have worried about the quirks of human behavior traditionally accompanying those milestones in our own culture.

Metaphysical conjecture on their part might more likely have been triggered by the lingering passage of Halley's Comet, the briefer plunge of a meteorite, or the flare of a supernova from a distance for which they did not possess a measurement. In responding to those events, they and we would have shared common tendencies.

Until we know how those long ago people experienced the flow of time upon this mountain-ringed circle, we cannot know who they were. Until we know how we measure the value of this place against our own conception of time, we cannot know who we are.

March 16, 1986

Early the morning that Stanton Englehart's current show opened at Fort Lewis College, I awakened to what sounded like thunder in the outer darkness. It was gusts of wind. Wet snow pelted the south window at the head of my bed. Inside the house there was an eerie silence—no muted hum of motors. The power was off. The night before I'd retired to the sight of the stars. The predawn storm was yet another reminder of the power and the whimsy of the sky which dominates this rugged land.

The storm lessened and a few hours later, after a quick lunch with Englehart and his wife Pat, I sat on the floor of the Fort Lewis gallery staring at the paintings while Englehart and artist Jim Whitfield hung the last of the show. The power of the new work is so great that I forgot the earnest dialogue of the two artists. Englehart's work is at that point, at last, where what Stanton has to say about it is irrelevant. The beauty on those canvases speaks for itself. Over lunch Stanton had said that his work was so consuming that he had no ego left. He is right.

The paintings cannot be described. They must be seen. Or more accurately, they must be felt, slowly and openly. They cannot be judged. If they are judged, then the only standard against which that can be done is creation itself.

I have never totally trusted my response to Englehart's work. I have come back to live only a few miles from where he grew up. I wander the same patch of fractured plateau with the same awe as Stanton. I've known Englehart for years. But as he hung the show last week, his amazement at what he saw seemed as great as my own. I'll trust his judgment if not my own; I've never seen him pleased before.

That evening the storms once again moved across this place, pulsing in from the west in towering, rhythmic waves. I could not stay inside but wandered alone down the ridge to the south. Curtains of snow—glowing in the setting sun—moved eastward across Mesa Verde. Black cliffs of cloud loomed in the west. The Sleeping Ute vanished, reappeared, then vanished again behind dark fogs. In the east the La Platas were a mound of silver vapor.

It was not a sunset of crimson brilliance but of somber, deep ochres beneath which the snowy far fields flashed a blinding silver in the last sun. There was no sound of any living thing, only the wind . . . or was it the sound of light? No matter, it felt good, very good, to be there.

Englehart is so consumed with his work that he sometimes will produce one of his smaller paintings in a day. This sky changes each second.

Englehart does not try to copy the merging of this rock with this sky, wedded by light, but in his newfound freedom from trying anything he comes close.

Stanton Englehart, at fifty-five, has been teaching and painting at Fort Lewis College for a quarter of a century. It is not hard to imagine him painting for another quarter century. Given the distance he's come in twenty-five years, there is no predicting where he'll be in the year 2011.

May 18, 1986

AFTER A LIFE OF GOOD FORTUNE it finally happened: I got skunked. The details remain sketchy. A disturbance on the front porch just as I was leaving for work sent me scurrying for the front door. I stepped out and nearly onto a small spotted skunk doing a dance at my feet. A dog, for whom I provide a sort of halfway house, raced past me into the house. I stumbled backward and slammed the door in the skunk's face.

The dog became a whirling dervish jumping against me and covering me with a slight dampness. The dog then sped into my bedroom and did a series of slow somersaults on the bed. From there she headed for my favorite upholstered chair to execute a series of rubbing circles. I grabbed the dog and tossed her out. Thirty seconds had passed since the initial encounter.

My first response, of course, was to look at the clock. Twenty minutes until my first appointment. It takes me fifteen minutes to get to work.

I have never been offended by the fragrance of skunk—at least of the roadkill variety passed at 55 miles per hour. This was sickeningly different. I smelt—and felt—as if I'd been drenched in a gallon of rancid garlic juice. And here I was, I thought, merely a secondary victim via the dog.

I raced to change clothes. Tuesday morning. I do laundry on Tuesday night. No clean clothes. I pawed through the laundry heap, stripped, showered, put on the most presentable of the dirty laundry, and made it to the appointment on time. The appointment was most notable for its brevity. For once, all day long, I had my own space so to speak.

That night I discovered that the shirt I'd been wearing that morning was splattered with yellowish spots. The skunk had scored a direct hit. I dumped the clothes—all the week's dirty clothes—into the washer.

Now for some free advice:

—Don't assume that an irritated skunk emits a visible stream of fluid.

—Don't let the dog in the house.

—Don't assume, once hit, that you can tell whether you've gotten rid of the odor. That's what best friends are for. People you thought you could count on will simply keep their distance and mutter phrases like "lemon juice" or "tomato juice."

—Don't go back in the house to strip. Do it outside and bury the clothes.

—On stepping out of the shower don't fool yourself into being glad you use Dial. Your Dial now smells like rancid garlic lying in wait for your next shower.

—Don't put the polluted clothes and the innocent clothes into the same batch of laundry.

—Don't use Tuesday morning's towel again on Wednesday morning. You still don't know what smells like skunk and what doesn't.

—After putting on "clean" clothes, don't sink into your favorite chair. Bury the chair.

—Call the office and tell them you're experiencing a meltdown in the microwave and, given a few days, you're perfectly capable of controlling the situation without outside help—even if, like me, you aren't.

June 15, 1986

"Up on the roof" is the title of an ancient (sometime in the sixties) song by the Drifters. It's not my favorite Drifters song, but it does come to mind on these long June evenings. At sunset, that's frequently exactly where I and one or both of my sons can be found: up on the roof.

From the peak of the roof we can see the Abajos in the west, the La Platas in the east, Lone Cone to the north, and Mesa Verde in the south. They are the edges of a vast circle catching the last light washing against the sky, cloud, forest, and earth.

Historically June is the driest month of the year here. This June, however, is acting more like late July. Huge banks of thunderheads boil above the La Platas and spread westward spitting lightning and rain upon the windswept land. Often, in the last moments before sunset, the sun appears beneath the clouds in the west.

It was at just such an instant last week that Jonathan and I watched a perfect double rainbow arc over the shadow-blackened La Platas. A golden eagle shot up from a nearby juniper into the brilliance of the rainbow. The sky darkened quickly after that.

The rains have brought an emerald lushness to the hay fields awaiting first cutting and to the pastures. The tall grasses are rippled easily by evening breezes and hide the sight but not the sound of pheasants and foxes on the ridge below my house. The wind is seen, too, upon the brimful ponds on every farm along these country roads.

At dawn now, less than a week away from the longest day of the year, the sun rises over the Wilsons far to the north of the La Platas. Next Saturday the point of the sun's rising begins to inch southward once more until, in the darkest winter it will be rising over Mesa Verde to the south of the La Platas.

Given the peaks, ranges, and ridges that encircle this vast place, and the subsequent ease with which the sun's changes can be tracked, it is no wonder that the architecture of the prehistoric structures that dot this landscape show an apparent solar orientation wherever the terrain allows. The Anasazi people who built these structures inhabited this region for a thousand years. Matching architecture to seasons requires a sensitivity that evolves over time.

That evolution—the matching of human work to the land and the seasons—is a fascinating subject to me. From my roof, when the light is just right, I can look west into the dryland fields and see the mounded ruins dating to Anasazi times here. The Anasazi were a dryland farming people, too. The knowledge encoded within those ruin mounds may eventually provide us with guidelines to a less costly and more prosperous relationship with this land.

August 17, 1986

A FRIEND SAID RECENTLY she'd given up introspection for the rest of the summer. I couldn't forget what she'd said. From the dictionary I learned that introspection is "an examination of one's own mental and emotional state."

My friend went on to say that since giving up introspection she feels better. Despite the contradiction contained in that self-diagnostic statement, I took her word for it.

Then I began to wonder how she could possibly feel better. Not only is knowing ourselves considered a major virtue in our culture, but it's a big industry as well. Social workers, counselors, therapists, psychologists, psychiatrists, authors, talk show hosts, advice columnists, film makers, astrologers, gurus, and our friends are all there to help us know ourselves, i.e., to assist us with introspection. Under the circumstances, is it really possible to give up introspection for the rest of the summer?

As I read the dictionary definition, I had the definite visual image of introspection: someone standing outside himself looking inside himself. A single person became two—the observer and the observed. The scene had the flat, dim tranquility of a medieval painting.

I recalled then an economics class from my college days. The professor, a self-proclaimed Marxist, insisted that a great advance toward human liberation was achieved when individuals first saw themselves in the conditions within which they lived, worked, exploited, or were exploited. I was eighteen then and not given much to introspection even of that most simple sort. It seemed a little like being able to walk on air—to step outside oneself. Still, it had a certain intellectual appeal. It was my first introduction to the concept of the observer and the observed.

At some point all this took hold in literature. Dostoyevsky and Joyce were the early masters who created narration that spoke of themselves, flatly, in the third person. Kafka and Camus quickly followed. In another discipline, Freud and then Jung told us what to expect to find beneath what we saw along the introspective path.

I began to wonder then if I could follow my friend's lead and give up introspection for the rest of the summer. What would the world look like if seen without the filter of "self"?

I started out by looking at a nearby thunderstorm in the evening. The northern sky was obsidian, the lightning molten platinum. Against that, the cottonwoods were silver. Flocks of magpies fluttered madly in the roaring wind.

Forgetting oneself for a few brief moments brings a liberation of its own. Now to make it last the rest of the summer.

October 5, 1986

I ARRIVED HOME LATE once last week to an odd sight: partially-consumed slices of bread littered the kitchen floor. On the table a new loaf of bread had been ripped open lengthwise and its contents scattered. I do eat hurriedly, and I'm not a great housekeeper, but I wasn't taking credit for this.

I blamed the cat. Then I remembered that the cat and dog had been outside the tightly-closed house all day and had come into the dark living room with me. In short, I had an unannounced houseguest, and that being was still on the premises. I searched the house. Nothing. But there are large, dark, and inaccessible nooks and crannies in the building. I went to bed assuring myself that it was certainly a squirrel and not a mountain lion that had helped itself to the bread.

On rising in the predawn darkness I renewed the search. Nothing. Well, something. On the floor where the bread had been were several empty chewing gum wrappers. Lions don't chew gum, I thought, not dwelling on the fact that squirrels don't either.

At sunrise there was a disturbance in the utility room. I approached carefully. Perched on the windowsill was an obviously irritated magpie. I was nearly to it when it flew past me into the large open area that constitutes most of my house. It flapped around in circles against the high ceiling a few times before settling on another windowsill. The cat and dog remained oddly unperturbed, oddly because they spend half their time chasing flocks of magpies here and there in nearby pastures.

I opened doors and windows to the frosty dawn, sure that the magpie would make a hasty exit. The cat and dog sauntered onto the porch. The perverse bird simply moved to a new perch on a nearby partition. It greeted my approach with open beak and curved tongue, the magpie equivalent of a Bronx cheer. It returned to the utility room. The bird lit on the sill of the closed window.

This time the magpie simply sat there until I picked it up. I expected a frenzied attack, but the bird, somewhat scruffy and old, just cocked its head and regarded me calmly with sparkling eye. I sat it on the porch railing. The bird sat there looking at me. The cat and dog sat on their haunches looking at it. Then it flew away into the crystal dawn.

On the way to work I began wondering just how long I'd shared my quarters with that magpie. First there was the accepting attitude of the four-legged creatures in the house. Then I remembered my absent-minded puzzlement at the disappearance of cat food on days I knew the cat was outside. I recalled that in recent days, with equal inattentiveness, I'd noticed other items of misplaced food; a grape on the carpet or a cracker next to my typewriter.

How did it get in the house? What do I do if it comes back? My cat and dog came to my household in unexpected ways. Do I draw a line at magpies?

October 12, 1986

THE AUTUMN BEAUTY of the Montezuma Valley is so great now that one tends to consume it in gulps. Detail gets lost. I became aware of that tendency driving home one evening. A pear tree, leaves turned the color of burgundy, stands alone in an emerald green pasture miles from my house. I must have seen it but made no note of its existence.

From my front porch at sunset I noticed, in the sea of color that stretched away in all directions, a single, isolated purple flame. Then I recalled the pear tree. That was what I could see there in the last light rays. Now I take note of it on my way to and from work. The pear tree has caused me to see other detail since.

From my office window I can see, set in the grassy floor of Crow Canyon, an ancient grove of golden cottonwoods. Fat Hereford cattle graze there beside the weathered walls of an abandoned homestead. In early light the ripening grasses are cast bronze.

Outside my kitchen window, in the east, is a slender young cottonwood with unblemished yellow leaves that tremble in the slightest breeze. Behind it are the snow-covered La Plata Mountains. The tree in the rising sun is translucent as stained glass against the silhouetted peaks. In the evening it is orange against the crimson mountains.

Again, at Crow Canyon, purple asters bloom among the sage and stands of scrub oak lend color to the rocky ledges. Yellow daisies and rabbitbrush mimic the color of the cottonwoods below the pond. The banks of the pond are imprinted with deer tracks. Flocks of Canada geese fly reconnaissance runs low over nearby fields. At night there is no sound but an occasional owl and, by day, the happy voices of scores of children. After breakfast the children gather on the porch to warm themselves in the sun rising above Mesa Verde.

One recent night I drove west a ways to an ancient ruin to sleep beneath the stars and view them from a different angle. I awakened looking through grass at the sunrise. In that light the grass glittered like blades of molten platinum. I walked up dirt roads bordered by tall, blooming sunflowers. Across the canyon the aspens on Sleeping Ute Mountain caught fire in the dawn. In the crystal air the mountain seemed near enough to touch.

November 2, 1986

READERS OF THIS COLUMN occasionally ask why I do not use this space to take stands on burning regional issues. I'm not sure I have an answer to that question, and my attention usually gets distracted before I discover the reason. It's never been a conscious decision. The column more or less evolved to its present state.

Recently a friend, an experienced journalist unafraid of taking well-informed stands on controversial issues, did not let me off so easily. The friend pointed out that it is a privilege to be allowed to regularly express one's views in print. With that privilege, the veteran journalist said, comes an obligation to inform readers about the issues directly affecting their lives and to take stands on those issues. Granted, I said, columnists do have that obligation. My friend wasn't letting me off the hook.

I've thought a lot about my friend's challenge. First of all, the older I get the less certain I am of just what my views really are and the more certain I am that there are usually at least two sides to all issues—not to all issues, but to most issues. I find it increasingly difficult to take a stand and to feel that my stand is right and all others are wrong.

A case in point: Not long ago I sat with others in a living room of a house in a tiny Four Corners community. We watched statesmen and TV commentators express their views on Reagan's performance in Iceland the day before. Everyone who was in that room wants the arms race stopped. There was, however, deep disagreement in the room over whether Reagan was right or wrong to reject negotiations on Star Wars. Was Reagan's action in Iceland part of a long-range strategy to end the arms race? I left undecided. Other than to see the unleashing of the massive U.S. and Soviet nuclear arsenals as utterly pointless, to say the least, I have no insights to offer. I do feel that Reagan has the greatest opportunity offered one man in nuclear history to bring about disarmament.

Let's hope he uses the opportunity on behalf of all of us and all future generations.

It is not just the apparently complex blurring of black hats and white hats into varying greys that contributes to my reluctance to indulge in moral self-righteousness. It is also that I find my attention increasingly drawn to the world I can see from where I'm located. I live and work in a place of indescribable beauty, the Montezuma Valley of southwestern Colorado. The word indescribable is not used lightly. For much of it there are no words and for the rest of it there are few words. It is a beauty that surpasses my grasp of the language.

To stay aware, in the press of daily life, of the beauty in which I make my routine is a challenge in its own right. It's not the beauty that dims, it's the awareness that dims. Then to write about the beauty is, I find, a more disturbing challenge than most verbal confrontations I can imagine.

No eagle, no turning leaf, no cast of autumn light on sandstone will ever voice a view on the future of the earth. Seeing them, however, may provide reason enough to all of us to want a future for this earth.

November 16, 1986

AND THEN IT WAS WINTER. That's how quickly it seemed to happen. I knew it when the phone rang very early last Sunday morning. The news was bleak: the pipes were frozen at Crow Canyon. Not a drop was flowing from any faucet on campus. On most winter Sundays that is a problem that can wait until Monday. Last Sunday, however, archaeologists were due to arrive from as far away as New Haven, Dallas, and Pullman. They were to be housed in the Crow Canyon lodge.

As I drove off into the frosty dawn, I saw the first ice of the winter around the stems of the cattails in the ponds by my house. The pastures along the country roads glittered beneath layers of crystal frost. A few cottonwoods still clung to their leaves—overnight the leaves had gone from golden to russet, the color of the soil around their roots. Canada geese stood baffled by ponds that had frozen in chillier valley bottoms.

Frozen water pipes rank second only to the common cold in calling forth the native expertise in each of us. Since the problem is so hard to locate, solutions are offered up with the greatest of ease. By the time I arrived, several other staffers were applying themselves to the problem. A full-blown seminar was under way around the kitchen sink. The cold water faucet was open. No water. Eventually we moved into the dining room. Discussions of that nature require table and chairs.

We talked briefly about going outside and looking around, but finally decided that that would be futile. What's to see? The lone dissident went out to look anyway. He soon returned to report that it was cold outside. Glad for any new information, we plugged that fact into the discussion. Having thoroughly discussed the immediate situation, we turned our talk to past frozen pipe episodes. Individuals in turn told about the time they got up one morning . . . As with the common cold, everyone has had a frozen pipe.

Then, for the first time, genuine worry worked itself into the conversation. No coffee was brewed. I suggested that everyone desperate for coffee avail themselves of the pond. "Frozen over," was the brusque response.

Someone left for the airport to meet the first incoming guests. Stirred to action, I called the plumber. No answer. I rejoined the seminar in the dining room. The discussion had turned to computer software. I wondered what that had to do with anything. Only moments before we'd been a SWAT team dealing with frozen water pipes. Discipline had vanished completely.

Frustrated, I wandered up the hill to the structure housing the water storage tank. The door was open. In the gloomy interior I could see a maze of pipes. For lack of anything else to do, I kicked one of them and headed back toward the lodge. I walked into an excited knot of colleagues gathered around the kitchen sink. Water was gushing from the cold water tap.

The kitchen was filled with self-congratulation. We'd fixed the problem. No matter that we were all a little tired from the unceasing effort. I kept my mouth shut and hoped that I hadn't sprained a toe.

That was when I knew winter was here.

November 30, 1986

Dawn the day before Thanksgiving came here with a simple kind of light from which all color was absent. Clouds in countless shades of grey hung low beneath the peaks and mesas. Juniper forests were black, as were fence posts, against dim white pastures. The only movement was slowly falling snow, white upon grey and black. Once again it was an Anasazi world of blacks and greys and whites.

Color—muted willow reds and grass tans—appeared here and there as the sky lightened. As I descended into Crow Canyon on my way to work, a deer stepped into the center of the road. The slight color in his wet coat matched perfectly that of the world at large.

The night before, as I headed up country roads on my way home, a great horned owl played leapfrog from post to post along a vast black field. The predator was an arresting sight as it lowered needle-sharp talons to grip the weathered wood. The owl's wings spread wide and powerful against the darkening sky. At home a very few stars glittered in the jet mirror that was the pond by my house. Fog and rain obscured the usual vista of the lights of Cortez in the Montezuma Valley far below. My house seemed a becalmed ship a thousand miles from land. There was no sound. From within the house, the windows were rectangles of grey in which were silhouetted the twisted black branches of nearby trees. For a while I could not bring myself to turn on any lights. The cat and dog stayed nearby, perplexed by this break in my homecoming routine. Neither did I turn on the heat, not wanting the system's low hum to break the silence.

The night before I'd gone to the home of neighbors for dinner. Their house, cheerful and warm, had contained that same welcome silence. The house is solar heated through a surprisingly small expanse of southern glass. The only other heat is a Russian fireplace containing a chimney that doesn't go straight up but winds here and there through a massive hearth before exiting. The last small fire had been built two days before. The hearth was still warm to the touch.

My hosts seemed far more aware of the cycle of the seasons, the movements of the sun, than I am. That, I thought, was as great a reward from solar heating as the cost savings themselves . . . that awareness and the silence of no motors.

When I arrived at work on Thanksgiving's eve, I was greeted by Durangoan Charlie Langdon. He and his son Matt had ridden over on ten-speed bikes the day before. Charlie's first comment was upon the silence that had lain over Crow Canyon through the night; I was glad that a friend shared an enthusiasm for this winter stillness.

December 7, 1986

IN LAST SUNDAY's *Herald* the comic character Ziggy experiences " . . . the first warning signs of acute living aloneness . . . " I laughed. The comic strip hit home. I've lived alone for much of the last two years—sometimes in fairly secluded places—and have more than once noticed "signs of living aloneness." If, unlike Ziggy, I've never followed up a sneeze with "God bless me," it's because I never follow up someone else's sneeze with "God bless you."

I have my own list of signs: the automatic checking and rechecking to make sure that all appliances are off upon leaving the house; the slight start at the sound of another voice when there's a guest in the house; the irritation at having to buy more than I can eat of prepackaged foods from bread to pork chops; raised eyebrows of houseguests upon discovering that I eat from paper plates—a fact that I always forget until it's too late to do anything about it; the required scheduling of business and shopping errands to town in order to get there before everything's closed; occasional astonishment that although more people live alone than ever before, our culture does little to accommodate us; and a growing tendency to forget to close the door when I'm using the bathroom.

I was glad that Ziggy used the term "aloneness" rather than "loneliness." There's a vast difference between the two. Two years ago when I left a familiar neighborhood to enter a state of "aloneness" well-meaning friends repeatedly warned me that I was setting myself up for the hellish tortures of loneliness. As I settled into my relatively remote surroundings, I steeled myself for the first painful symptoms of loneliness.

That time two years ago was one of anguish, but it had nothing to do with loneliness. That, in part, was due to supportive friends who stayed in constant contact; but then I discovered I liked my aloneness. I like it even more today. I may indeed be settling into "acute aloneness."

Why, in a culture that does nothing to accommodate aloneness—a culture where the fear of loneliness is a raging epidemic—do I prefer living alone in places apart from others? Even to me the answer seems paradoxical. It is because, in the end, it offers the opportunity for stronger relationships with other people.

When two or more people who live alone are around one another, it seems to me at least, there is less than the socially-acceptable level of pretense between or among them. Otherwise, they wouldn't be together or in communication in the first place. Living alone, too, gives one a greater ability to know when one's own presence isn't welcomed by another. Polite retreats are more possible than otherwise. It's a great deal easier than disentangling from someone with whom you live. One's energy is freed to go where one wants it to go.

It may sound like it, but I'm not an advocate of living alone. It's just that in my case it has slowly, to my great astonishment, become a matter of personal preference. I'm always delighted when one or both of my sons are staying at home, but they're so self-sufficient that the better qualities of aloneness remain intact. It's nice to know they're there because they want to be, not on some pretense. We do manage to be very much ourselves around one another.

My favorite moments alone have come to be after dark when I can walk in a direction where no lights are visible among a thousand soft sounds with no thought of returning at a given time. It may sound self-centered, but such moments seem to exist for me alone. Time loses its artificial meaning.

January 11, 1987

CHRISTMAS DAY, 1986. The sun was setting behind the legendary Kaiparowits Plateau. We made camp at the foot of its snowy ramparts. In the final moments of twilight we watched as a thick frost began to grow on our sleeping bags. I awakened often that night, always in the hope that I would see the first light of dawn in the east. That light was a long time in coming. When, at last, it arrived I arose to find our water supply, totally contained in plastic, frozen solid. There was no way to melt the ice without melting the plastic first. The only solace was the sight of the new light upon vast vistas of ice-laden sage.

The ice vanished beneath the first warm rays of the sun. We turned our backs on the Kaiparowits and headed east into a place that appeared to be a land of unbroken dunes frozen into salmon-hued Navajo Sandstone. That perception proved deceptive. The trace of a trail, marked by few recent tracks, subtly descended between these dunes and then the next. Soon we walked not between gently sloping mounds of slickrock but into a narrow fissure bounded by vertical stone. Shadow replaced sunlight. Damp seeps firmed the dry sand that shifted beneath our every laden step. The seeps gathered into a stream. The fissure grew into a dim meandering canyon cut deep into the stony crust of that place. I began counting the times we waded the ice-crusted stream as it bounced first off the south canyon wall and then the north. I soon abandoned that line of research. There are certain things in life one is better off not knowing. Soon, too, I decided not to try to keep track of the days of winter wilderness that lay ahead.

There are times when time itself is best forgotten. That place, without time, took dominion.

Direct sunlight became a precious commodity. For the most part, even at noon, it was limited to a thinly visible slice high on the north canyon wall hundreds of feet above our heads. We—my son, a friend, and I—walked slowly and in silence. There was little point in words.

One evening we made camp at the point of a sharp meander.

The canyon wall did not rise straight above us but sharply over us to form a great alcove. The melodious stream which flowed against the back wall of the alcove was covered with thick fronds of maidenhair fern green as June. From our camp the sky was a thin horseshoe of starlight wrapped around the curve of stone that was the opposite canyon wall. At one end of the alcove a soaring stone arch provided a view on down the canyon. Just before dawn a thin curve of moon, followed by Venus, rose to fill the arch and alcove with a chill, silvery light.

Late one day we approached the mouth of the canyon to find that the stream filled its floor from wall to wall. Islands of ice slowed the water's flow. We waded down the stream in the fading light to be stopped at the canyon's mouth by a river with a much greater flow than we'd expected. A tiny wet sandbar was our only refuge from the cold water. We debated about whether to cross the river. Far across the inky water was a high, dry beach that seemed to offer the perfect camp. We waded, knowing that our only exit would be to wade back the way we'd come.

The day before we left that country, we stood in a shadowy glen beside a pool that mirrored the encircling rock. Thick patinas of desert varnish, deep cobalt blue, plunged into the water. Lush golden grasses curved over to brush the water. Gnarled hackberry caught the reflected light from above. The place contained the essence of the canyons of the Four Corners Country.

January 25, 1987

THE RECENT STORMS HAVE MADE IT EASIER to plot the movements of the foxes that share the narrow point of land on which I live. At first I found it difficult to separate the maze of fox trails from those left behind by coyotes and by my dog and her occasional visitors. Then one morning I glanced out a north window at dawn and saw a fox not far away. It stood, its gaze fixed straight ahead. Then the fox moved, walked slowly between stands of cattails toward a juniper-covered knoll glowing in the first light. I made careful note of its course as it wandered into the long shadows of the grove and vanished.

Within minutes I was outside and hot on the fox's trail. The tracks led beyond the knoll, detoured briefly toward an abandoned fruit cellar, headed toward an ancient, deserted house, and vanished through its open door. On the floor inside, the fox had left snowy tracks leading into another room. I swung the door shut behind me, waited for my eyes to adjust to the darkness, and tiptoed—a little nervously—through the house. I searched every corner. No fox. I went back to the door and looked outside. Had the fox come and gone before I got there? I saw only one set of tracks, and it clearly led in the door. No other tracks were visible. I searched the structure again. No fox. I didn't want to, but I abandoned the search. I was already late for work.

It was dark when I got home that night, so I couldn't pursue the mystery of the disappearing fox. I set my alarm a half hour earlier so I could take my time at it in the morning. I awakened to the alarm and the sound of a high wind buffeting the house. Visibility was zero outside my window. A blizzard was raging. What the snow had brought, the tracks of foxes, the snow had taken away.

If anything, I had an extra half hour to ponder the mystery of foxes. Why do they command my attention so? My house is surrounded by wildlife: raccoons, coyotes, bobcats, prairie dogs, badgers, and even gophers—or especially gophers. The foxes are my favorite. Some of the others are rarely seen.

Foxes are fully as stealthy as coyotes, but lack the air of sneakiness sometimes exhibited by the latter. Foxes seem to be more playful. At times they literally bounce in circles, appearing to rise straight up, spin, and fall to earth again. Other times they run in great leaps, their long, bushy tails straight out behind them. Sometimes they vanish into the ditches here and emerge there. I have never seen one sit or lie down.

My dog guards the southern approaches to my house from a sunny deck. I've never seen her chase a fox, but the foxes do cast a wary eye in that direction when they appear in the south pastures. They're much bolder on the north side of the house where the dog rarely goes—for some inexplicable reason—unless I go too. That's where I'll try tracking them once more.

In the meantime I can only wonder about the mystery of the vanishing fox. All traces of its magical act have been erased.

March 15, 1987

Beneath an ancient juniper outside my kitchen window there is a brilliant emerald green patch of grass. It is an island in a sea of winter white and brown. I look at it each day in the muted light of dawn and check it once more in the crimson light of dusk. That circle of green is growing, expanding by inches with each passing day. There is a neon fluorescence in the green. It is a sign saying "Spring Starts Here." I think of Dylan Thomas's phrase, "Fire green as grass."

It is a time of extraordinary light in the place where I live and work. One chilly evening, as a snow storm ended, I drove north toward home at sunset. The sun was a fiery orb beyond vapors of ice crystals. A single column of translucent rose-hued light shot straight up from the sun. The western horizon claimed the sun itself, but that pillar of light remained until near darkness, bisecting the known universe, reflected in the steaming surface of my pond along with the first stars.

There is a saddle between Mesa Verde and Sleeping Ute Mountain through which, from my living room windows, I can see the Chuska Mountains astraddle the New Mexico–Arizona border. One March storm came up that range, blotting it from view before funneling through the saddle. Next both Mesa Verde and the Ute vanished in the storm. Then snowflakes the size of silver dollars began floating dizzily down upon the pastures and woods around my house.

Low on the western horizon a window opened in the clouds and the sun shone through it and through the falling snow. The light illuminated the boiling bottoms of the black clouds.

The light was dazzling platinum on the fallen and falling snow.

My son Geoffrey grabbed a camera, plunged into the storm of light and snow, and, until the light failed, clicked away like a paparazzo who had just crashed a royal wedding.

It is this light and this place and more that is contained in the paintings of Stanton Englehart who grew up here. Englehart, a Fort Lewis College professor who is gaining widespread recognition for his work, has his annual show this week in the Fine Arts Gallery at the college.

Earth, light, and sky sometimes collide here with awesome force. At other hours they coexist in gentle harmony. That is the way they appear on Englehart's canvases. I'm looking forward to seeing Stanton's show. His work teaches me to see this place more clearly.

April 12, 1987

It was raining. Two herons dropped slowly from flight, long spindly legs outstretched, to alight upon a skeletal cottonwood snag above Longenbaugh's pond. Behind them the dawn brushed the low, wet clouds pewter and bronze. Minutes later I sat looking north from my office window. Three deer, touched by the soft light, stared back from the grassy, damp valley floor. There was no sound.

It rained most of the day. At dusk I drove north up the Lebanon road toward home. There was a hint of turquoise in the dripping, new-leafing sage. The marsh grasses in the valley floor below Russell Martin's house glowed deep russets in the gathering darkness against black, forested ridges. Where I turned east across yet another of the countless valleys and canyons hidden upon this vast and deceptively gentle plateau, stands of willow were blood red at the edges of quicksilver ponds.

I built a fire to chase the chill from the house and walked south along the highest ditch into the gloom. The juniper smoke from the newly made fire poured down over the eaves in that heavy atmosphere and kept pace with me as I went. The clouds broke and lifted in the west. The sky was ruby crystal, the moon a thin crescent sliver.

Not far to the west of my house is an old Greek Revival style country schoolhouse recently restored to its original white splendor. Adjacent to the school is a weathered country church with a high narrow steeple. In that light both were black silhouettes with only the belfry and the steeple rising above the peaks of the pink, snowy Abajo Mountains fifty miles away.

From high in the branches of a cottonwood just behind me, the scream of a red-tailed hawk broke the silence of the first western stars. Feeling like an intruder, I turned back into the fragrant smoke toward the house. I had wandered into the hawk's hunting territory. The hawk had company. From a rocky rim on one side came the sharp bark of a fox. From a juniper stand on the other floated the first call of an owl. Inside the walls of my house was the only territory I knew to be mine. I took refuge there for the night.

Dawn came to a clear sky. The sun rose north of the Sharkstooth in the La Plata Mountains. When I left for work my dogs were yipping excitedly at the edge of the pond beside my house. In its center, safely out of reach, were two Canada geese floating in slow, complacent circles. Their feathers were silver upon the silvery water.

April 26, 1987

Part of being middle-aged—as I am—is to contemplate voluntarily or involuntarily the approaching time when one's parents are both dead. This is usually thought of as a process of self-preparation if not self-preservation. This is not an unhealthy process. Among other things, it reminds one of one's own mortality at exactly the time one ought to be reminded to pay a bit more heed to the accelerating hands on the biological clock. One thinks, too, that advance contemplation of a parent's death allows much of the grief to be released in advance, thus lessening the blow when the inevitable becomes reality. I'd pretty much completed that whole process some time ago.

Or so I thought . . .

Two weeks ago I found out differently. Except to put words in one's own mouth, thinking through such matters in advance is an exercise in futility. The death of a parent—particularly, perhaps, of a sole surviving parent—is a profound event in the lives of the next generation.

In the past two weeks my thoughts have returned frequently to my mother's life. Oddly, to me at least, I don't think back to childhood moments or even to her many quiet accomplishments. I think most upon the final months of her life . . . for more reasons than merely that they were the most recent months of her life.

Last autumn she underwent major surgery for a particularly virulent form of cancer. She went into the surgery weak, ill, and frightened. Hours later she emerged weary but lucid, smiling, and doing her best to reassure the crowd of family that had gathered in the hospital hallway during those hours. A day later, in a frank session, her doctors told her that the cancer probably had spread before surgery and that if it did not reappear it would be just short of miraculous. She didn't flinch.

She recovered with remarkable speed. The sparkle returned to her eyes brighter than ever. She gently pushed away her hovering children, asserting her capability—and her right—to take care of herself. She returned to her daily routine. I hoped for that miracle. It didn't happen. Two weeks ago she quietly took her leave.

In those final months, she radiated more than her usual contagious cheerfulness. She seemed to move in the center of an almost tangible field of calm. I came away from visits with her feeling as if I'd unconsciously absorbed some of that calm into my own life. I would have thought my mind was playing tricks on me had not many mutual friends commented on their own similar responses to her presence in recent months. The only time that calm was ever broken was when she felt that someone was questioning her capacity for self-reliance and independence.

Physically, in her final weeks, she faded almost perceptibly. She changed in other ways. She seemed always to believe that she would be known for her deeds alone. Her deeds were her identity. At the end she seemed to put even that aside as a matter of no great importance. Finally, for some strange reason, I stopped thinking of myself as "her" son or of her as "my" mother. Even those possessives, those identities, had slipped away.

Her final days, I believe, were spent in preparation for departure. Her cherished independence—the quality of her life—had ended. She simply took her leave, in the darkness before dawn, from the town and from the country she loved.

My response, I must admit, is not grief. It is more a feeling of wonder. Who was this woman? I feel as if I'd never met her until last autumn and was fortunate that she was there through one more winter into spring.

In recent months this column had become something of a weekly letter to that woman. She never failed to read each one and to comment upon each one. I shall miss that.

May 3, 1987

A VERY LARGE COCK PHEASANT—the largest I've ever seen—has staked out my yard as its territory. Its raspy call has the quality of two toots on a steam whistle. It struts along the borders of its kingdom at dawn and at dusk, pausing occasionally to rise on its toes, flap its wings, and let forth that two-tone crow.

The dogs, at first, shot off wildly on hearing the ventriloquil call, running back and forth across the pasture as if in pursuit of an echo. The pheasant would crouch and vanish beneath the tops of the spring grass. Now the dogs have grown bored with that pursuit and the pheasant walks its circle unperturbed. Whether the foxes will adopt the nonchalant attitude of the dogs is another question.

The dogs, too, have come to ignore the meadowlarks that populate the pastures and fence lines that surround the house. Spring fever has so leveled the dogs, in fact, that they show little interest in moving objects except for the magpies that flap down in surprise attacks on pans of dog food and the gophers that burrow along beneath their very noses. The dogs freeze, gaze at an apparently blank spot, then lunge and dig straight down. The effect has been to rid the immediate area of those little subterranean beasts. I don't regret the gophers' absence. Maybe this year I'll be able to get water across the lawn rather than down a hole.

For a while, as the ponds filled, the dogs hunted awakening crawdads along the edges of the water. They've stopped that, too. The result, I suspect, of painful encounters. The crawdads bite back.

In evening, against the setting sun, my son Geoffrey hunts along the edge of the pond, netting minnows for transfer to the pond at Crow Canyon where he's trying to establish a population of the translucent creatures. The Crow Canyon pond already boasts catfish, bass, and a reclusive rainbow trout. Hundreds of minnows have joined them.

Another avid fisherman at Crow Canyon reports that he's had good luck catching rainbows from his secret spot along the shores of McPhee Reservoir. With the longer daylight hours, Geoff and I have resolved that after work we'll start heading for McPhee and trying our luck at catching larger fish than minnows.

May 17, 1987

TEMPERATURES NUDGED THE EIGHTIES HERE. I tried to ignore the thin patch of snow remaining on the north face of Ute Mountain. I really couldn't quite see it from the corner of my house, I told myself. Then, in disregard for local legend, I stuck half a dozen tomato plants into a protected southern nook. Anyway, I thought, the plants cost only nineteen cents apiece.

Within the hour, chill, quilted clouds moved down the sky from the north. A breeze from the west became a wind from the east. Banners of petals flared out from blooming apple trees in a forgotten orchard below my house. Sheets of cold rain, punctuated by lightning, lashed out from all sides. The weather has been changeable lately, I assured myself, trying to forget the admonition that one *never* starts a garden before *all* the snow has vanished from Ute Mountain. Then, by twilight, the sun warmed this place once more. Six tomato plants, I decided, must have added up to a minor transgression. Nevertheless, I set the marigolds inside for the night.

The weather has in fact been whimsical here in May. By noon the warmth is pushing the upper levels of comfort. By evening, on arrival home, I build a small fire to take the chill off the house. In the morning small flares of frost cling to the windshield.

The chill dawns have not touched the wild asparagus along the fences. On weekends families from town advance along country roads gathering the delicacy until forced to retreat before the lightning-laced afternoon storms. The more persistent asparagus lovers return in the late afternoon light. They take away huge batches of the stuff. My own ventures into the world of asparagus are limited to seeking it out in evenings on the rocky slopes within my own domain. I eat as I go. Not one stalk of asparagus has yet made its way into my kitchen.

Those same slopes that produce widely scattered stalks of asparagus are now covered with blooming cliffrose, patches of scarlet gilia trembling in the evening breeze, and clumps of yellow composites that match the setting sun. When I turn homeward, it is the mounded forests of lilacs around old, deserted farmhouses that match the evening sky. The ancient silver wood of the houses reflects the light of the sky and the lavender flowers.

How long this whimsical season, caught between winter and summer, will last is impossible to predict. One recent year I followed all the rules. The snow vanished from Ute Mountain before my tomatoes went into the ground. Two days later I fell asleep to the sound of a warm May rain. I awakened the next morning to the sight of Ute Mountain asleep beneath a blanket of new snow.

May 24, 1987

MESA VERDE IS AN ENCHANTED PLACE this time of year. One recent evening Crow Canyon's Roberta Leicester and I went into Park Headquarters to view a group of newly restored Native American paintings now on display in the museum there. Showers washed the forests and rocky ruins. Shafts of sunshine lit the grassy valley bottom, and towering cumulus boiled up from the Great Sage Plain to the north of Mesa Verde. It was an appropriate approach to the paintings.

The canvases were discovered rolled up in storage in the Park nearly a year ago. They had been there for a half century. Park Superintendent Bob Heyder immediately recognized the unique value of the art works and Park curator Allen Bohnert took them to Denver for expert restoration.

The mural-sized canvases and a sand painting were done by Pueblo, Kiowa, and Navajo artists at the Santa Fe Indian School and presented to Mesa Verde National Park in 1935, according to Doug Caldwell of the Park staff. They were exhibited briefly before World War II and put in storage until discovered last year. The restored art is now permanently exhibited in the auditorium of the museum on Chapin Mesa.

My first reaction was to be struck by the size and the simplicity of the paintings. It takes a while just to scan them and begin to comprehend them. The one I was drawn to most was "Corn Dance" by Romando Vigil of the San Ildefonso Pueblo. Black and white dancers, reminiscent of harlequins, stretch across the ten-foot width of the canvas against a backdrop of a few isolated spectators. All the figures appear isolated upon an expansive, flat background. It is almost as if the dancers and spectators are suspended against the sky of late dusk.

Even more fascinating, if one scans the dancers from one end of the painting to the other, each figure seems to be frozen in motion to a continuing drumbeat. The first figure to a single beat, the next to a subsequent beat and so on. One can almost hear the drums. The paintings fill the walls of the auditorium, a space that feels like a small Spanish colonial church in a New Mexico pueblo. It is a perfect surrounding for the paintings. Because the paintings contain timeless symbols of Puebloan culture, Mesa Verde seems their most appropriate permanent home. Bob Heyder is to be congratulated for assuring that the paintings are now a permanent part of the Mesa Verde experience. Seeing them is to understand more about the remarkable peoples who built the beautiful, humane communities preserved in the National Park.

As we departed Mesa Verde, the last rays of sun lit a solid bank of clouds over Red Mesa and the La Plata River Valley in the east. Lightning flickered in the clouds. It was easy to imagine the black and white dancers moving to the claps of thunder against the awesome backdrop.

June 14, 1987

O`N RECENT EVENINGS I HAVE WALKED` with my son Jonathan in the late light. Our wanderings have a vague sense of purpose. We are searching for a few acres to buy, a place to build a house. Neither of us seems very particular; we've liked every place we've seen. We're in no hurry. We've scheduled the project for next summer when, we hope, we'll have more time.

One such expedition began near the bottom of a densely wooded draw. We crossed a small, rushing brook bordered by wildflowers and fought our way up a steep, brushy slope. Water dripped from every rock outcrop. Suddenly we found ourselves in a flat, grassy meadow ringed by trees. On one side the land rose toward the La Platas, hidden by a storm. On the other a small cliff plunged into a valley filled with tall grass. In the distant west we could see the Abajos against the dimming sky. There were the songs of a thousand birds.

I forgot that I was standing on a piece of ground that was for sale. There was a quality to the moment that could neither be bought nor sold . . . nor owned. I thought of a phrase used by a photographer friend, Philip Hyde, "When the light says now." It was the first time I'd ever tried to imagine light saying anything. In that place last week the light was saying everything.

When I got home later that evening, I looked up "light" in the dictionary. I've always thought that the longer a dictionary definition the less definable the word. "Light" has one of the longest, if not the longest, definitions in the Random House Dictionary: "1. something that makes things visible or affords lumination. 2.a. electromagnetic radiation to which the organs of sight react . . . " I quit reading there. The definition continued on down the page.

I tried to imagine what kind of house would be appropriate for the spot I'd seen earlier that evening. The house itself would almost have to be of light. Anything else would be too heavy and obtrusive, an invading alien, in that place.

It was then that I remembered another definition of light I'd stumbled across a few months ago: "Light is the gods." There are times when that definition is quite adequate.

June 28, 1987

I OBSERVED THE SOLSTICE this year by going with my son Jonathan to a remote spot in Hovenweep National Monument. There, carved into the face of a huge, tilting boulder, are two sets of concentric rings several feet apart. We were not the only ones there. A small crowd gathered in the dawn. One woman said she'd driven seven hundred miles to be there that morning.

At sunrise a thin band of light creeps across the face of rock. It cuts through each set of circles just below center. There was a silence so great that one would have thought the assembled observers had stopped breathing.

I've thought back on that moment ever since. In a sense, it is a purely natural phenomenon: a juxtaposition of boulder and overhang, a juxtaposition of light and shadow. The boulders were not put there by the ancient ones, and the sun was not made to rise at that point on the horizon by the ancient ones. Taken alone there is very little that is remarkable about the phenomenon. Light and shadow occur all around us every moment of every day of the year. We ignore it.

What is remarkable is the act of human intervention required to carve those spirals into the rock at the point that they would indicate to observers a significant instant in the natural world—the summer solstice. The fact that the band of light strikes the circles just slightly off center is easily explained. The massive boulder is precariously perched on a steep clay slope. A fraction of an inch of settling on the downhill edge of the boulder would cause a shift in the position of the rings. Over the centuries such a shift has probably occurred.

The individual or group responsible for creating that solar calendar would have to have known the seasonal shift of horizon to sun. Someone would have to have noticed the band of light itself on or near the summer solstice—an awesome observation in a place where light and shadow upon rock are everywhere, every moment. Finally there was the act of pecking the circles into the stone at just the right spot. The creation of the simple circles was a simple act. Their placement was not—it required the accumulation of unknown generations of human observation and knowledge . . . the knowledge that the sunrise apparently changed position on the horizon in harmony with the seasons.

The result of that ancient act of human intervention is so magnetically powerful that even today, many centuries later, it pulls us, aliens in this land, to that spot from hundreds of miles away.

The rediscovery of that ancient solar calendar occurred only a few years ago. That in itself should be considered remarkable.

There is nothing at the spot to tell anyone of its significance. I left there at sunrise certain that we yet see only the smallest fraction of the remarkable prehistoric imprint upon this place we now call the Four Corners Country. It is our own power of observation, our own ability to accumulate knowledge, that is now challenged. We have yet to glimpse this place through the eyes of those departed ancients.

July 26, 1987

"What we are trying to find out is who we are."

The speaker was Andy Contiguglia, a high school student from Denver. Contiguglia was one of forty students in their fourth week of the High School Field School here at Crow Canyon. The students gathered here from as far away as Pisa, Italy, and a score of other cities from Manhattan to Los Angeles. One of the most outstanding students was Margaret Sluss of Durango.

Contiguglia's statement came during an evening roundtable discussion at which archaeologist Mark Varien and myself had asked the students whether the pursuit of archaeology was useful to our times or merely a luxury. The students broke into small groups. The ensuing discussion was so lively, sometimes heated, that the National Geographic film crew on campus at the time hopped frantically about trying to keep up. The students seemed oblivious to the film crew.

When they came back together, it was quickly apparent that no group had reached consensus on the question of the usefulness of archaeology. A majority in each group agreed that archaeology was useful, that we can learn from the past how better to cope with today's problems of population growth and resource depletion. A minority in each group held to the opinion that archaeology is a useless luxury because we are so arrogant about the supposed superiority and sophistication of our own times and culture as to be incapable of anything but disdain for other cultures and times.

One student came up with the ultimate argument for the irrelevance and uselessness of archaeology. "We're all going to get blown up anyway, so why worry about learning from the past?" he asked. I winced as usual when hearing an adolescent express that profound nuclear despair—and in this case the speaker was an unusually bright and disciplined thinker. Being, inescapably, a member of my own generation, I tend to view pessimism as tantamount to defeat. That view, however, may be its own path to destruction.

To my surprise, thirty-nine voices responded in a near chorus of disagreement with the nuclear nihilist. It was then that Contiguglia stood to say, "What we are trying to find out is who we are."

The next night, alone, I watched the sunset reflected in the pond by my house. The nighthawks boomed in a darkening sky. The last dove songs rose toward the first stars. I began to think that what I'd heard the night before was something of an affirmation, an expression of hope and faith. Our chances, it seems, might be strengthened by a pursuit of who we were, are, and will be.

August 2, 1987

THE SUMMER STORMS ARE HERE AT LAST. Now in early afternoon, hundreds of grey-bottomed cumulus clouds fill the sky. By early evening the clouds have joined forces, gathered into black and bronze thunderheads boiling thousands of feet above the La Platas and other mountain ranges encircling the Great Sage Plain.

The first lightning does not touch the earth but flickers deep within the twilit clouds themselves. In last light the peaks vanish behind curtains of rain. Lightning dances down the mountain slopes across the rocky crust of the vast plateau. Then, from all directions, the rain comes to wash the Great Sage Plain.

In the darkness the light flashes and the thunder crashes without end. Gale-like winds lash the cottonwoods in the pasture below my house. The dogs run wildly into the storm seeking the noisy intruder from the sky. The normally aloof cat hops into my lap but does not purr. I stay on the front porch until the cold spray of rain drives me indoors.

The dawn comes in cloudless skies of golden crystal. There is no sound but that of a single, startled killdeer. Then, as the sun floats free of the grip of the La Platas, there is a piercing attack call of a kingfisher diving at the pond. I look out to catch a glimpse of the marauding bird but see only a set of concentric waves where the fisher hit the water. The still surface of the pond is afloat with leaves liberated by the storm in the night.

November 22, 1987

THE FIRST SNOWFALL in this place came in the night.

I awakened to a world full of darkest silver. Fingers of cloud dipped to touch stilled pastures. The night snow had ended. I walked from my house into a dripping dawn. Here and there clouds parted beneath the last stars.

A cock pheasant, roosting high in a juniper, was startled into flight when I passed beneath. Deep in stands of cattails, sleeping flocks of blackbirds rustled into wakefulness at the sound of my step. Red apples, sweetened by frost and still black in that light, hung low beneath crowns of snow. I munched as I walked. Breakfast.

Juniper smoke from the chimney of my house drifted through the living junipers like perfumed ghosts. The clouds lifted from the Montezuma Valley revealing and bronzed by the distant crescent of light that is Cortez from my angle. Beyond that the ragged rockfalls beneath the cliff of Mesa Verde were gentled into white triangles in the growing light. My pond mirrored the first color to touch the sky. A rooster crowed on some far farm. Night had ended. I turned back into the juniper smoke toward home. The sun rose. That first snow vanished.

The next morning I followed the smoke once more into the woods, this time beneath a sky thick with coldly glittering stars. The frost on the grass and sage sparkled in that chill light. An owl called from the slope across the valley. My footsteps cracked upon the brittle earth. The frost was crystal, hiding the lichen, on the then treacherous slickrock encircling this thin finger of land. An owl glided across my path. I turned away.

It is in these dawns that the return of wildness to these rocky spits of land between near canyons is almost tangible. The stubborn farmers who cleared the narrow pastures and tended the now-deserted orchards have vanished. They eked an existence from a thin blanket of red soil upon rock. The surviving farmers are now found on the vast expanses of deep, fertile soil not far to the west.

My wandering takes me over fallen rail fences, humble crumbling houses, and weathered barns. I sometimes stop, hold my breath, and listen hard for some faint echo. A child's laughter, a woman's song. Nothing. The farm families are gone. At my feet, in a front yard, juniper and sage seedlings have taken root.

It is that time of year when the snows and the crystal days follow each other across this place like slow waves and troughs. Perhaps humanity follows the same, if slower, rhythm across the land.

November 29, 1987

"WE SHOULD NOT BE ASKING why the Anasazi left here, that's obvious; but why they came here in the first place, to this godforsaken country?" I didn't react much to that remark by an acquaintance at the time I heard it. Later it came back to mind. It was as I left Crow Canyon for a journey south.

A bitter wind was blowing. The evening sky was leaden. The Sleeping Ute was hidden beneath colorless cloud. At the mouth of Mancos Canyon sheets of sand and tumbleweed hurried down the highway in front of me. Not long after I entered the Navajo reservation I saw an elderly woman in traditional dress herding sheep through the gloom. She turned this way and that, keeping her back to the shifting, cold wind. It was then that I thought my acquaintance's cynical question might have been well put.

In Shiprock a Navajo service station attendant pointed to an ancient cottonwood that had lost a large limb in the gale just moments before. He said that if it snowed—and snow was in the forecast—it would be a killer storm with drifting snow. He laughed and said he wouldn't go home that night. He'd sleep on the floor of the station. As I passed Shiprock Peak, snow was already gathering in phosphorescent-looking drifts in the great coves high atop that dark pinnacle. I had the wide, smooth highway to myself and the wind. The tumbleweeds were no longer bouncing along beside me but crossed my path in front of and behind me.

The sun, just as it slipped behind the Chuska Mountains, broke beneath the clouds. Light bounced from earth to sky and back again. The sun vanished, and the clouds glowed deep crimson, then flickered out. In the ensuing blackness the wind gusted with renewed force. Wet snow splattered against the windshield. Windshield wipers reduced the snow to curving streaks of mud. Later I fell asleep in a neatly deserted Gallup motel to the sound of rattling windows and shrieking wind.

The next morning, headed south once more at dawn for an early appointment at Zuni Pueblo, the world seemed new. There was no breeze. The air was crystal. Towering pines were glittering white with new snow that had been blasted against them by the night wind. Rose colored cliffs glowed beneath a turquoise sky.

It was not a piece of country then that anyone would want to leave for long. It was, in fact, easy to understand why people had come here in the first place.

December 13, 1987

I WAS ASKED RECENTLY just what I mean when I use the phrase Four Corners Country. My simple answer was, "The area surrounding the point where Arizona, Colorado, New Mexico, and Utah meet." The next question was, "How big an area?" That question stumps me.

Geographically speaking it would be easiest to define the Four Corners Country as the San Juan River Basin. That region, stretching from Wolf Creek Pass to Navajo Mountain and including vast drainages to the north and south, is large enough to accommodate several small modern nations. The problem with that definition is that if residents of Del Norte, Ouray, Gallup, or Dolores were asked if they lived in the Four Corners Country, they would probably answer yes.

The residents of the modern pueblos of Arizona and New Mexico, all of which are located outside the San Juan Basin, feel such deep ties to ancestral places in the San Juan Basin that they consider it to be a part of their homeland, even now. That pushes the cultural boundaries out even farther. The first modern explorations of the Four Corners Country were launched from Spanish Santa Fe, and the cultural links are still easily apparent to anyone glancing at the place names on a map of the region. Those first Spanish explorers were heavily dependent upon Ute guides. The first official U.S. explorations were heavily dependent upon Spanish maps. Tens of thousands of Navajos now live in the San Juan Basin, but their lands extend far beyond it.

In the end one might conclude that the Four Corners Country is less a place than it is a state of mind created by timeless natural and cultural circumstances. Its borders could be defined as encompassing the outermost people who consider themselves residents of the Four Corners Country.

I sometimes remember T. Ralph Bennett's attempts to have the Four Corners Country secede from Arizona, Colorado, New Mexico, and Utah, efforts that sometimes seemed on the verge of actually going somewhere. The state capitols, he said, were too distant to address the needs of this place. As a high school student I was always ready to join the secessionists. Those state capitols did seem a long way off. Now they seem much too close.

As I think now of my definition of the Four Corners Country, I would say it is rooted in a certain tilt of stone, a certain cast of light, a certain human stubbornness. Nothing more.

December 20, 1987

THE SUN NOW RISES into a silver lace of cottonwood branches obscuring Mesa Verde. The south faces of the La Plata peaks glow in that light. It sets, flaming, into the peak of Ute Mountain. There is a brief interim of blue snow-light before darkness and the glow of planets through thin clouds. At noon I look into long shadows cast by ancient trees. Solstice light.

It is that time of year when stillness, a certain slowing of all rhythms, is the most perceptible dimension of life here. Herds of deer move slowly across sage slopes. A bald eagle glides in circles with no visible movement of its wings. Magpies on my porch rail lower their voices to hoarse whispers. Ice has stilled the song of water. Snow muffles the sound of foot on earth and stone.

In this dim stillness of winter solstice I sometimes imagine that the light one sees is radiated from things themselves rather than being the reflected light of the distant, fleeing sun. The color of stone, where it is not hidden by snow, seems more of time than of matter. The vast fields gently rising to meet the western sky halfway are the soft pewter of space itself rather than of earth.

Walking at night beneath cloudy, moonless skies, I listen in vain for the call of a single owl, the bark of a single fox, the yip of a single coyote. Nothing. There is a spot where I can find sound. My path goes along thick stands of cattails. The ringing silence of the inky darkness is interrupted, when I am by the cattails, by what seems to be the muffled beat of a thousand wings. My dogs lunge and then pull back. I puzzle over the sound.

One morning I saw hundreds of blackbirds rise from the cattails and then, as quickly, vanish down into them once more. Then I knew that as I walked near them at night, I disturbed their slumber. They beat their wings in protest. Now I walk past that spot quickly. Though knowing there is still life on the planet is somewhat comforting to me, if not to the blackbirds.

Soon the sun will be drawing near to this place once more. Sunrise will move away from Mesa Verde toward the La Plata peaks and beyond. Sunset will depart from the Sleeping Ute toward the Abajos. The stillness will be shattered. Owls will call in the darkest moment before dawn. Blackbirds will sleep in the treetops.

December 27, 1987

OUTSIDE MY KITCHEN WINDOW is a wintry scene. Snow, driven by a south wind, is plastered against the glass. The door rattles in the gale, the eaves wail. Inside the window, buds on a young lemon tree swell toward bloom. Though separated only by a thin pane of glass, the exterior and interior landscapes function as if a thousand miles apart.

Later, in my office at work and surrounded by windows on three sides, the falling snow blots out the near world. The wind shifts with such ferocity that snow clings to all the windows. Nothing changes inside the office. Once again there seems no connection between the exterior and interior landscapes. If the storm abates even for a moment, I feel a slight twinge of regret.

A good blizzard never fails to set the imagination free. It makes it nearly impossible for me to actually get to a favorite cliff dwelling a few miles to the west. Thus, I can do little but imagine this snow swirling against those stone walls, settling on sills and drifting into dark interiors. Or I can envision the storm crashing into the rocky, forested rim of Yellowjacket Canyon forcing owls deeper into their dark crevices in the chill stone, the depths of the canyon itself hidden by the flying flakes.

The only problem with these flights of the imagination is that before long I'm anxious to experience the real thing. I'd rather be at that cliff dwelling or on the rim of that canyon in the storm. It is then that I become most aware of the "inside-outside" phenomenon that accompanies a good winter storm.

I am left then to wonder at all the life-forms that do not have what we call houses. Hawks, for instance. I have seen them at the onset of storms standing on fence posts facing into the blowing snow. Do they shift directions, like weather vanes, with the wind? Or do they ultimately take refuge in some sheltered spot?

In the end I am rewarded with one New Year's resolution for 1988—in addition to all the usual ones. I'll keep a closer eye on weather forecasts, and the next time we're about to be blessed with a good winter storm, I'll be outside in some sheltered spot with sleeping and cooking space. Then I'll know what it's like to be outside rather than inside.

January 24, 1988

MY DOGS HAVE SEVERAL DIFFERENT BARK STYLES. Most of them I am able to ignore. One of them is generally sounded after dark from the front porch. It is amiably conversational in tone. From a neighbor's a quarter mile away another dog barks back. The dogs are probably exchanging a mildly juicy bit of gossip. Another bark is less friendly. This tone is used to talk back to some distant coyote or fox. A third pattern of bark starts on the front porch and recedes down the lane. I know then that someone is coming to the house. I usually have time to get the dirty dishes in the sink.

One recent night I heard the bark that is impossible to ignore. It was a yipping, growling bark somewhere near the house. This generally translates itself in my brain into "skunk." I lock the doors and hope the car windows are rolled up. I have learned the hard way that rejected canines, dripping with skunk, will spend the night curled up in the driver's seat when accessible. I have learned, too, that it is unwise to wait until a good fight is in progress to make a dash to check out the car windows. Certain truths are best confronted at dawn.

This particular night I checked the locks—one dog can open, but not close, the front door herself—and peered out into the moonlit snow scene. The unfortunate creature dancing between the snouts of the lunging dogs was either a skunk from another planet or no skunk at all. It was as large as the dogs. I cautiously went outside for a closer look. A huge porcupine, puffed up for full battle, was doing a sort of whirling dervish in the snow. The dogs showed no signs of retreat.

I grabbed a stick from the porch and entered the war solidly on the side of the certain winner. In the end the porcupine would lose a fistful of quills and the dogs would be the losers. Or, more truthfully, I would be the loser. One sharp stroke at each dog's nose and each dog retreated. The offended porcupine headed up into a small apple tree. Not willing to let it go at that I poked once at the porcupine with the stick. Its tail hit the stick with the force of a mightily swung baseball bat. Quills were embedded deep into the wood.

I got the dogs—they were OK—into the house and went back to look once more at the porcupine. Its quills were then flat along its back and tail. It peered quizzically down at me. There, against the moonlit clouds, it had a beauty of its own.

January 31, 1988

THE VAST FIELDS that rise to the western sky here are now choppy seas of dazzling white, the deep snow drifted like waves from forested canyon rim to canyon rim. At dusk the fields dim to a translucent rose then to pale blue before sinking from sight into deep cobalt. The surface glazes then to reflect Venus in the dark western sky.

Those drifts have little respect for human progress. They block country roads with amazing speed. One morning I awoke to find a house-high drift extending along the north side of my house, obscuring views and preventing exit through the back door. When I returned home that drift was gone without a trace but further up the hill to the north a new, subtler drift arced like a crescent moon from lane to pasture fence. I regretted not having taken the day off to watch the drift's progress.

I tried to ignore the effect of a succession of storms and drifting winds upon the long, narrow lane ascending to my house. I would start up the lane at high speed and hope that momentum alone would carry me through the drifts and to the house. The one hazardous maneuver came at the top of the lane where a right angle turn had to be taken close to the inside or I would face a fifty-foot free fall into a lower pasture. This tactic succeeded for a couple of weeks. One night when it was snowing too hard to see the morning's ruts, I came to a halt right above the bend.

I walked out to a crossroads the next morning and caught a ride to work. I had difficulty in getting around the crosswise car even on foot. It was not difficult to imagine the vehicle blocking the lane until the Easter thaw at least.

I called a neighbor who had a snowplow and explained my dilemma in hopes that he could clear the lane as far as the car and I could dig it out. All day long I wondered about his progress. When I got home that evening, prepared to shovel into the night, I found a cleared lane between two huge snowbanks and my car, nicely swept off, sitting on a level spot well up the lane.

The neighbor explained that the job had been too much for the plow, and he'd resorted to a front end loader for much of the task.

"Next time," he said, "call sooner."

Now in the sub-zero mornings there are new drifts in the lane. I do not crash through them. They are like concrete. I more or less nose over them, expecting to bog down and high center. I think about calling my neighbor. This time he'll probably have to resort to dynamite.

I reassure myself that I'm learning a lot more about the formation of dunes.

March 27, 1988

THERE IS A TIME HERE each year when at noon feathery clouds spread like lace across the sky. They are the sign that afternoon winds will soon rise to buffet the frosted canyon rims. The winds are warm. They are whimsical. Their song in the trees is suddenly broken by motionless, ringing silence. Then comes another gust from another direction, and the voice of the wind is heard once more.

Sometimes no breeze stirs the grass where I am standing but the roar of the wind may still be heard from around a rocky bend, a choir of natural voices. In this wind two golden eagles spiral, plunge, and rise in the swirling air above Crow Canyon. The light glitters on the darkness of their wings. They swoop crazily among the treetops, then shoot once more into the air. Rabbits freeze in the speeding shadows of those eagles.

In the late afternoon there is the movement of deer against the last few banks of shadowed snow. As the light moves toward evening, the winds relent and the song of the birds takes rise over the dying windsong. It is then that the deer walk westward into a great field of tawny grass and weeds. Black in the last light, an owl glides across the path of the deer. The deer are there at dawn. In the first sun they move back into the trees.

The world of morning here is breezeless, silent. A gopher pokes his head from a ring of new earth near the pond. Prairie dogs chase one another in joyful circles in the meadow. The air is filled with the sound of meadowlarks and robins. Cottontails hop through stands of young sage. It is that bright, carefree moment after the silent flight of owls and before the whistling scream of hawks.

Then it is noon once more, and the first lace of cloud floats like a feather across the sky.

It is that cycle, that rhythm of each day, which marks this time. It is seen in shifts of light that can always be predicted but are never the same. It is seen in reflection, at the end of day when the clouds have thickened and the light dims. It is a rhythm not seen but not forgotten.

April 10, 1988

As I was donning my Levis one morning last week, I felt a quick scratching sensation against my right ankle.

I thought nothing about it until I glanced down and saw something that looked like a black marble beside my bare foot.

I'm still a lot more nimble than I'd assumed. I hopped backward to crash into the wall. The spider stayed put, wrapped up into a tight, venomous ball. I scooped it up on a dustpan and tossed it out the door into the dawn.

I spent the next half hour keeping an eye on the ankle and trying to remember the symptoms of a black widow bite. If a rapid, pounding heartbeat is a symptom, I concluded, then I was a goner. Half an hour later I began to feel like an alarmist fool and decided to drive to the office rather than to the emergency room. By noon I'd even overcome my determination to henceforth turn my trousers inside out before putting them on. By evening I'd forgotten the incident.

About midnight that night I awakened suddenly, knowing that something was crawling on my skin. My hop this time, I think, sent me crashing into the ceiling. My life did not flash before my eyes. Recollections of three friends who had been bitten by black widows while sleeping did occur to me before I hit the floor.

I groped for the light switch. Then I saw a tiny, agitated moth fluttering in circles on the sheet. While trying to get back to sleep, I thought about spiders. They do have a way of eliciting powerful responses from human beings, at least from me.

Spiders, I realized in the midnight darkness, are really quite tolerable creatures—as long as there is at least a minimum distance kept between self and spider. Even black widow spiders are so numerous in the slickrock country that they seem an inseparable part of the natural landscape. They are also incurably shy.

I thought about the place of spiders in the mythology of the Old World and New World. They are wise and creative creatures. On that reassuring note I fell asleep. The next morning I didn't turn my trousers inside out. I did give them a pretty healthy shake.

May 1, 1988

LIGHTNING DANCED ACROSS THE EARTH in the middle distance just beyond a forest of towering spires. The shadows of those great monoliths were cast dark upon whipping curtains of gale-driven rain. The lightning flashed, the shadows flickered. Thunder exploded with such force that the flame of a nearby candle trembled. There was an immense wildness to the storm, a sense of near total isolation from all things human.

I was not witnessing this storm in some remote desert valley studded with sandstone monuments and buttes. I was instead, one night last week, high in the tallest building on earth having dinner with friends in a private club. It would be hard to imagine a more urban setting. The thicket of nearby towers were the skyscrapers of downtown Chicago.

The Sears Tower, where we were gathered, may be one of the most technologically advanced structures in existence but, as the intensity of the storm grew, the wind seemed to work its way through a crack alongside a huge plate glass window. A heavy drapery billowed outward pushing china across a window table. The room cooled perceptibly. The tempo of our conversation slowed until we were finally reduced to silent spectators of the storm.

We might as well have been gathered in a cave in Monument Valley. When the storm broke, the difference was apparent. In Monument Valley there would have been the blackness of wet stone below and the flash of a million stars above. From the Sears Tower there was the blackness of wet sky above and the flash of a million city lights below. The storm forgotten, the tower seemed once more invulnerable to the forces of nature. We took up talking again.

I stayed at a friend's home overlooking Lake Michigan. Later that night I was awakened by the din of the storm returned, by thunder echoing down skyscraper canyons. Between rolls of thunder there was the hollow roar of waves crashing against storm walls. There is a sense of great permanence to the wall of buildings hard against the lake in that section of Chicago. But, listening to the roar of the storm-whipped lake, it was easy to imagine the city gone and the waves running far into the tall grass of a boundless prairie.

The next morning my friend spoke softly of missing the unpeopled expanses of the Four Corners Country. I asked if she had heard the lake in the night. No, she said.

May 15, 1988

I REALLY SURPRISED MYSELF. I bought a house in town. For a year I've been exploring the spectacular canyon rims of this country looking for a few acres where I could build a house. The house I imagined would be small and in a natural setting that required little care. After living for two years in the midst of treeless pastures with beautiful but distant vistas in every direction, I longed to look out a window and see something close at hand.

Cortez Realtor Alyne Eakins seemed to grasp all of the above at once. She directed me to several rural properties, some with houses and some without. All of them were appealing. I was in no hurry. Throughout the process I avoided looking at houses in town. I wanted that natural setting.

Then I learned about a house in town in a natural setting. Alyne took me there. The entire living area of the house is contained within a single small room. It sits on an acre of land covered by piñon and juniper and stepping down lichen-etched sandstone rims. The acre adjoins the town limits.

I went back several times alone or with my son Jonathan. One morning at dawn the air was filled with the melodic songs of canyon wrens. Those birds sold me on the house. So now, after several years of country living, I'm a town dweller once more. After living in a house that seemingly enclosed vast space, I'm settling into one small room. It's a white, bright room, just about exactly what I would have built for myself. I've already heard an owl at dusk and jays stealing cat food from the deck at dawn.

The best reward is to have neighbors close at hand, neighbors who chose this neighborhood because they too value its natural beauty. They are neighbors who have already demonstrated that they care about one another. I'm pleased, too, because I'm now within easy walking distance of two superb restaurants and a great bookstore.

So far my only walking has been at dusk along the edge of a cliff just below my house. Aside from the songs of night birds, the only sound is that of a stream in the canyon bottom far below.

It's good to be home at last, and that home is Cortez.

June 12, 1988

ONE RECENT EVENING an enormous thunderhead towered above the motionless face of the Sleeping Ute. The shape of the cloud changed with each blink of the eye as if it contained—imprisoned—some great energy seeking escape. As the shadowed western horizon rose further against the light of day, lightning flickered from deep within the glowing cloud. Then, so distant it was only a speck against the thunderhead, a nighthawk wheeled and dove, visible there until darkness claimed it.

There was in the solitary aerobatics of that single frail bird a simultaneous sense of overwhelming vulnerability and of daring against the fleeting mood which possesses this place at dusk in summer. It is a moment when the inorganic—cloud, stone, wind, light, sky—take such powerful dominion that all life seems a brief act of courage.

I went inside and latched the western windows against what I thought was the approaching storm. It never came. The cloud evaporated beneath the flashing stars. The breeze died. Life once again stirred in the darkness. Owls' calls floated up from the blackness of the canyon. Day birds chirped sleepily from perches in the taller sage. A deer's hooves were a slow staccato upon the rimrock. My dog Chaco sprawled on the deck, her legs twitching, chasing the deer in her dreams.

I sometimes wonder about the character and quality of beauty in such moments. We all know by now the answer to the ancient question, "If a tree falls in the forest . . . ?" Of course there is sound, because we know that sound is a physical event independent of the presence or absence of the human ear. But beauty—is beauty present in these moments at dusk without the presence of human aesthetic perception?

Somehow, I think the nighthawk knew.

July 31, 1988

I WENT IN SEARCH OF A CIRCLE and found a square.

The circle I'd seen once several years ago set in an aspen grove high on a divide between two deep red rock canyons. It was about twenty feet across and made long ago of stones since fused together by a lace of green lichen. The circle was so perfect in shape that it surely was a human creation.

It was late afternoon when I made camp and set out to find the circle. The divide is narrow but flat-topped. Points jut out into surrounding canyons. The canyon walls plunge steeply on all sides but, on top, the walking is easy. I had initially stumbled across the circle while hiking, had spent a few minutes examining it, then walked on. Now, years later, I tried to recall any surrounding landmark that would serve as an indication of the circle's location.

At sunset, thin pink clouds glowed through the western aspens; I returned to camp. In the darkness, with no fire, I did nothing but look at flashing stars. All I could remember about the location of the circle was that it was in a clearing on a slight northward slope.

At dawn I set out to find the clearing. By midmorning I'd catalogued several clearings, all north-sloping. I knew I wouldn't find the circle. When I'd first seen it, cattle had grazed the grass to the soil. Now there were no cattle, and the thick grass was waist high. The circle was hidden.

In the afternoon I explored the head of a nearby canyon. A steep slope plunged nearly a thousand feet to the rim of the canyon cliffs. The rim itself was another thousand vertical feet above the canyon floor. On the slope, I traversed this way and then that on ancient game trails etched into red earth. Towering pines, far beyond the lumberman's reach, shaded the arid earth.

Trails seemed to converge. I rounded a bend and found a spring and pool set in a narrow shelf on the slope. That was reward enough for the effort. I turned back.

When I was nearly back to camp, back up in the aspen once more, I stumbled upon another spring. Next to it was an ancient, small corral built of aspen logs. It was perfectly square. The corral had been built to keep an animal in, I assumed, but, forgotten over the decades, had served to keep all animals out. Within its barricades was a tiny, lush jungle of native plants beyond the reach of deer, elk, and cattle.

That night, stargazing from camp once more, I realized that I'd come looking for neither the lost circle nor the found square. It was solitude, silence, and stars I'd sought. I resolved, however, to return soon in search of that ring of stone. It seemed as good an excuse as any.

August 7, 1988

THERE ARE THOSE RARE AND FLEETING MOMENTS when the equilibrium within the cosmos reveals itself in the world that meets the eye. I glanced out the window before dawn one recent morning and saw the full moon floating above the folded arms of Sleeping Ute Mountain. I forgot about the morning routine of preparing to go to the office and sat out on the deck.

The moon floated behind thin wisps of grey cloud in the early light. There was a deep blue silhouette in the crystal, rain-washed dawn. A quarter of an hour later the mountain had risen to touch the bottom of the moon. The bands of cloud changed from ash to glowing pink. As the moon vanished behind the mountain, the first rays of sunlight touched its highest peak.

There was in that instant an almost tangible sense of all things fitting together, earth and sky, night's end and sunrise, light and shadow.

A balance had been struck between sun and moon.

With the sunlight, the sage-fragrant silence was broken. Jays swooped in to steal the cat's food. A hungry jay is incapable of respectful silence. The first jay was soon joined by ten noisy colleagues. My cat and dog, who prefer fresh food for breakfast, simply sat by while the jays attacked the prior day's leftovers. I turned back toward the morning routine.

Then, out of the corner of my eye, I saw a flash of russet plunge into the midst of the jays, then vanish as quickly as it had come. It wasn't the cat. He sat looking baffled. The jays scattered screaming with indignation. One jay remained, cocked its head this way and that, and resumed its feast. Suddenly the remaining jay flew straight up. This time the russet invader collided with the jay. A few feathers drifted down through the early light. The jay reappeared, relatively intact, on a nearby cottonwood branch.

I walked to the cat's dish and looked up into another small cottonwood. A sparrow hawk stared down at me. The jay hopped forlornly further back into its tree, silent at last. The hawk viewed me with disdain and flew off.

The attacks by the hawk had come less than a minute apart. There was an undeniable, deadly violence to the encounters, though the jays had escaped. I thought back a few minutes to the setting moon and rising sun. Had the magic of that moment been destroyed? No. Instead the morning had offered two insights instead of one.

August 14, 1988

I WAS AWAKENED by the light of a half moon as it rose from the top of a canyon wall a half mile above me. The stairstepping cliffs of the opposite canyon wall were a dark red in the cool light. A few silver clouds floated against the thin band of stars visible between the canyon rims. There was no sound but that of the stream a few yards away.

It would be hours until dawn, but I was thoroughly awake. I got up and set off walking downcanyon. A rain shower an hour before had left little trace but droplets on the grass and sage sparkling in the moonlight. When I entered the shadow of some pinnacle or promontory on the east wall of the canyon, I slowed and stepped gingerly, fearful of snakes. I reminded myself that the nearest emergency room was in Cortez, hours away.

Ahead of me the canyon rounded a hairpin bend before resuming its northward course. My route left the canyon floor and headed toward a saddle in the point formed by the bend. Once I had reached that ridge, I could look down in either direction and see the moonlit stream hundreds of feet below me. From that height even the stream was silent.

The moonlight had the effect of magnifying the heights and depths around me. The silence seemed to add to that effect, particularly to expand the starry sky above. Such moments of total silence, I think, are quite rare, even in wilderness. Almost always there is at least a whisper of a breeze, the clatter of a falling rock, the call of one night bird to another more distant. I had stumbled onto a moment of pure silence.

I returned to camp and slept until the first streaks of dawn lit the sky and the half moon floated directly above, suspended midway between the canyon rims. I went to the stream and fished, returning one young catfish after another to the churning waters. The sound of the stream echoed from the rock hanging above it. I thought of the silence of the night before and was glad when my sons joined me to fish in the brightening dawn. The silence receded in memory.

October 2, 1988

THE NORTHERN FACE OF MESA VERDE has turned from green to a soft tapestry of crimson, gold, and orange. Stands of aspen are golden near the peak of Ute Mountain and on the rugged west slopes of the La Plata Mountains. The cottonwoods along Crow Canyon Creek are still a deep green but splashed with scattered leaves of gold. New snowfall shines silver on Lone Cone in the earliest light of dawn.

Mountain brooks are clear as crystal at timberline between tundra-gentled banks. Bronze leaves, fallen from willows, whirl in the liquid eddies before cascading on downstream into the dark shadows of fir forests. At dawn meadows glisten beneath frost.

It is a season when I try to imagine the people who were here thousands of years ago. There were no farms. The people moved with the seasons. In the summer they would have been in the mountains. In autumn they would have moved to and across the mesas and toward winter, having waited for the obvious sign, for the frost on the tundra. Or would they have sensed the coming changes before they could be seen or felt?

They were a people with few barriers between camps in the basins and canyons.

I wonder about the signs they heeded as summer slipped from the peaks and it came time to turn toward lower country. Would they have themselves and nature? They moved with nature and were essentially a part of nature. As I think of those people pursuing their seasonal round between high country and low, I wonder, too, just how much we really differ from them in the end. We have placed more barriers between ourselves and the elements, and we have trained the land to produce more or less. Thus, we can settle into one spot and stay put.

I'm not sure the differences go much beyond mobility and staying put. We haven't really removed ourselves from nature. That may be why, in autumn, something tugs on our souls as if the time had come to move on.

February 26, 1989

THE DAWN SKY, but for a band of deep purple in the west, was steel grey. A thin band of clouds stretched just above the horizon. The full moon slipped behind the clouds, then emerged. The first sunlight struck the snow on the mountains. The moon vanished, a pale disk, into the junipers.

I walked across frozen ground in that first light. Frost glittered on every surface, but there was in the clarity of the dawn a hint of spring, a sense that a hard winter was slipping effortlessly away.

Later I glanced across a snow-covered field. Four coyotes, perfectly equidistant from one another like points on a diamond, stood facing west. They were absolutely motionless. From the west, very slowly, a fifth coyote approached the quartet. I felt as if I had inadvertently stumbled across some coyote ceremony, as if the four were preparing to meet some very important emissary from a coyote clan in the west.

In the canyon below my house, the stream has vanished beneath a crust of ice, and snow has broken free and now runs a deep golden brown, lashing at the willows lining its banks. The stream grows wider and deeper with each sunlit hour. By noon, on country roads and trails, the frozen earth has given way to soupy mud. Sheets of water trickle down sandstone ledges.

I find myself willing to accept this illusion of spring as irreversible. I tell myself that the fragrance of wet earth will soon be replaced by the smell of sun-dried soil. But then I glance up from these warming mesas to the towering peaks. To do so is to glance backward into a winter far from ended.

Winds in that thin air whip banners of snow southward from the frozen peaks. Sometimes the peaks themselves vanish in those icy gales. There is a warning in that chilling sight. Winter has retreated from the mesas and canyons to the mountains.

Those mountains are not so far away.

March 26, 1989

IN 1874, THEN AGAIN IN 1875, noted photographer William H. Jackson ventured into what is now Montezuma County.

Jackson's account of the expedition, a part of the report of the Hayden Survey, was first published in 1876. It contains detailed sketches of ruins in this area.

Last Sunday an archaeologist friend and I, with the Jackson Report in hand, set out in search of some of the ruins in the sketches. We walked up slanted beds of cream and rose-colored Navajo Sandstone toward distant cliffs of the same. It was a leisurely stroll.

My friend stopped frequently to examine a ceramic fragment or piece of worked stone before putting it back where she found it. Her description of the artifacts along the way created strong images of the vanished people whose ancient homes we were seeking.

Before long we came upon one of the sites sketched in the book. It was identifiable only by the surrounding rock formation—which was depicted with amazing accuracy. Not a stone was left standing intact. Houses that had stood for six centuries before Jackson's arrival had been mindlessly destroyed in the last century. The same was true of the next sketched site we located, and then the third.

We stopped by a small cliff dwelling for a picnic lunch. The midden beneath the ruin was pitted with recently dug holes and crude trenches. We were on public land where such vandalism and looting is illegal but ugly, mindless destruction goes on and on.

As we continued our walk, my friend would approach standing stone walls to satisfy her professional curiosity. I found myself holding back. I preferred to view the ruins from a distance great enough to mask the recent graffiti and traces of looting.

A couple of evenings later, at the vernal equinox, my friend and I went to a nearby spot to watch the sun set behind Monument Valley and Navajo Mountain—visible on the very distant western horizon. Between ourselves and those distant buttes was the vast expanse of the Four Corners Country explored by Jackson in 1874.

I found myself wishing my friend and I had been with Jackson—before so much of the past of this place had been so viciously mutilated.

April 9, 1989

I DIDN'T KNOW WHERE the winding, narrow road was taking me. On one side, Wingate Sandstone cliffs rose into the southern sky. On the other, the Colorado River sparkled in the late light through thickets of willow and tamarisk. In the yards of occasional farmhouses, fruit trees bloomed and daffodils leaned in the breeze.

The pavement ended. The road turned away from the river and into the mouth of a side canyon. A small stream wound through the shadowy depths. On its banks, ancient cottonwoods wore the soft green of new leaves. At a place where the canyon widened, I abandoned the vehicle and continued along the road on foot. There was no sound but the wistful songs of canyon wrens.

I was not far from Moab where I'd gone to watch my son Jonathan and Durangoans including Brent Brown and Ned Overend compete in the annual Moab Stage Race. Moab was crowded with tourists and cyclists. The canyon seemed a world away from that bustle.

The next morning, on my way home, I stopped on a high sandstone bench for another walk. The springtime world of the canyons was behind me. A chill wind whipped down from the Abajos. The air, swept by that wind, was clear. Distant peaks shone in the early sun. Crows played in the turbulent sky. The wind whistled through tawny grass. Fifty yards away I saw an antelope, motionless as the stone, looking back at me. I stopped. We stood staring at one another for as long as I could stand the wind. As I retreated, he turned and, somewhat disdainfully, walked in the other direction.

Now, back in my office, the springtime canyon and the antelope are fragments of memory. Here there are the constant songs of meadowlarks in the meadow, the crowing of cock pheasants at dawn, and the shrill warnings of a pair of Canada geese keeping interlopers away from what has become their private pond. A mountain lion is sometimes heard at night in the rocky ledges across the meadow.

It is springtime in the Four Corners Country . . . a time of warmth, of cold, and of change.

May 28, 1989

"Air in motion" is a dictionary definition of wind. This spring, to the inhabitants of this place, wind has become much more than that.

It is a dimension of the natural world in which it is harder and harder to find beauty.

The air is unseasonably hot, unseasonably dry, and constantly in motion, sometimes with gale force. Last week the wind did not begin until afternoon. This week it is a growing presence within an hour or two after sunrise. By dusk it is whistling around and buffeting every exposed surface of soil and rock. Sheets of airborne dust spin along country roads. Whirlwinds catch the last light. Even the clouds do not build into the great towers of evening but are fanned out and dispersed by the wind.

People here who do not have to go outside do not now go outside. People who have to work outside become weary and look baffled by their weariness as if they have not yet fixed the blame on the unceasing motion of the air. There is something about this wind that strikes below the level of constant consciousness. Maybe we find it difficult to acknowledge a presence over which we have no control. Or maybe it's merely resignation.

This wind is more than uncomfortable. It is becoming a peril. Builder Dick Glasco, who is working at Crow Canyon, found no soil moisture at the bottom of four-foot excavations. Dryland farmers have completed the first cutting of alfalfa early in hopes of salvaging some of it. They are worried about the winter wheat. Beans have not yet been planted, and no one knows what will happen after they are.

Wind is always a part of springtime here. One has only to glance across this landscape to see that its principal sculptor is the wind. This shaping process has been going on for millions of years. This year it seems as if the wind wants to get the job over and done with.

June 4, 1989

FROM MY OFFICE WINDOW I can see a brief slope that rises to meet the near southern horizon. The red earth of the slope is concealed in most places by groves of piñon and juniper and stands of sage. What little stone is visible is covered with ancient lichen.

It is not unusual to see deer moving through the shadows. Rabbits emerge from the sage to seek food in the sparse grass. Mourning doves sometimes join the rabbits. Once I glanced up to see a tawny animal moving with grace and speed across a clearing on the slope. At first I thought it was a coyote but it moved in a different way. I suspect it was the elusive mountain lion whose voice is heard from the rocky rims along Crow Canyon.

When I do not want to stare at the piles of work tumbled across my desk, I stare at the slope instead. I imagine myself following the tracks of deer through shadows and sage. I tell myself that this idleness may indeed be productive, that when I look back at my desk, the problems will have rearranged themselves into solutions. That does happen sometimes.

I can look north from my desk, as well, across an abandoned farmstead up Crow Canyon to the place where distant fields rise to the edge of the Dolores Canyon on the northern horizon. I cannot see the Dolores Canyon but can see across it to the Ponderosa forest on the Glades . . . another good place to let the imagination wander.

It is to the east window of my office that I turn my back. That window overlooks Crow Canyon and the rocky rims across it. Beyond those ledges rise the La Plata Mountains and the scalloped edges of Mesa Verde. The temptation looking east is not merely to let my mind wander, but to let the rest of me wander with it.

It would probably be stretching it to convince myself that wandering off into the aspens on those near mountains would clear the work from my desk.

June 25, 1989

LAST WEEK I DESCRIBED my first two days as a participant in the weeklong novice program at the Crow Canyon Archaeological Center. Although I've been on the staff of the Center for several years, I'd never completed the participant program. After a day of introductory activities overseen by staff educators Lew Matis and Beth Wheeler, I assisted with the excavation of a probability square at Sand Canyon Pueblo for a day.

On Wednesday I joined other novices for a day in the Crow Canyon research laboratory under the watchful eye of Margie Connolly, an archaeologist and educator. We learned to distinguish worked stone (lithics) from unworked stone shaped by nature alone. We were shown, too, how to identify ceramics from the different periods of Anasazi occupation of this region. Then we sorted bags of artifacts according to such broad categories as lithics, ceramics, and animal bone. The preceding exercises made that sorting a process of discovery in itself. We ended our day in lab by washing artifacts coming in from the sites. It was fascinating to see patterns emerge after centuries of concealment.

Thursday and Friday we were back excavating with archaeologists Bruce Bradley—who oversees research at the massive site—and Jim Kleidon. I also worked with Cindy Paul in another probability square. Bradley assigned me to the 1000 Block, an architectural unit containing a kiva, adjoining rooms, and a D-shaped tower. My task was to continue removing fallen rock from the upper level of what remained of the tower. Bradley showed me what to watch for—"corner stones" that had fallen from windows or doors in the semi-collapsed tower. These, when found, were mapped according to vertical and horizontal position before being removed. All of the fallen stone was then stacked in a manner that would allow measurements indicating the original height of the completed tower. I concluded my participation in Crow Canyon's program by spending a day with archaeologists Mark Varien—who heads the small site testing program at Crow Canyon—and Kristin Kuckleman. Through test excavations of small sites in the Sand Canyon Locality, Varien hopes to gain a greater insight into their relationship to Sand Canyon Pueblo and, thus, into Sand Canyon Pueblo itself. One of the sites is located atop a ridge with magnificent views in every direction and another at the base of a colorful sandstone cliff. All of the test sites contain the potential—as does Sand Canyon Pueblo—for contributing to a better understanding of what was happening among the Anasazi in the final decades leading to the ultimate abandonment of this region by those prehistoric farmers.

I was sorry when my days as a Crow Canyon participant were over. Not only had I made new friends among the participants, but I had a better understanding of why hundreds of people come to Crow Canyon each year to assist with the painstaking reconstruction of an ancient and remarkable culture.

A trowel, I learned, is not wielded lightly, and excavation is just an initial brief step in the process of archaeological research. The greater the appreciation of the Anasazi produced by research, the greater the humility with which the trowel is applied.

July 2, 1989

I WAS STANDING ATOP a pile of rock on the crest of the McElmo Dome west of Cortez talking about the more favorable farming conditions there created by deep, wind-deposited soils and greater rainfall. Suddenly I was hit by a strong gust of dusty wind and a spattering of raindrops. I began to topple from my perch. Dr. Alfonso Ortiz, standing on firmer footing next to me, grabbed my elbow and kept me from blowing away. The wind was gone as suddenly as it arrived.

The people to whom I had been speaking began to laugh at nature's perfect timing and the effect it had on me. That was the end of science for the evening. I was relieved and, I suspect, so was my audience.

The gust of wind was followed by perfect calm. We wandered silently for a while among small, thirteenth-century ruins and then to a rocky rim overlooking a deep canyon opening to the west. The air was filled with dust as the sun sank toward Elk Ridge on the flanks of the Abajos. Familiar, distant landmarks were obscured by the dust. The setting sun was a crimson disc departing a surreal land. I thought about the few raindrops earlier that evening. They were the first I'd felt since February.

Time seems a bit warped in this drought-stricken place. Early summer has the look of autumn where fields of alfalfa stubble have turned brown, offering no hope of the usual second cutting. The leaves of native shrubs on the high mesas hang limp as if struck by frost. Except for rare moments, the dust-laden wind never ceases.

Droughts are to be expected here. They have visited this place time after time in the fifteen hundred years since the first crops were planted in this fertile soil. They leave their mark first on the outer landscape, then droughts begin to shape the inner landscape of the mind as well.

July 16, 1989

AT NOON ON SATURDAY, as viewed from Cortez, the forest fire manifested itself as a thin spiral of smoke rising from beyond the scalloped ridges that form the northern rims of Mesa Verde. As time passed, the smoke thickened. Sunday afternoon, as firestorms exploded on the mesa, the smoke grew into a thick, seething, black column miles across. The sun dimmed to a deep orange. Flakes of white ash drifted down on Cortez. The fire jumped the ridges and flames were visible from town, thousands of feet below.

People came together in groups to stare at the spectacle. They said very little to one another. It was an awesome, indescribable event of nature that spoke for itself. It brought a sense of helplessness and ineffectiveness to all who saw it. While the fire posed no physical danger to Cortez, to see it was to see the essence of danger in nature.

That night the flames, viewed through the smoke, were strands of fire suspended in the southern sky. The flames had a beauty of their own.

For seventy-two hours Mesa Verde National Park Superintendent Bob Heyder probably saw very little beauty in the fire. The fire was a threat to human life, efforts to contain it threatened irreplaceable archaeological resources, and the future of the local economy was put in doubt. Under the severe pressure caused by a rapidly exploding fire, Heyder made all the right decisions.

Containment efforts were begun the instant the fire was discovered. Archaeologists were made a vital part of the fire fighting effort, assuring sensitivity to archaeological sites. The Park was closed when it was obvious the fire would spread in the prevailing hot, dry, and windy conditions. The decision to close the Park assured the safety of thousands of park-bound tourists and freed park personnel to concentrate on fighting the fire.

Without those difficult decisions, the fire would probably still be raging, and people probably would have been injured or killed and the Park's priceless attractions and buildings marred or destroyed. The local economy would have suffered a major, lasting blow.

As it turned out, the fire's most lasting effect will be as a reminder of nature's powerful potential for shaping our lives.

July 30, 1989

THE SONG CAME from deep in the throats of the men as they danced. There were no words, just the sound of thirty singers in such perfect unison that it seemed an amplification of a single, deep voice. Their movements were equally in unison. The kachina dancers wore high tablitas on their foreheads above collars of spruce boughs covering their faces and shoulders. Each wore a fox skin draped down the lower back and a turtle shell behind the knee which clicked with each brief step. Inside the crescent of kachinas were more dancers dressed as women. They used instruments which mimicked the sound of grinding corn. The sound of the dance was mesmerizing.

I was in a Hopi village with Katina Owen and Mark Varien to see the Niman, or home-going, dances of the kachinas on their departure for the San Francisco Peaks to the south. The dance also serves as a call for rain. We joined several hundred other spectators on the ground and the rooftops surrounding the plaza. As the dance progressed, thick clouds formed beneath the sun. Then a few raindrops splashed to the earth.

At sunset, many miles to the south of the Hopi mesas, we visited a kiva being excavated by Chuck Adams in one of the prehistoric Homolovi villages. Against the brilliant bronze of the western horizon, the San Francisco Peaks were looming silhouettes. The people of the village where we'd witnessed the dance that day regard the Homolovi villages as ancestral. I wondered if the Niman ceremony had once taken place in that large, square Homolovi kiva where we stayed late into dusk.

Among the sites we visited the next day was one on a flattopped, high butte rising from the barren purple landscape of the Petrified Forest. It was nearly a thousand years older than the villages of Homolovi. Slightly discernible circles of standing slabs were about all that remained of that ancient village.

There was a striking similarity between the modern Hopi village, the Homolovi villages, and the village atop the flat butte. All are located in settings which strike our eye as barren and uninviting. All are located where it would seem that nothing would grow, in places that farmers should shun. Each of the settings, however, has a haunting beauty of its own and in each of them the hypnotic song of the Niman seems very much at home.

August 27, 1989

MY DOG CHACO loves electrical storms. The first distant flash of lightning has her leaping at the door to get out. She awaits the first drum roll of thunder and goes barking after it. As the storm nears, she works herself into a near frenzy, moving fast in every direction without a moment of silence. For some time I allowed myself to believe that she saw herself as protecting me against the approaching storm because, whenever there was a quiet interval, she would return to the door as if to tell me she was responsible for the moment's calm.

Lately, on closer observation, I've concluded that her storm ritual has nothing to do with me. What Chaco is in fact doing is calling down the rain. With the first drop of rain she returns to the deck and plants herself there with nose straight into the wind and tail straight away. She stays that way until thoroughly soaked. Lightning and thunder may crash around her but the dog remains motionless after the rain begins to fall. Once drenched she comes inside, runs to me, shakes herself, and hops onto the couch.

I don't know whether it was Chaco or the storm itself that awakened me one recent night. The dog was barking at the door and threatening to go into her rainmaking routine inside the house. The room was lit by a continual bright flicker, lightning across the canyon. At the thought of the wreckage that would ensue if Chaco remained inside, I resigned myself to stumbling to the door and freeing the dog.

Chaco's efforts quickly produced results. The rain struck in horizontal sheets, delivered upon house-shaking gusts of wind. I was sleepy but decided the show was too good to miss. I sat looking out the west window into the teeth of the storm. The house was encircled by a curtain of lightning. Worried about the proximity of the strikes, I managed to coax a somewhat disappointed Chaco in from her perch on the deck . . . by which time I was as drenched as the dog. I toweled myself dry and fell back into bed.

The next day, in the first cobalt light of dawn, Chaco stood at the west window looking out and making small sounds. Two mourning doves had lit beneath the window beside a ripe clump of Indian rice grass that had been flattened by the storm. The birds breakfasted there until the sky brightened to gold.

It was one of those still, crystal mornings that visit this place in the wake of nighttime storms.

September 10, 1989

LAST SATURDAY MORNING I stood on a knoll overlooking the Rio Puerco in Arizona. Surrounding me were the remnants of a large prehistoric pueblo dating to approximately A.D. 1100. The pueblo was encircled by an earthen berm several hundred feet in circumference. Through two openings in the berm, traces of prehistoric roads could be seen leading into the high desert landscape.

I was with archaeologists Andrew Fowler, John Stein, and Mark Varien. For several years Fowler and Stein have been giving their own time to mapping large sites in northern New Mexico and Arizona and classifying the ceramic sherds scattered across them.

Later in the weekend we visited massive thirteenth-century sites in remote, canyon-creased areas of New Mexico. These abandoned pueblos—like the pueblos of the time periods before them—exhibit characteristics unique to themselves in terms of architectural and ceramic design and, yet, also share characteristics that are common to hundreds of pueblos scattered across the vast Anasazi world from the Rio Grande to the Grand Canyon and from the San Juan Mountains to the Mogollon Rim.

At the end of the thirteenth century the common characteristics shared across that great expanse began to disappear. Far more regionalized cultures, each more distinct in itself, began to appear across the former Anasazi world. At the same time, long-occupied areas were abandoned and sparsely populated areas began to gain population.

Virtually nothing is known about the vast cultural framework or processes, which stretched through time and space and which enabled Anasazi communities in any given time period to simultaneously share architectural and ceramic designs and other common characteristics. Thus, nothing really is known about why those shared characteristics began vanishing when they did. It is to addressing such questions that Fowler and Stein will make a contribution.

At sundown Sunday I was back in the world of the living, standing on a crowded rooftop with Mark Varien looking down into an enclosed plaza in Zuni Pueblo. The plaza was filled with masked dancers moving in unison to their own song. They seemed as bound together by some intangible concept as had been the deserted communities of the Anasazi.

We still know very little about these ancient living communities and their prehistoric predecessors.

September 17, 1989

THE RAIN CLOUDS COME and the rain clouds go. I was awakened recently by a clap of thunder. I listened in the darkness for the sound of rain. It didn't come. I drifted to sleep and awakened later to the flash of stars in early dawn. The drought that has gripped this place since February—briefly broken by early August rains—continues to cause plants to wither and die.

The exception came one night last week when Duane Smith was to give a lecture under the stars in Mesa Verde National Park. At sundown a massive cloudbank moved in from the west obscuring the Sleeping Ute behind curtains of rain. Soon the wind whipped the rain in horizontal sheets against the northern ramparts of Mesa Verde. Duane's talk was moved into an area protected from the rain but not the cold. He shivered during his brief lecture. We can only guess how much more we would have learned had the evening been a mellower one.

On the La Platas the clouds do leave traces of snow, and the mountain mahogany and Gambel oak are turning in the upper foothills. Asters and coreopsis are a blend of purple and gold along the road between Cortez and Durango. Rabbitbrush is blooming a pale yellow beside the grey sage.

At nightfall now there are the autumnal calls of owls and at noon the screams of hawks over Crow Canyon. In the early light of morning, flocks of Canada geese cry out against a lightening sky.

At any time of day there is the chorus of coyotes again and again announcing the demise of a hapless rabbit or squirrel.

The drought is an unwelcome presence here, but otherwise the seasons march on without hesitation.

September 24, 1989

THERE WAS A BRIEF RAIN SHOWER an hour after dawn. From my west window I could see a perfect rainbow arcing up from the canyon floor. Through the rainbow, Ute Mountain was ablaze with autumn color. Streaks of golden aspen streamed down from the stony peak to touch the bronze oak and mountain mahogany on the gentler lower slopes.

I recalled a recent evening after work when I went with an archaeologist to a large prehistoric site on the lower slopes of Ute Mountain. From that perspective that isolated mountain range we call the Sleeping Ute was more a series of sharp ridges and deep valleys, dominated by the peak, than the usual familiar silhouette of a reclining giant against the western sky.

The ruin is a looming, multistoried structure with massive masonry walls more than two feet thick. Only the tops of the remaining walls are visible above the mounded fallen stone of the upper walls. This ancient structure is surrounded by later, lower structures on three sides—a thick crescent of decaying architecture opening onto the floor of the South Valley to the east. A few yards below the ends of the crescent is a large, walled square surrounding a circular great kiva.

There is an astonishing formality to these straight lines, rectangles, squares, and circles when contrasted with the rugged mountain range against which they stand. Archaeologists across the

Southwest are addressing the question of what information might be encoded in the architecture of prehistoric ruins. The more I visit sites with archaeologists, the more interested—and perplexed—I become. How did the people who created these communities conceptualize them before construction began? Does the answer to that question exist in the archaeological record today? If so, how can it be discerned?

We wandered through the ruins until the sun had set behind Ute Mountain and a chill breeze came down those slopes. In the east the great cliffs of Mesa Verde reflected the last light. A distant arc of peaks, from the La Platas to Lone Cone, were lavender beneath bronze thunderheads.

It was time to go home. I left reluctantly.

October 8, 1989

THE MOUNTAIN COLORS are fading now and the brilliance of autumn is beginning to advance across the mesas. The cottonwoods in Crow Canyon have gone from green to golden, and the asparagus along the fence lines is a deep yellow adorned with scarlet berries.

Recently I traveled along Elk Ridge west of Blanding from the Bear's Ears across the Notch to the Chippean Rocks and the Causeway. We stopped at the head of Arch Canyon to look down across slopes of blazing aspen into the pink depths of that chasm. There was no sound but the soft song of mourning doves.

Later, in the last light, we wound our way among the Chippean Rocks. The Utah maple groves were splashes of deep crimson, pink, and pale yellow against the white stone. Far below, across the Great Sage Plain stretching from the Abajos to the La Platas, town and farm lights began flickering on in the lengthening shadows of western mountains.

That vast expanse between the Abajos and the La Platas, between the Dolores Canyon and Mesa Verde, is gashed by deep canyons cutting toward the San Juan River. When looking across it from mountain viewpoints, one is impressed with the apparent lack of a human imprint upon the land. By day one sees a crescent of farmlands arcing from Cortez in the east to Monticello in the west. At night there is the sparse sprinkling of lights that conforms to the same crescent.

It is only when wandering through the piñon and juniper forests and sage parks of that expanse that one begins to realize that the human population is concentrated in a much smaller area today than it once was. Deserted prehistoric pueblos are found far to the west of modern fields in the arid lands where the mesas stairstep and crumble into the San Juan Valley.

It is easy to wonder then why different cultures interact so differently with the natural landscape.

October 15, 1989

I STEPPED ONTO MY DECK one recent morning to hear the owls call up the dawn. The air was crystal clear. Orion floated motionless in the central sky. Deer hooves clicked on the rimrock below. A thin line of cloud above the La Platas in the east caught the first light. The frozen air soon drove me back inside.

The sounds of owls calling along the canyon reminded me of the grotesque death not long ago of an owl of whom I'd become rather fond. When driving along a certain country road in the evening after sunset, I'd see the owl perched atop the same power pole near the crest of a hill. Sometimes, before sunrise, it would be there in the morning. Occasionally I would slow to a stop, and the owl would cast a cynical glance in my direction before turning back to the more significant task of scanning the roadside for a meal.

A week ago I looked at the pole and saw the owl. It was not perched but hanging from a power line by one foot. The bird was dead. It had probably touched a parallel power line with a wing tip and been electrocuted. It was a sad way for that proud bird to die.

A day later I encountered an owl in broad daylight. It flew up from a cave in a small cliff along which I was walking. The owl glided to a landing in a patch of shade beneath a nearby tree. It glared at me warily, angrily. I left its territory as quickly as possible.

I can never think of owls as friendly or cute. They are imposing and somewhat fierce creatures. There is a certain charm, however, in their calls to one another along the canyons in the first light of day.

December 17, 1989

I WENT WEST A WAYS last Sunday to a narrow finger of mesa top between two deep canyons and found more than I'd set out to see. I was caught unawares by a certain chill slant of light. Solstice light. It is that distant, dim light—seen only in December—in which color grows more deeply brilliant.

I walked along a cliff edge, stopping now and then to warm myself in some stony refuge from the wind. The wind screamed through sharp breaks in the rock. Snow flurries whipped across Ute Mountain but left no trace of white on the peak. The Abajo Mountains played hide and seek behind their own turbulent bank of clouds.

I found what I'd gone to see—a thirteenth-century pueblo gathered around a small canyonhead. In the shadows below, spring water dripped onto ice. There was no other sound but the wind in the standing remnants of curving stone masonry walls. It was a face-numbing, cold wind.

I had gone there to see those ancient walls but ended up seeing, instead, the light upon them. At noon the walls cast long shadows across the sage. I was alone and was, in that low light and the song of that wind, more aware of my aloneness than usual. Again, I sought refuge from the cold in the ruins and found it there.

In a few days, I thought, the sun's long retreat will end and its return begin.

The clouds were gone from the Abajos and the Ute when I left the ruin and walked south into the sun, the wind at my back. I departed reluctantly. I could return to the walls at any time. It was the light on the stone that would soon change.

I was glad I was alone when I came across the solstice light. That light itself had enough to say.

December 24, 1989

THE CLOUDS THAT APPEAR each day in the west over Ute Mountain and spread to the east over the La Platas now seem to taunt the land below. They offer the hope of snow but vanish on their eastward journey leaving only dry earth below.

A friend who is working on a doctoral dissertation on the relationship between precipitation and crop productivity here in the Montezuma Valley recently wrote me saying, "My numerical data indicate especially dry years in the recent historical period as being 1896, 1899, 1902, 1904, 1946, 1951 and 1959."

This year may end as the driest year since official weather records have been kept here. Less than half the average precipitation has fallen thus far in 1989. The drought has already taken a heavy toll in the dry farming areas of the county.

My friend's research will cover not only the historical period here but every year since A.D. 700. I look at the distant peaks covered only by traces of snow and wonder how many times in the past so much mountain stone has been visible at the winter solstice. How many times in the past thousand years have the farms of the Montezuma Valley been parched by drought?

In the historic period here, at least, excessively wet years have followed not long after each unusually dry year. Because of my friend's research, we will soon know if that pattern holds for the past thirteen hundred years.

With more feeling than ever, here's wishing one and all a very white Christmas.

December 31, 1989

MY FIRST RESPONSE to what I saw was a sense of loss. With my son Jonathan, I had hiked to a petroglyph panel in a nearby canyon—a panel I'd first visited several years ago. The panel stretched nearly a hundred feet across the nooks and crannies of a blocky sandstone cliff.

On my return to the panel, I discovered that a huge chunk of the inscribed stone had fallen face forward and shattered upon the talus slope below. Many of the petroglyphs I wanted to see were beneath fragments of the fallen block of cliff, fragments weighing several tons each. The event had occurred so recently that trees felled by the crashing stone were still slightly green and limber.

One of the questions I had hoped to answer in returning to study the petroglyph panel was whether each single marking had any apparent relation to the hundreds of others in the panel as a whole. By removing the center of the panel—a substantial part of the center—nature had made it impossible ever to know the answer to that question or even to speculate upon it in any reasonable way.

Part of the cultural legacy of this region had been irretrievably taken by the destruction of a segment of the petroglyph panel. It took me awhile to get over my indignation and my search for someone or something to blame. Nature had taken its course without any regard for my particular priorities or for the thousand-year-old legacy of an ancient Four Corners Country people. Someday, I reminded myself, the entire petroglyph panel would be gone as well as the entire canyon that sheltered it and the mountain that loomed over that canyon.

Still, something significant had vanished from this place, taken by the elemental forces that shape the beauty of these mountains, mesas, and canyons.

January 7, 1990

It finally happened at dusk last Tuesday—it snowed here.

All day long the clouds had gathered and thickened. At times they threatened to break and vanish as they had so many times before. Then they would close beneath the sky again. A golden eagle returned several times to fly low over the meadow at Crow Canyon. It seemed less conscious of human presence than usual. I took that as a sign.

Later, at home, I watched the same eagle—I think—fly low over the rimrock below my house. The light began to dim. The Sleeping Ute vanished behind curtains of snow. The storm moved closer. The eagle took its usual perch just across the canyon.

Soon, great white flakes were striking my west window. The far wall of the canyon disappeared into a white blur.

I did not turn on lights in the house but sat watching the snow as night fell. It was a sight I had not seen in nearly a year. The next morning, in the predawn darkness, I looked out the window. About an inch of snow had fallen in the night. That may not be much, but it was a reassuring sight—an indication that perhaps, once again, storms would visit this place.

The clouds dimmed the dawn but broke later that day. At last the visible world had the look of winter. Brown fields were white. Flocks of Canada geese crisscrossed a chill blue sky. Distant peaks emerged from low cloudbanks to glisten white for the first time this winter.

On New Year's Eve and on New Year's Day I had explored nearby mesas and canyons with my sons. It was impossible to ignore the sight of dust where usually there is snow or frozen earth. That made Tuesday night's small storm more than merely welcome; it was a sign that 1990 could be a wetter, better year here.

January 21, 1990

ON WEEKENDS, when the weather is favorable, I try to spend at least a few hours at one archaeological site or another in the vicinity of Cortez. I am drawn to them for no particular reason other than that they are in settings of great natural beauty and often are surrounded by sweeping vistas stretching into four states. These ancient, silent villages are great places to wander and to regain some perspective on the apparently pressing problems of the moment.

One of those sites, located on a gentle sage-covered ridge northwest of Cortez, has become a frequent destination of mine. To arrive there one travels across rolling fields, through piñon and juniper forests, and along deep canyons before breaking into the sage. The site is a cluster of parallel mounds running along the ridge. From the highest of these mounds, it is possible to see

Navajo Mountain in the west and the LaSal Mountains in the north. The La Platas are in the east and Ute Mountain, beyond two deep canyons, looms in the south.

At the ruin there is, as is the case at many of these sites, a sense of tranquillity which I cannot explain. This cluster of mounds seems to gather the surrounding landscape around itself in such a way as to become the center of that circle of earth and stone, forest and field.

While there I find myself alternating between looking at the landscape beyond the ruin and then tracing the outlines of the fallen stone walls surrounding me. I can never see the land as the builders of that pueblo saw it, and I can never hear the voices of the builders. Still, there in that place, enough of their legacy remains to speak with a voice of its own.

January 28, 1990

AT DAWN LAST SUNDAY most of the world was gone, taken away by fog. The only shapes visible from my window were the vague, black outlines of a few nearby junipers.

By noon the fog had gone, but moisture in the air magnified familiar landscapes. Mesa Verde loomed like a mountain range above the Montezuma Valley. My resolve to get some work done vanished like the fog. I drove off into the countryside, where junipers were mounded with frozen snow, in search of a place to walk. I found it in a canyon.

Red slickrock tilted into the canyon floor. The snow had melted from the stone. Its color was deepened by the moisture. Pools of water shimmered in pockets in the stone. As I climbed the rock, there was no sound but that of sheep bells floating up from somewhere downcanyon. I was only minutes from home but in an entirely different world. I did not stay long.

By evening the fog had returned. The sun was a barely visible disk through the vapor. Icicles formed on the trees. They glittered in the last light. Darkness fell quickly after the sun had set.

By midweek the fog had retreated to the mountains. Mesas shone beneath cloudless skies. The fields and forest floors were a welcome white.

There is here, though we have winter at last, a subtle sense of change. The light lingers longer each evening. The color of willow thickets along the creeks has shifted from dormancy. What we can hope for now is that the usual heavy snows of late winter will soon come our way. The last storm was a good beginning.

February 4, 1990

It is that time of year when seed catalogs begin arriving and my thoughts turn to planting. I dream up incredible gardens. In general, these fantasies begin taking on reality sometime in late May when I go to a local garden supplier, buy seeds, and get them into the ground. By August or so the weeds have taken over and little survives of the fantasy garden.

Last year I managed to get a cantaloupe to about the size of a tennis ball—that cantaloupe by then was the garden's sole survivor. One night in late August some creature ate half the cantaloupe. The next night it came back and finished off the melon.

Nevertheless, my thoughts now turn once more to summer gardens.

Old dreams die hard. The fact of the matter is that when I bought the house where I now live, I virtually eliminated the opportunity to massacre gardens year after year. Much of my acre of land is lichened rimrock, stairstepping its way down toward a cliff. Where there is soil there are junipers, piñons, sage, and saltbush. Lack of soil isn't the primary barrier to a garden in my future. Lack of water poses greater problems. A truck delivers a few hundred gallons of water each month to the cistern beneath my deck.

To water the cantaloupe I dug a ditch from the rain spout to the plant. It didn't rain. In July, in order to keep the melon alive, I was watering it each morning and night. That adds up. I could have bought a cantaloupe a week with the money I was pouring into that single, ill-fated melon. Traditional perennials are no better than annuals. They die of thirst.

With four surprising exceptions, the only non-native plants on my acre now are what most people would consider weeds—and there aren't many of them. The exceptions are four young cottonwood trees planted by the previous owner. Cottonwoods love moisture. I stubbornly refuse to water the trees in the hope that they will maintain some sort of balance with their setting. They continue to flourish. There must be water in that bedrock somewhere.

So, seed catalogs notwithstanding, I'm learning to let go of my yearly garden fantasies. Now it's more a matter of checking out the acre on a regular basis. Even in winter something changes every day. Nature is a better gardener than I'll ever be.

February 11, 1990

TRAVELING NORTH FROM MONTICELLO toward the Colorado River at Moab, one descends from the feet of the Abajo Mountains to an expanse of grassland encircled by colorful sandstone cliffs. While traversing that grassland at this time of year, it is impossible not to glance ahead at one of the more memorable vistas in the Four Corners Country—the sight of the chill, snowcapped LaSal Mountains rising above one stretch of those warm cliffs.

I went that way last weekend en route to an appointment in the ski village of Beaver Creek near Vail. That vista set me thinking once more about the tremendous ecological diversity these isolated ranges lend to the Four Corners Country. The Abajos, the LaSals, and the Sleeping Ute—unlike the larger mountain chains of the region—can each be circled by car in a few hours' time, but they dominate the rugged lowlands from which they rise.

It can be winter on the peaks and summer below. There is not a great deal of space nor time separating these seasons. On the LaSals and the Abajos one can descend by foot from tundra through shadowy forests to sere desert canyon floors in a single day.

The influence of these ranges extends beyond the ecological diversity they make possible here. They gather the weather about them—in the case of the Sleeping Ute, in a manner which is legendary—casting rain shadows across the land on their leeward sides. Without the mountains, moisture up from the Pacific might pass over the surrounding lowlands unimpeded, never falling to earth.

Nestled against each of these island ranges is a single human community—Towaoc beneath the knee of the Sleeping Ute, La Sal at the south foot of the LaSals, and Monticello by the Abajos. Each of these communities looks to the nearby mountains for sustenance.

Those of us here who do not live against those mountains look to them, too. There is a place not far from Cortez where all three ranges can be seen at once. I go there when I can, just to see those mountains.

April 22, 1990

NEW-LEAFING SERVICEBERRIES now catch the last light on the slopes below my house. They are a translucent green against the lichened stone at the canyon's edge. In the canyon, apricot trees bloom beside the creek.

At dawn each morning a pair of ducks flies up the canyon. At dusk a pair flies down the canyon. I do not know if it is the same pair, but the flights seem precisely timed to the first rays of sun in the morning and the last of the evening. The ducks fly at the top of the canyon walls. They follow the canyon's curving course through the stone.

The last snow will soon be gone from Ute Mountain—a signal to Montezuma Valley gardeners that it's time to get to work. Somewhat early this year, the leaves are appearing on a cottonwood in my yard, and the first shoots of mariposa lilies are visible on the slopes below.

Recent showers have washed the dust from the sage and enhanced its smell. At dawn, when the ducks fly up the canyon, the air is filled with the calls of mourning doves floating up from the stony rims on that fragrance of sage.

It's a good time of year here.

May 13, 1990

Because I had a late flight home from O'Hare last Sunday, I had time to join a group of friends for a day of playing softball in Chicago's Lincoln Park. It was the perfect spring day. Two days of gale-driven rains had cleansed the city and the air. The sparkling lake shone lavender, green, turquoise, and blue. At the south end of the park, one of the world's tallest and most varied skylines caught the morning light.

By noon the park was crowded with Chicagoans of all ages coming to the zoo or to play or simply to stroll beneath new-leafing trees. Their voices nearly drowned out the roar of traffic on Michigan Avenue. It was with reluctance that I left the park and headed for O'Hare and a flight westward into evening light upon the greening Great Plains.

At Stapleton a near-full moon rose over the east end of a runway. The plane to Cortez departed at dusk, and that moon rode a wing tip over the snowy Rockies.

It was pleasant stepping off the plane into the darkness, the silence, and the fragrance of sage and to see the stars that are no longer seen in cities.

At home, the silence broken only by an owl calling from the canyon, I sat awhile in the cool night outside my house while some internal mechanism slowed from the rapid pace of cities and planes to the surrounding tempo of stone and stars.

A city of millions of people is powered by the masses. The place where I sat takes its energy from some less definable source. As I sat there in the darkness, I was glad I do not have to choose one place over the other.

May 20, 1990

Along the dirt roads across the Great Sage Plain patches of foxglove are pink and lavender against the sage. Cliffrose is in bloom along broken rims, and mariposa lilies bow in the breeze on sandy canyon bottoms. The stony rubble of ancient, ruined villages beside the creeks blazes with cactus flowers.

Around my house pale blue flax are here at dawn and gone by noon. White and yellow daisies dot the slopes, and clumps of paintbrush are crimson fire at dawn. Across the canyon, the pale green of new-leafing aspen creeps higher up Ute Mountain every day.

A bonus in this season of lengthening days is that there is time to stroll before work in the first light beneath the last stars, among the last calls of owls. As the sky lightens, the first mourning doves are heard but not seen. Crows awaken then, too, to begin their aerial play above the cliffs.

If there is a jarring note in this place now, it is the wind which begins rising at noon and does not die until well after dusk. The sun sets into a haze of red dust. Even then the wind is warm and dry. But it is not a warmth that invites evening walkers into the open. Instead one becomes a prisoner of built spaces, staring out into the falling darkness and gusting wind.

Not every spring is windy here, but one learns to live with the ones that do occur. It may be the wind that makes one treasure the stillness of dawn.

May 27, 1990

THE HELICOPTER LIFTED OFF into the still dawn and headed north from Crow Canyon over green fields. The aircraft's owner, Archie Hanson, was the pilot. Archaeologist Mark Varien and I were the passengers. Hanson had generously donated his helicopter and his time to allow us to do aerial photography of major archaeological sites in Montezuma County. We hoped the photographs would reveal traces of prehistoric roads and other earthen features reported to exist in the vicinity of some of the sites.

Three-and-a-half hours later, mission accomplished, we landed back at Crow Canyon. We had circled and photographed twenty-five sites along a thirty-mile axis from north to south. Of those sites, there was only one we had not visited and examined on the ground—a project we've been pursuing for more than a year on weekends and evenings after work. To see all of them in less than a morning's time made an overwhelming impression on me. The prehistoric cultural imprint upon this place is lasting and complex.

It was during that flight that I was overwhelmed by another realization: archaeologist Bob Lister is going to be missed by all who knew him and thousands more who did not. Bob, with his wife Florence, was one of the most prominent and able interpreters of the remarkable natural and cultural landscape we had just viewed from the air . . . and of the greater Southwest as a whole. Bob and Florence Lister's books have reached tens of thousands of readers and given them an appreciation of the ancient people of the Southwest and of their material legacy. Most of those readers are, like myself, not archaeologists. Bob opened many windows upon the past for me and thousands like me.

In the normal course of events I would have discussed my perceptions of what I'd seen from the air with Bob. With his typical gentle wit he would have corrected any of my misperceptions and then, more firmly, have suggested where I should look next.

Bob, in the past, has not only told me where to look, but he proved invaluable in assuring me access to sites. More significantly, he assured that I was better informed and better organized in my way of looking at them. Bob personally and unselfishly gave his time and attention to hundreds of people in the same way he gave it to me.

Bob was fortunate in having a wife who shared his passion for archaeology. Each made an equal contribution to creating a national and international appreciation of Southwestern prehistory.

Florence, I am sure, will continue to be an authoritative voice in her field. I am glad she is nearby. I know where to turn when I need inspiration and a fresh way of viewing the world around me, past, present, and future.

June 10, 1990

THERE HAS BEEN AN UNUSUAL CLARITY to the evening air here lately. I can sit in the shade at the east end of my house at dusk and scan the crags and cliffs of distant peaks lit by the last sun. I imagine streams of cold, crystal water flowing from snowbanks turned crimson in that light.

This is a refreshing, renewing exercise in that particular setting, the location of my house. There the earth is so hot and dry that even many of the weeds are dying. I've taken to pulling up some weeds so that others may live until the next rain. The orange mallow, which I leave, is surviving. So is the native flax. They are proving the exceptions. Now even the piñon pines are showing stress. They've lost their sheen and are turning dull and brittle. For a while, in April, there was hope here that the drought had ended. But the rains ended then and were followed by the wind. Now, unseasonable heat, ironically punctuated by killing frosts, is taking its toll. The soil is turning to powder.

It is said that drought is a cyclical, recurring phenomenon here and that even in a single lifetime one is destined to experience several of them. In short, drought is normal weather. But, as this drought deepens, I find it influencing my daily routine.

By midafternoon, when the breeze becomes a hot wind, I am suddenly surprised by the unexpected brightness of the light. It has, to my eye, a harshness which deadens the color in the landscape—as in an overexposed photograph—and renders it featureless. My thought processes seem soon to follow suit. At home, in the evening, I can hardly wait for the sun to set. Then I open the curtains and windows and go outside to watch that last light on the cool, distant mountains.

I go to bed as soon as it is cool enough to sleep. That enables me to get up at first light, when the mountains are a jagged black in the east, and enjoy a couple hours of coolness before the heat and light return. I resolve then not to complain about the drought. My existence here is independent of the weather. Many others here are not so fortunate.

July 1, 1990

Now, IN THE HEAT OF AFTERNOON, thunderheads build and cast shadows across the shimmering land. Thin curtains of rain fall from the sky but never reach earth. Lightning flickers between cloud and mesa.

It is difficult to describe the particular natural phenomenon that is occurring here now. One can see the effects of heat and drought, but the two themselves are not visible. They defy four of the senses and can only be felt.

The drought does heighten one's awareness of certain things. I find myself looking, almost without conscious thought, at the natural setting of my house. I see the ancient junipers that crowd against the sun-cracked wood of my deck and the large piñon pine that reaches across the carport. I gauge the thickness of the native grasses that have flourished beneath the trees this year and look at the dead wood accumulating in the grass.

I can see the scar of a fire, two decades old, that raced up the canyon wall not far from my house. I recall articles I've read about fire prevention in natural settings. One recommended removing all trees within fifty feet of the house. I dismiss the articles from my mind. Those old trees have more claim to that place than I.

At times, without premeditation, lists form in my mind of things I should remove from the house to a less vulnerable setting. The lists evaporate before I act. I tell myself in the morning not to park in the carport, but habit makes me forget when I return home at night.

If anything, I'm gaining a better understanding of people who live in floodplains or atop the San Andreas Fault—people I've always wondered about. Ignoring reality is easier than it might seem.

July 8, 1990

A LIGHT HAS GONE OUT AT CROW CANYON.

Last Saturday, Shelly Runck, a valued part-time member of the Crow Canyon laboratory staff for the past three years, died in her sleep. She had just turned twenty-nine.

I admit to being skeptical when approached three years ago by Angela Schwab, Crow Canyon lab director, with a proposal to employ Shelly and others from the Cortez Sheltered Workshop. I expressed that skepticism. Angela responded firmly that she wanted to go ahead. I said OK. For the first few days of the new program, I felt sure that my skepticism was justified.

What I slowly came to realize as the months passed was that it was not a concern for Crow Canyon that was at the root of my reluctance to have Shelly and her friends here. It was in fact a private fear of my own discomfort at being near disabled persons.

It was only with the greatest effort that Shelly either walked or talked. Words exploded from her at five-second intervals, intervals that seemed an eternity. I'm sure that Shelly sensed my discomfort. That did not deter her.

As time passed, I began to hear what Shelly had to say. I was astonished to discover that beyond that apparent inarticulateness was an incredibly sensitive, inquisitive, and intelligent human being. I discovered, too, that although she walked with great difficulty, in many other ways she possessed physical discipline and grace.

I began to look forward to my brief encounters with Shelly in my daily office routine and to seeing her while doing errands in town. She was an avid follower of national and global events and managed to keep me up on the news. She was never opinionated in her accounts of happenings large or small. Shelly's enthusiasm was infectious. People valued that in her. Her contribution to work at Crow Canyon became substantial.

Last winter Shelly began to weaken. Her almost uncontainable energy was ebbing away. She seemed more accepting of that than those of us around her.

It is said that we live in an age without heroes. Shelly's life was heroic. She proved that the disabled offer remarkable gifts, and it was Shelly's determination that made me understand that.

July 15, 1990

W<small>EEK BEFORE LAST</small>, in less than ninety-six hours, more than two-and-a-half inches of water accumulated in my rain gauge at home. Most of that water came in brief, intense, lightning-laced cloudbursts. The break in the drought lifted the spirits of everyone here. Partly, I think, because the cooler evenings allowed everyone a good night's sleep.

In my yard, chicory, asters, and coreopsis appeared and bloomed almost overnight. The blue, purple, and yellow flowers were a welcome relief from the drab dryness that had prevailed since May. Next, a young cottonwood I'd given up for dead due to drought, put out new leaves. The flowers were early and the leaves were late. Drought does odd things to the plant world, just as it does to the human world.

A few days before the rain began, with two archaeologists—Allison Hoff and Mark Varien—and my son Geoff, I visited a fourteenth-century archaeological site, Grasshopper Pueblo, in east-central Arizona. The trip brought home the vast extent of the drought. Grasshopper Pueblo is located in an area on the Mogollon Rim forested by Ponderosa pine, live oak, and walnut trees. I travel through the Mogollon country at least twice a year. It has always struck me as a lush region of the Southwest.

When we left Show Low headed for Grasshopper fifty miles to the southwest, the haze from the Payson fire was visible. Just ahead of us another fire raced through the tinder-dry forest. At Grasshopper, the forest floor was hot dust.

In midafternoon it began to rain. The forty students and professors gathered there for the University of Arizona Archaeology Field School didn't seek refuge, they stood out in the brief shower. Lightning danced along nearby ridges. I began making mental notes on escape routes. By early evening White Mountain Apaches in fire-fighting gear were patrolling the forest around us looking for fire.

The next day, on a knoll overlooking Grasshopper Pueblo, archaeologist J. Jefferson Reid, who directs research at Grasshopper and has been associated with it for more than twenty years, talked about evidence of drought in the prehistoric record there. It had had a devastating effect on all life in those mountains.

That is why, when the rains began on my return home, I went outside and sat on a ledge until I was soaked to the skin. My dog Chaco looked at me as if, at last, I'd acquired good sense.

August 5, 1990

THE LAST RAYS OF THE SETTING SUN vanished as we wandered through the ancient stone pueblo last Saturday. Remnants of rooms, kivas, and towers were strung around and atop two small buttes. Across a shallow canyon cut into white sandstone were the ruins of a much earlier village. Clouds turned crimson in the last light.

At the archaeological site with me was Michelle Hegmon, a research associate at Crow Canyon and a postdoctoral fellow at the Smithsonian Institution. Michelle took me to a large rectangle of stones she'd been shown on an earlier visit. It was another of the prehistoric features I've come to think of as "architecture with no apparent function." We'd spent the entire day in San Juan County, Utah, looking at such features on the landscape.

These features—including linear earthen berms and swales, stone circles and rectangles, low stone walls that would keep nothing in or out—are at or near many prehistoric Puebloan archaeological sites. There are a number of them here in Montezuma County. I now find myself consciously looking for them and increasingly fascinated by them. Unlike architecture intended to provide housing or storage space or indoor space for community activities, these features beg for explanations but offer few clues.

Some of the features, such as stone circles and rectangles, could have been constructed with little effort. Others, such as linear earthen berms and swales stretching hundreds of meters in some instances, would have required a considerable investment of time and energy. At Chaco, where they go on for miles, these features are called roads. North of the San Juan River, however, they rarely seem to connect archaeological sites—or if they did, long segments of them are now obliterated. Thus, it's difficult to think of these long linear features as roads.

Aided by Michelle and other archaeologists, I'm accumulating a long list of these various features. As we drove from feature to feature last weekend, I wondered what it is about them that interests me. Short of arousing sheer speculation, they don't offer much as a topic of conversation. Discussions of them tend to be brief.

But as the sun set on that rectangle of stones, I realized one thing about these inexplicable features . . . every single one of them is in a spot I want to visit. So, I'll just keep looking for them.

August 19, 1990

It was evening. Swallows darted beneath pewter clouds. Drops of water clung to wet junipers. The fragrance of sage floated up from the canyon, bringing with it the calls of mourning doves. I walked a muddy path along the canyon rim. The rain came again.

At moments like that I am glad to be alone. Thoughts unravel. The mind loses its focus. It is possible then to absorb the smaller events of a place without giving them names and putting them into categories. That can be done later.

The sun set beneath black clouds lined with silver. I turned toward home.

The next morning clouds hung low over the Montezuma Valley, obscuring the northern ridges of Mesa Verde. Dawn was a bronze glow through curtains of gentle rain. I walked then, too. Again, glad for no company other than my unusually pensive dog.

The weather forecast, at the time of this writing, is for clearing. Once the sky is blue and the sun reappears, I'll be glad for human company once again.

These welcome rains, however, seem to make time for solitary meditation.

August 26, 1990

Sometimes sunsets can provide surprises. A spectacular sunset is usually the one where western clouds change hue from white to golden to pink to crimson. The clouds then darken like dying embers. Night falls.

One recent evening, however, the sky provided a different spectacle. A group of friends had gathered on my deck before sunset. Even at that early hour the sky had our attention. One large section of sky, directly overhead, looked like an enormous rectangle packed with straight rows of cotton bolls. The linear effect was distinctly unnatural. The rectangle was surrounded on three sides by black, ragged, wind-whipped clouds. On the fourth side, the east, the entire landscape was invisible, blotted out by a black storm. The wind was unseasonably cold. No one retreated indoors.

The sun vanished across the western canyon. The cotton bolls shone a pale, translucent green. The ragged clouds were blacker yet, edged in bronze. The east remained impenetrably black. From the deck, all eyes were on the sky. Conversation slowed to a near halt.

Lightning bolts struck nearby . . . one so close that static crackled around the house. Gusts of wind shook the junipers. The first pink touched the green clouds. A fast-fading crimson spread across the sky. The darkness did not come at once. The sky held a dim light for much longer than usual. Nighthawks boomed into the canyon.

We moved inside then. Slowly, conversation resumed.

September 2, 1990

I WOKE UP ONE MORNING last week to the realization that sometime in the night I'd turned fifty years old. The odd thing about reaching the half-century mark, I thought, was that people weren't wishing me a happy birthday. Instead, they were offering condolences. Those are, I hope, tongue-in-cheek sentiments.

I won't underestimate the psychological impact of turning fifty. For weeks before, the event intruded, unsummoned, into my thoughts. Those thoughts, to my surprise, were entirely positive.

I felt as if I were approaching an instant of liberation. The last three decades of my life have been busy, sometimes hectic ones. They've been geared not only to my own desire to succeed at this endeavor or that but to the perceived needs of others.

Now I find myself with two grown sons who are determined to be self-sufficient whether or not I'm willing to regard them as so. And I would be hard put to say that others near me, in fact, really need me. Therefore this sense of liberation.

I'm free now to choose what I will do with my life. If I don't pursue my choices or if I fail to make them real, the responsibility for that is my own.

Suddenly the world around me looks different. The day before I turned fifty, a friend and I walked across a stretch of red rock landscape. We've known one another for nearly thirty years and our mutual interest has been world events. Our conversations have always sounded as if we could shape those events. This time we talked and laughed about how aging changes the way we see ourselves and our values. Self-importance wanes. The ability to control our own lives, much less the lives of those around us, seems less and less certain. Things we thought we knew all about we now doubt we know anything about.

I had walked across that red rock place many times before, each time as if it would be the last. This time it looked like home, a place I can revisit at will.

To the friends who sent me the flowers with a notecard bearing the words, "Thirty's the worst," I would say, "Right on." So far, at least, fifty's the best. Another friend, a scientist at the National Laboratory of Tree-Ring Research, sent me a cast-off cross section of a thousand-year-old bristle cone pine missing the forty-ninth ring denoting its forty-ninth year of life. Not only that, it smells good, too.

September 9, 1990

CHACO, THE DOG who headquarters at my house and is generally more civil to visitors than I, recently designed a test of my sanity. I've probably failed the test.

It is an ingrained routine of mine to make sure she's in the house when I go to bed. If I fail to do so, Chaco waits until she's certain I'm at the deepest level of sleep and then begins scratching and barking at the door. This has the effect of getting me out of bed in seconds wondering where I am and what's going on. Sleep does not then return easily.

One night last week, I went through the routine of calling Chaco in from the dark and then quickly went to sleep. At

11:59 P.M., according to the bright red numbers in the clock, I awakened to Chaco's insistent bark, let her in the door again, and finally got back to sleep. At 3:48 A.M., I found myself at the door once more letting the dog in. The light of a full moon streamed through the windows. I gave up on sleep.

It had rained in the night, and the air was warm. I went for a walk. Somewhere along the canyon rim it occurred to me that I'd let the dog in twice during the night. When had I let her out? A coyote's howl got my attention, and I dropped the question.

That night at bedtime I called Chaco in. I was slightly tempted to put a note on the door saying, "Yes, I called the dog in before I went to bed." I didn't. I should have. At 12:22 A.M., I was at the door letting the dog in. She seemed a bit sheepish. I slept until 3:32 A.M. before she was outside the door, barking to get in.

I went for another moonlit walk.

I told myself, and I hope I'm right, that Chaco's figured out how to get out the window, not out of one of three locked doors. The cat's good at getting out the windows. This would, however, take some doing for a dog. In the meantime, I'm learning to like those 4 A.M. strolls . . . and debating whether to try locking the windows at night. Not yet. There are some things I probably don't want to know.

October 7, 1990

EACH MORNING NOW a thin wisp of cloud is draped at dawn over the peak of Ute Mountain in the west. Soon after sunrise it vanishes to reveal the golden aspen and bronze and crimson oak, translucent hues in that early light, colors that are advancing down the mountains below timberline.

New snow is etched silver on Hesperus Peak in the east and shines in the crevices of the Wilsons and Lone Cone farther north. Splashes of yellow in the valley cottonwoods are a sign that autumn will soon spill over from the high country onto the mesas below.

There is, I think, a certain autumnal cast of light across this place. A couple of weekends ago, my friend Rina Swentzell and a number of us, visited prehistoric pueblos along the forested canyon rims. On Sunday, at noon, the clouds were black across the sky. Ancient junipers were burnished pewter against that darkness.

Rina, a Pueblo Indian, feels a deep reverence for these places that most of us view from a more detached perspective. Even during her characteristic long silences, she communicates that feeling to all around her. Rina, by training, is an architect, but she points beyond the fallen pueblos to the distant landmarks—the mountains and mesas—as the defining elements of "community" for her people.

Perhaps someday, a thousand years from now, they will have the same meaning for our own descendants.

October 21, 1990

THE MOON, when I arrived at work one morning last week, was a thin sliver above the first streak of light across the eastern horizon. That moon floated on the still surface of the pond at Crow Canyon. Once in my office, I found it hard to turn my back on that scene and tackle the piles of paper on my desk. More than once I glanced back at the clarity of that dawn. The first rays of sunlight, through golden cottonwoods, were welcome in the chill morning.

I thought back to a couple of weeks before when I took a group of Crow Canyon participants to Monument Valley to watch the sunrise. We arrived an hour early when autumn constellations still flashed above us and the monuments were black megaliths against the western stars. As that place slipped into the light, and the colors emerged around us, one woman told me she'd never before seen the sun rise. She was an advertising executive in her middle sixties who lived and worked in mid-Manhattan. Her admission brought a similar one from another participant. Yet another member of the group was so skeptical that we'd be able to actually see the sun clear the horizon that it seemed she'd never seen it rise either. Surely, I thought, they'd been out at dawn before but were merely unconscious of the sun's rising.

When the first sunlight struck the monuments and warmed the frosty air, the three treated it as a religious experience.

I believed them then. Dawn is so much a part of my life, as is dusk, that I find it hard to imagine life without them.

As we turned to leave Monument Valley, the full moon was setting over Navajo Mountain. That, too, was a first for some of them, to see the full moon vanish into the western horizon. Later, as we wended our way homeward, over mesas and around canyons, I listened closely as my fellow wanderers chatted about their own lives.

Each of their lives, I thought then, has its own equivalents of dawns and of dusks.

December 9, 1990

RECENTLY, I WATCHED a near-full moon set across the canyon from my house in the first light of dawn. As it set, a string of Canada geese flew across it headed north. A few minutes later three ducks hurried south against the first pink of thin western clouds.

The evening of that same day, from an adobe-walled compound, I watched the moon, full by then, rise into a cold cobalt sky over the Sangre de Cristos east of Santa Fe. The mountains caught the last crimson of dusk that gave them their name. I walked through the narrow, winding, unlit streets surrounding the house where I was staying. The fragrance of piñon fires drifted across the town. A cold breeze soon drove me back indoors.

It was not long before the breeze became a gale. I was alone in an unfamiliar house. I awakened more than once in the night and got up looking for the source of sounds . . . the wind rattling windows, the wind driving leaves against the walls of outdoor courtyards, the wind coming down chimneys to shake the glass doors of adobe fireplaces in the corners of the rooms.

I recalled then a fragment of a line I'd read earlier from Claude Levi-Straus, "Until we comprehend the primitive within, our civilizations cannot progress." Levi-Straus was not the first to say that, but he may have said it best.

Levi-Straus was not talking about the forces of nature, but the forces of humanity. Still, a wind-haunted night in Santa Fe was the perfect place to recall his thought. Since Levi-Straus made that observation, he's been joined by a growing number of artists and anthropologists who believe that our great civilizations, by seeking to separate themselves from the primitive that preceded them, have alienated themselves from the energy that drives civilizations.

I don't know. I'll be pondering that for a while. I was glad though that the wind in Santa Fe called it back to mind.

December 16, 1990

LAST MONDAY I went with Crow Canyon archaeologist Mark Varien to visit prehistoric pueblos in a not-too-distant canyon. The sun was just clearing the horizon when we set out, skirting the heads of intervening canyons in the plateau country to the west. An hour later we dropped into a side canyon that provides access to the canyon that was our destination.

The road switch-backed steeply through the thick layers of buff and grey Cretaceous sandstones and shales to the warmer rock of the upper Jurassic. The Abajo Mountains vanished from view in the rearview mirror, as did Ute Mountain ahead, as we descended into the shadow, frost, and stone at the narrow canyon's floor.

Another hour later, after passing through modern farms so removed from the world that I wondered if they simply stored their harvests for winter consumption rather than trying to haul them to market, we spotted the sage-covered mounds that are the current manifestation of the ancient villages we were seeking.

We walked to one of the mounds in a bone-chilling breeze that cut through the early sunlight, stealing its warmth. Apple orchards and vineyards were the mark of the modern farms we'd just traversed—horticultural options not available in prehistoric times. Had those ancient Puebloans farmed here at all, or had these silent villages served another purpose? . . . Questions for Varien, not for me. I don't know where to look for the answers.

Hours, and several thirteenth-century villages later, we climbed a small mesa as the western stone rims rose to meet the late sun. Here the canyon broadened into a valley. From atop the mesa we could once more see Ute Mountain and the Abajos. Even in that late sun, the mesa was warm, its back turned to the downcanyon breeze.

It was easier to imagine Puebloan crops growing here in this shimmering landscape with nearby water—a more livable place than the ones we'd visited earlier.

I continue to wonder if some of those ancient villages served purposes other than farming towns.

January 6, 1991

As of this writing, my house has been without running water for a week. A week may be long enough to meditate upon the power of nature to thwart the wants of mere mortals.

Since I don't have a conventional water system, it is impossible for me to simply turn on a tap and hope that it will be trickling when I get home from work or get up in the morning. My water system requires that I get more actively involved in solving the problem—if a solution exists.

My water arrives in a tank truck and is stored in a cistern beneath a deck on the south side of the house. A pump in the crawl space pulls the water from the cistern—through a plastic pipe—then forces it up through more plastic into the house. The problem is in the outdoor, underground pipe between the cistern and the crawl space. The day after Christmas it was frozen solid.

Plumbers here, already overwhelmed by an epidemic of frozen pipes, tell me on the phone there is little they can do that I can't do. Focus heat on the pipe where it comes through the foundation, they say, and eventually it will thaw.

My action-oriented sons spent our holiday time together digging through frozen ground to get at the outdoor pipe. Now heat is being applied all along it. About once an hour—when I'm home—I go outside, enter the crawl space, plug in the pump for five minutes and wait hopefully.

This process gets me outside later at night and earlier in the morning than usual. On an almost rhythmic basis I plot the progress of stars, moon, and planets across the night sky. Twice I have seen a ringtailed cat checking the scraps I throw out for the birds.

Without frozen pipes, I would not have seen these things.

July 7, 1991

NEARLY A YEAR AGO I decided to leave my job with the Crow Canyon Archaeological Center to resume my career as a writer. That transition was recently completed. I will miss Crow Canyon—it's a unique place staffed by committed, wonderful people—but I'm also enjoying the new routine emerging in my life.

I learned a great deal about many things while at Crow Canyon. The most valuable lesson was learning new ways to see and appreciate the pre-European archaeology of the Four Corners Country.

I grew up among these ruins. My first awareness that a "vanished people" had once flourished here came with a school trip to Mesa Verde nearly forty-five years ago. I was six. Those first views of Cliff Palace, Balcony House, Far View, and the pots and tools in the Chapin Mesa Museum made a deep impression on me. In ensuing years I visited countless archaeological sites here.

My youthful view of these places was that of an incurable romantic. I simply made up stories about them. I peopled these silent villages with imaginary men, women, and children living peacefully in an idyllic pastoral world set mostly in spectacular sandstone canyons. As time went on, and I became interested in writing about the archaeology of this region, my romanticism was somewhat tempered by reading general interest texts based on professional archaeological research.

It was not until I began working at Crow Canyon—where it was not my job to be an archaeologist, I'm not—that I first became aware of the ways in which highly disciplined archaeological scholars gain new knowledge about a people who left no written account of daily life. I found the complex, painstaking research process, from excavation through analysis through publication, as fascinating as the new knowledge being gained in that process. It was while at Crow Canyon, too, that I first visited local archaeological sites with Pueblo Indians, the modern descendants of the pre-European inhabitants of the San Juan River Basin surrounding the Four Corners. Those visits, with scholars such as Alfonso Ortiz and Rina Swentzell, made me see these deserted hamlets and villages as deeply connected to the natural landscape in which they are set and from which they can never be viewed as separate.

Educators at Crow Canyon have developed excellent methods and materials for communicating both of these views of the local past.

So, as I departed Crow Canyon a few weeks ago, it was with gratitude for the new, enriched view it gave me of this place where I live . . . a view that will influence my writing in the years to come.

July 21, 1991

ON ONE SIDE OF US the stream rushed from deep turquoise pools through tumbled boulders into more deep pools. On the other side the canyon wall, stairstepping red cliffs and steep talus slopes, rose two thousand feet to the narrow slot of sky above. My son Jonathan and I rode our bikes along a dirt road shaded by box elders and Gambel oak. The streambank was graced with brilliant green patches of poison ivy. Ponderosa pines towered over all other living things there.

Looking up the canyon wall I could see the work of rivers, oceans, and winds which, for one hundred million years, had laid down the beaches, deltas, and dunes, now stone, into which the stream had cut this gorge. The narrow terrace, between canyon wall and stream, along which we rode was Triassic Wingate Sandstone deposited as windblown dunes nearly two hundred million years ago when this place was a Sahara Desert on the Colorado Plateau. The canyon rims, so far above us, were the legacy of a Cretaceous sea that crept across this region and then retreated about a hundred million years ago. Jurassic Navajo and Kayenta sandstones were sandwiched in between the Cretaceous and Triassic. Alongside us the stream continued to cut its way down, backward, through time.

Later, homeward bound, we emerged from the canyon directly into vast, rolling fields of ripening winter wheat, a golden carpet beneath an azure sky filling with the towering thunderheads of afternoon. Curtains of rain hung from the clouds but did not touch the earth. Though we traveled country roads along its rim, we could see no evidence that the canyon was there at all.

The next day I saw canyons in a different way. With a group of friends, including Cortezans Michelle Hegmon, Ricky Lightfoot, Steve Sloan, and Mark Varien, I followed a small, dry arroyo across a hot mesa top covered with fine red soil. The arroyo gradually deepened until it revealed the white sandstone beneath. We were walking then atop what had been, two hundred fifty million years ago, a white sand beach brought there by the currents of a Permian ocean. A broad groove began to cut into the stone. Suddenly it dropped away, plunged briefly, to become the canyon we sought. Pools of clear water held thousands of toad and frog eggs waiting to hatch. Three miles down that canyon, after dropping several hundred vertical feet, we found a thirteenth-century cliff dwelling constructed as much of logs and twigs as of stone.

That evening, on the same mesa and in the same stone, we parked in the bottom of a canyon and walked up it. Ponderosa pines and Douglas firs reached to the canyon's rims. Clematis concealed the lower stone. Clumps of manzanita anchored new dunes in place. A pair of hawks nesting in the crown of an ancient Ponderosa circled and screamed at our approach. We were trespassers. We visited another small cliff dwelling and turned back downcanyon.

A short time later and a few miles to the east we stopped to watch the sun set behind a western ridge. The mesa on which we'd spent the day spread out before us, but I could see no sign of the canyon we'd just walked.

Canyons can be the surprises of the Four Corners Country. They vanish into the mesa tops, unseen until they are stumbled upon. They can teach us much about the ancient past of this place we call home.

September 22, 1991

A FAVORITE AUTUMN PASTIME here is driving to farms down McElmo Canyon to purchase exotic crops ranging from okra to sun-ripened melons. McElmo Canyon is the only place in Montezuma County where many of these crops will grow to maturity.

The drive down the canyon is spectacular. Just west of Cortez, McElmo Creek begins cutting into buff Cretaceous sandstones. The stream winds along emerald fields of new-mown hay. Suddenly the buffs give way to the pinks, reds, and whites of older Jurassic sandstones. Not far beyond legendary Battle Rock, the brighter rocks once more dip beneath the canyon floor and the Cretaceous resumes.

Near Battle Rock the north wall of the canyon is nearly fifteen hundred feet high. It is at this point, near Battle Rock, that west-running McElmo Canyon cuts through the axis of the McElmo Dome. In the bottom of the canyon are the small farms producing crops that require a warm, long growing season. On the top of the canyon wall to the north, the McElmo Dome is blanketed with vast fields of winter wheat, dryland alfalfa, and pinto beans—crops that produce in cooler, shorter growing seasons. These higher elevation crops need less intensive cultivation than those on the canyon floor. The canyon floor and the canyon rims are two different agricultural worlds separated by a mere fifteen hundred vertical feet of elevation.

McElmo Canyon, cutting through the McElmo Dome, provides a great study in agricultural specialization in order to adapt to specific growing conditions.

Every time I travel through McElmo Canyon or through the fields above I wonder if this crop specialization was practiced centuries ago by the pre-European Puebloans who farmed this area for more than a thousand years. Their pueblos are plentiful both near the canyon floor and along the rims high above. They lived in both places at the same time. Did they grow one type of crop on the canyon floors and another type of crop along the canyon rims?

Did the people come down from the rims with beans and corn to trade for squash and other tender crops grown on the canyon floor? By foot, the distance is not far.

Such questions are easy to ask. I do it all the time. They are not easy to answer. I certainly cannot answer them. Some method would need to be devised to find the answer in the archaeological record found in the canyon bottom and along the higher rims.

I pose these questions to Dr. Karen Adams, director of environmental archaeological research at the Crow Canyon Archaeological Center. She listens carefully despite the demands posed by the projects and analyses she already has under way at Crow Canyon. Fossil pollens found in sites on the rims might be compared with fossil pollens recovered from sites on the canyon floor. But, Adams explains, pollens cling to harvested plants and can be carried along with them—and pollens can survive better in one environment than another. Plant remains pose the same dilemma. It would take a lot of time and a lot of material information to begin finding concrete patterns in the data recovered from sites.

Another question about whether people living on the canyon rims *traded* crops with those on the canyon floor is raised by Crow Canyon senior research archaeologist Mark Varien. He wonders if the same people might have lived both places and moved back and forth tending crops both along the rims and on the canyon floor. He and other archaeologists are seeking ways to determine if particular sites were occupied year-round or only seasonally.

I'll leave the hard work, developing methods to find the answers, to the archaeologists. Questions come easier. I'll stick with them.

September 29, 1991

THE ARCHAEOLOGICAL SITE, more than a thousand years old, sits on a narrow terrace hundreds of feet above the canyon floor. Getting to it is no easy task. Getting back down from it is just as difficult. Except for one narrow crack allowing human access, the site is surrounded on three sides by a sheer cliff. On the fourth side, the arid canyon wall stairsteps up another fifteen hundred feet to the canyon rim. The nearest water is on the canyon floor. It's hard to imagine carrying a fragile ceramic water jar up and down the challenging route between the site and the stream. The location of the site defies logic.

I went to the site with a friend last Saturday afternoon while it was being mapped by a group of archaeologists from Boulder and Cortez who were volunteering their time to do so. Though I'm not an archaeologist I was asked by Richard Wilshusen, who is overseeing the project, to help an archaeologist from Crow

Canyon determine whether some outlying mounds were cultural or natural and whether, if cultural, there were mappable architectural features in the mounds. That sounded easy enough, and I welcomed the task because I was in a somewhat contemplative mood and not eager to join the focused, disciplined team working in the areas of the site where architecture was most obvious.

It did not prove to be an easy task. The mounds are located on a section of the terrace where it narrows and is no longer flat. Talus and soil had tumbled down from above and sloped from the foot of the cliff above us to the top of the cliff below us. A thousand years of erosion had severely smeared what cultural features may have been constructed on that slope.

The archaeologist I was assisting has worked for several years on sites located on talus slopes. Such sites pose special problems because of their vulnerability to almost every erosive action possible. It is often hard to tell a cultural feature from a natural feature. It is hard to know whether a cultural feature is now located where it was originally constructed or whether it has been moved downslope by nature in the intervening centuries following abandonment. It is hard to know whether entire elements of the site—middens, for instance—have been completely removed by erosion.

This particular archaeologist has recruited geomorphologists to look at sites on talus slopes and to help him understand the dynamics of slope erosion in this region. As a result of this experience, he can, to a degree, play the processes in reverse and reconstruct an image of what the site may have looked like immediately following abandonment. His way of looking at sites on slopes turns my way of looking at sites on its head. I learn to see in new ways . . . not always an easy task in its own right but worth the effort. I've started seeing not only sites but slopes differently.

While on sites, he often talks aloud to himself, and I've found that by eavesdropping I can acquire interesting information. For instance, last Saturday he counted pottery sherds as we stepped over them—probably accounting mentally for the sherds that had washed over the cliff along with walls, stone tools, and refuse—and arrived at estimates of how many pots of each particular type had been broken while in use at the site . . . fifteen of these, twelve of those, seven of another. This is not an idle pursuit but a method he uses to hypothesize about the intended function of the site and the number of years it was occupied. He is a constructor of patterns folded within patterns folded within patterns within which are revealed manifestations of human behavior that illuminate my own understanding of the enduring human spirit. I enjoy going to sites with this particular archaeologist because he is usually tolerant of my compulsion to tell stories about why sites are where they are and what people did there. He is also tolerant of my short attention span and my tendency to look up from the ground and focus on the landscape around the site.

What I saw Saturday afternoon was the opposite canyon wall towering above us to meet a deep blue sky. The Gambel oak that blanketed its upper reaches was turning—it was a patchwork of crimson, gold, and green, translucent as a stained glass window. It was, I'm sure, what the residents of that ancient pueblo saw on autumn afternoons more than a thousand years ago.

October 6, 1991

I WAS ONLY TWO HOURS from my home in Cortez but I was, in a sense, at the beach. Around me were fossilized dunes, the remains of a white sand beach left there by an ocean two hundred fifty million years ago. Rainwater had recently collected in the pockets between the dunes. In those pools were small freshwater shrimp, clams, fish, and snails. I know very little about these creatures but it is my understanding that they are the descendants of similar saltwater dwellers left behind when the last ocean retreated from here one hundred million years ago. They have adapted to the loss of their permanent saltwater habitat and now lead brief freshwater lives. They hatch, mature, breed, and lay eggs in the mud at the bottom of the pool during the short periods when there is water.

When the water evaporates, the creatures die, leaving only eggs behind to hatch the next time it rains enough to form pools on the arid stone ... which is not often. When I looked at the hollows between the dunes a couple of months ago, they were bone dry with thin, cracked, dusty soil on their bottoms. Now they are teeming with life. The creatures in them are a testament to the ability of species to survive even the most drastic changes in the environment surrounding them. The changes must have come very slowly or the species would not have had time to adapt.

There are half a dozen of these pools in the spot I visited last week. The pools are set only a few feet apart in the white stone. But, for the shrimp, fish, and clams in one pool, the other pools must be like galaxies beyond the reach of light, their existence unknown and unsuspected.

The pools are a few yards from the edge of a cliff from which it is possible to look down on the San Juan River a half mile below. At that point the river canyon is cut deeply into a vast, flat, arid sweep of limestone bounded on the east by the mesa upon which I stood and on the west by the towering monoliths of Monument Valley. The perseverance of the river in getting to where it wants to go reminds me of the persistence of the creatures in the nearby pools. Not only has the river swept that great saucer of limestone free of the sandstone that once lay thousands of feet thick across it, but it has cut a canyon more than a thousand feet into the limestone. The river is now cutting through stone nearly a hundred million years older than the white, fossilized dunes strung along the mesa's edge where I was standing.

I thought back to where I had been a couple of evenings before I arrived at that mesa's edge. I was in an aspen grove at sunset on the west slope of the La Plata Mountains. From that point it is possible to look across the Great Sage Plain and see the mesa where the pools are located. As the sun vanished in the west, a full moon rose above Hesperus Peak in the east. The cosmos seemed superbly balanced in that instant. The aspens around me were turning from green to golden so rapidly that the transformation seemed almost visible. A small, clear brook ran through the aspen grove, reflecting the pink of the sky in its rippling surface. It was a different world than that on the distant western mesa which had just claimed the sun.

Shrimp, fish, and clams in ephemeral pools on fossilized beaches; a river cutting deeper into ancient stone; aspen leaves turning before my eyes . . . these were things I'd seen in less than forty-eight hours and could have seen in a single afternoon if I'd been willing to hurry from mountain to mesa and glance into the canyon. But, for once, I was in no hurry.

October 20, 1991

It was easy to allow myself to believe, for a moment, that I'd stumbled upon a mass landing of little alien spacecraft not far northwest of Cortez. The sun was just clearing the eastern horizon. The field, set against the darker backdrop of Sleeping Ute Mountain, was filled with bright, silvery, luminescent spheres, thousands of them, each about a foot-and-a-half in diameter. I pulled my pickup over and stopped. I stared uncomprehending. My passenger reached for her camera and slowly opened the door of the vehicle. So far she'd only muttered one syllable, "Wow!"

When she was done photographing the glowing objects, I asked her what she thought they were. She looked at me warily, as if considering escape routes, and said, "Pumpkins, they are pumpkins." I blinked and looked again. That time I saw a field filled with ripening pumpkins. The first shiny, platinum rays of sunlight had reflected from the sheen of the pumpkins; a moment later the pumpkins reflected the blended green and gold of their skins. My companion's "wow" was an expression of her excitement about the photogenic quality of the sight, not a response to an illusion that we'd encountered space aliens.

I was, frankly, a little disappointed. As a child I always kept the corner of one eye alert for the sight of a ghost or an elf. As an adult, staying on the lookout for UFOs has had to do. Pumpkins, unless they are of the Great Flying variety, are something of a letdown. Nevertheless, the sight was a beautiful one, and I have journeyed several mornings lately to look at the field of pumpkins glowing in the light of the rising sun. They are now a deep orange and are being harvested. Wagons loaded with pumpkins are orange rectangles against the golden cottonwoods of the Montezuma Valley. My pumpkin encounter of the first kind made me start thinking about the effect of light upon the human experience. For me, thinking about light comes easiest between the autumnal equinox and the vernal equinox when the slant of light upon this place of exposed, fractured stone more readily reveals the shape of the landscape than when it is flattened by sunlight beating down upon it—and me—from directly overhead.

In his book, *Art and Visual Perception: A Psychology of the Creative Eye,* Rudolf Arnheim says, "If we had wished to begin with the first causes of visual perception, a discussion of light should have preceded all others, for without light the eyes can observe no shape, no color, no space or movement. But light is more than just the physical cause of what we see. Even psychologically it remains one of the most fundamental and powerful of human experiences, an apparition understandably worshipped, celebrated, and importuned in religious ceremonies. To man, as to all diurnal animals, it is the prerequisite for most activities. It is the visual counterpoint of that other animating power, heat. It interprets to the eyes the life cycle of the hours and the seasons."

It was light that tricked me, created that optical illusion, by that field filled with pumpkins. And it is the autumnal slant of light now that sets afire the yellow leaves of the serviceberries among the junipers on the canyon rim by my house. That slant of light on turning leaves tells me that our spot on earth is turning away from the sun and that light itself will be more precious now and for the next few months . . . along with its sensual counterpart, heat.

October 27, 1991

As I wander around the deserted Puebloan villages in the San Juan River Basin of the Four Corners Country, my mind keeps returning to what I now think of as the Columbus dilemma. How should one regard the journey of a man who set sail for one continent, ended up on an entirely different continent, and proceeded to dub its inhabitants as Indians . . . a misnomer they've been stuck with ever since?

As a schoolboy I was taught that Columbus was, without question, a hero of mythic proportions. I am still willing to concede that Columbus was a man who possessed the courage of his convictions. I think, too, that Columbus is getting something of a bad rap, that he is being blamed for wrongs committed by those who followed him. Columbus, after all, did not set out on a mission of conquest; he set out to establish ocean trade routes to the East Indies to replace existing slow, dangerous land routes.

One thing is clear, however: Columbus did not "discover" this continent in 1492. That had already been done at least twenty thousand years before Columbus. By the time Columbus got here, the continents now known as North and South America had as many as one hundred million inhabitants, the majority of whom were probably enjoying a better quality of life than were most inhabitants of Columbus's native Europe of the time. To his death, Columbus never conceded that he'd arrived at the wrong destination. Thus, he never took credit for "discovering" anything except a new seagoing route to the East Indies. Other Europeans, however, quickly grasped the significance of Columbus's error, and within less than thirty years the conquest of the societies of these two continents was under way.

In 1540, less than fifty years after Columbus's first voyage, the first official European expedition into the Four Corners Country made contact with the Puebloan people of the upper Rio Grande and Little Colorado river basins. Just more than a century after 1492, in 1596, the first European settlement was established in the Four Corners Country near what is now called San Juan Pueblo at the junction of the Rio Grande and Chama rivers. It is not a date likely to be celebrated by the descendants of the Ute, Navajo, Apache, and Puebloan peoples who inhabited the Four Corners Country in the late sixteenth century. These people, however, did not suffer as a result of Columbus's intent as much as from his willingness to risk sailing off the edge of the world.

Why have we made a hero of Columbus? It is because we have made him a symbol of our own western European culture. His arrival on the wrong continent triggered the expansion of our western European culture onto two continents theretofore unknown to western Europe . . . but intimately known by a hundred million relatively well-adjusted human beings living here at the time. When we celebrate Columbus Day, we celebrate the expansion and survival of our own culture. It is no wonder then that the descendants of the first people on this continent have come to regard Columbus as the ultimate antihero . . . somewhat in the same way as we regard Atilla, though the comparison isn't apt.

Now when I wander the deserted villages of the Puebloans in

the San Juan River Basin—villages that were last occupied two centuries before the arrival of Columbus—I hear the voices of my Pueblo Indian friends and of archaeologist friends from my own culture. What I am beginning to see around me is the material manifestation of an ancient social genius perhaps peculiar to the Four Corners Country.

I wonder then if, here in the Four Corners Country, the approaching five hundredth anniversary of Columbus's first journey should not only be a celebration of European culture—which it certainly will be—but also of the virtues of the cultures into whose homes and ancestral lands Europe entered uninvited.

November 3, 1991

RESIDENTS OF THE FOUR CORNERS COUNTRY are more likely to become involved in the controversy surrounding the celebration of Columbus's 1492 voyage than are residents of other regions of the United States. Nowhere else in the United States are American Indians as powerful a force in daily affairs as they are in the Four Corners Country. The descendants of the Ute, Navajo, Apache, and Pueblo Indians who were here when Columbus first sailed are here now. The descendants of the Spanish conquerors who, fifty years later, brought Europe to the Four Corners Country are here now. The descendants of the Anglo-Americans who took the Four Corners Country for the United States are here now.

There is probably no place in the Four Corners Country where the Quincentenary will be more hotly debated than here in Santa Fe. I arrived here three days ago and have not had a single conversation since where the subject has not come up. The discussions range far beyond the issue of Columbus himself.

The very relationship of cultures to cultures is being examined here. It is easy to understand why. The visible manifestations of intercultural contact and domination are everywhere in Santa Fe and environs. These are not limited to a dead past; they are found in everyday life, present, and probably future, in this turbulent community and its environs.

My first day here I went to Pecos National Monument to visit a friend who is on the staff and does research there. Pecos Pueblo was occupied at the time Coronado's expedition arrived here in 1541 and became a headquarters for Coronado as he and his men branched out in search of the legendary Seven Cities.

The history of Pecos Pueblo from that time until it was abandoned is one of cultural conflict, of religion against religion, of violent overthrow, and of reconquest. It is also a history of growing cultural interdependence and synthesis.

While I was at Pecos, my friend took me to another nearby pueblo that was constructed, occupied, and abandoned centuries before Coronado arrived at Pecos. We walked through piñon groves and across a small river valley to arrive at our destination. En route we paused and he pointed out a remnant of the ancient Santa Fe Trail. All that was visible was a cut through a small ridge. For me, the Santa Fe Trail has always been a romantic symbol of an idealized American West. To see it, to actually stand in it where it cut between two ancient pueblos, was to sense something more. The Santa Fe Trail, under some other name, probably had been there long before Columbus first sailed. Our European cultures simply followed a route developed by the Puebloans and nearby Plains Indians to meet their own needs.

It is that fact, the influencing of the path of European culture here by the more ancient cultures native to this region, that is getting lost in the increasingly embittered polarization over the Quincentenary observances. The day after I visited Pecos Pueblo, I traveled through the old Hispanic villages along the winding "High Road" between Santa Fe and Taos. It is there that one senses what most Hispanic community life must have been like before this region was reluctantly ceded to the United States. What one asks one's self while in those villages is: Are these European communities or pueblos in the Indian sense? My feeling is that they are a synthesis of Europe and Pueblo and that without the adaptation by Europeans to Puebloan ways of dealing with an ancient Puebloan environment, those new settlers here would not have survived and prevailed for long. Either they took the Puebloan path or the land itself would not have nurtured them.

The American Indians who are angered by the Quincentenary are, in many ways, too eager to concentrate on the exploitation and victimization of their peoples since Columbus first sailed in 1492. They portray themselves as losers. What they could do, instead, is turn the tables. They could point to the way in which their cultures have prevailed since 1492 in the face of terrible odds. They could rightfully ask if our culture would have succeeded in the same way. When in the Four Corners Country, one realizes that the dynamics which began in 1492 are far from history, they are present and future. We should abandon the win/lose rhetoric and use the Quincentenary as a time to examine the multicultural future of the Four Corners Country.

November 10, 1991

A FEW MILES SOUTH of Bloomfield on Highway 44, I passed a hitchhiker. I caught a glimpse of his disgusted expression as I sped by on my way south. After an unnerving experience with a hitchhiker when I was in college, I stopped picking them up unless they were obvious victims of car trouble. I had hitchhiked a few times myself while in college, the result of reading too much Jack Kerouac, but stopped after a couple of drivers left me feeling distinctly uncomfortable about their emotional stability. I gradually began to view drivers who picked up hitchhikers in the middle of nowhere as being as suspect as hitchhikers on roadsides in the middle of nowhere. I did, in fact, regret my loss of innocence. Kerouac had made it all sound so . . . intellectually enriching.

A short time after I'd passed the hitchhiker south of Bloomfield, along what must be the most deserted stretch of Highway 44, the engine of my aging, foreign-made pickup stopped. It stopped without warning, without a cough or a sputter. I pulled onto the shoulder and coasted to a halt, got out into a cold wind, and lifted the hood. I hoped to find a loose wire dangling there somewhere that could simply be reconnected and I'd be on my way. No such luck. I checked every connection I could find. All OK. Bloomfield was the closest town. I had no choice but to cross the highway, walk north a hundred yards to a wide spot in the shoulder, and start sticking out my thumb at the occasional passerby. Half an hour later and twenty speeding cars later, I was still there. I was to meet my son in Santa Fe in a few hours, and the rest of the day was tightly scheduled. The more likely alternative, a night in a Bloomfield motel if I ever got to Bloomfield, wasn't appealing. I walked back to the pickup in a last desperate hope that I could find the problem and fix it. This time I removed the distributor cap. The rotor had shattered into tiny fragments. My pickup wasn't going anywhere without a new rotor.

I remembered the hitchhiker then. He'd been walking south along the highway. In a short while he would catch up with me. At best he'd be amused, glad to see that there was, in fact, poetic justice. At best. I was replacing the distributor cap when a pickup stopped across the highway. The driver, a young Hispanic man, walked over and asked if I needed help. I explained the problem. He would take me to Bloomfield.

On the way he told me that he was going to an auto parts store and then driving back south again. He doubted, though, that the store would have the part I needed, and I'd have to wait for it to come from Farmington. He explained, too, that the shattered rotor could be a symptom of a more major problem. We passed the windblown hitchhiker.

The parts store had the rotor. On the way out of town, the driver stopped at an auto mechanic's shop with a tow truck parked out front. He told the proprietor where my pickup was and that, if it couldn't be fixed, he'd radio for the tow truck. Back at my pickup—I had not seen the hitchhiker on our return journey—I replaced the rotor and the motor ran perfectly . . . but for a squeaking alternator belt. The man tightened the belt and departed. I had been extremely fortunate. I regretted not asking his name. The clerk at the parts store and the mechanic had both greeted him only as "Candelaria."

I waited a minute before pulling onto the highway. I wondered if the hitchhiker had walked past my vehicle and was somewhere along the road ahead. What would I do? What should I do? A trusting stranger had just saved my day. Could I do the same for another? But nowhere, in the vast, barren, beautiful landscape ahead, was the hitchhiker to be seen.

December 1, 1991

THE EXCELLENT *Durango Herald* series by Electa Draper on the changing ethnic composition of the population of the Four Corners Country has been on my mind ever since I read it. In Part Two, Draper cites U.S. Census Bureau predictions that within less than thirty years a majority of the population here will be American Indian and that the ratio of Hispanics to Anglos will increase. Anglos will become an ethnic minority in the Four Corners Country. For the San Juan River Basin as a whole—in contrast to individual communities—that will, in fact, probably occur before the end of this decade, given the population explosion occurring among the Navajo Indians.

The implications of this are profound for all of us living here— Indian, Hispanic, and Anglo alike. The fact that the Anglo population here is headed for minority status does not make us unique. The same has already occurred in major urban areas of the United States. There *is* something happening in the Four Corners area which does make us unique. The ancestors of the soon-to-be majority ethnic group—American Indian—arrived here many centuries before the Anglos did. The ancestors of the growing Hispanic minority arrived in the Four Corners Country more than two-and-a-half centuries before the Anglos did. This is in marked contrast to many areas of the country where growing non-Anglo ethnic groups are recent arrivals in the United States. In short, in the Four Corners Country, Anglos *are* the most recently arrived ethnic group.

That means that the Navajo, Ute, Apache, and Pueblo cultures— and the indigenous Hispanic culture—are far more blended with, and adapted to, the region's environment and landscape than is the Anglo culture . . . Indians and Hispanics are not strangers to this land. They are at home here, and that strengthens those cultural elements, which are many, that arise from having lived in one place for many centuries. For that reason alone it is both shortsighted and futile to demand that the earlier, older cultures here forget their pasts, their languages, their traditions, and their values and embrace the past, the language, the traditions, and the values of the most recently arrived ethnic group, the Anglos. It won't work. Unlike other areas of the nation where the Anglo populations can say to recent arrivals, "We welcomed you here, now live according to our terms," the Anglo population here must begin adapting to a multicultural, multiethnic Four Corners society and economy.

As is pointed out in Draper's series, the place to start is in the schools. The schools should do more than promote and nurture the potential of minority students. The schools should do more than include more minority teachers on their faculties. The public schools must do the above, but they also should be teaching courses in Ute, Hispanic, and Navajo culture and language to Anglo pupils. All students in the Four Corners Country, including Anglos, deserve to be educated for living successfully in the emerging multicultural society of this region.

Fort Lewis College has great potential—far from fully tapped—for becoming the central institution in the emergence of a multicultural society and economy here. Fort Lewis College can educate the professional, business, and artistic leaders of all local ethnic groups in ways which prepare them to develop the strengths and overcome the weaknesses of the emerging society of the Four Corners Country.

In Cortez, where I live, it is now a common occurrence in larger retail stores to stand in a checkout line and hear a clerk speaking Navajo to the customer ahead of me . . . and then to have that same clerk address me in fluent English. I like it when that happens; it makes my town seem a richer place to live. But it is only the first step in a very long journey that needs to be completed in a very short time.

December 22, 1991

TODAY IS MY FAVORITE DAY OF THE YEAR, winter solstice. I am not sure whether this is because it is the shortest day of the year or because tomorrow will be a longer day than today. It does have to do with light. The light now brings out the color and depth of the stony spot where I live, in contrast to the more direct light of summer.

Outside my window, fog has covered everything with a thick layer of frost. The fog has lifted some since dawn but still obscures the sun. A jay is huddled deep in a juniper tree next to the house. Three deer, two does and a large four-pronged buck, nibble on the tips of sage. The buck walks with a slight limp. Two crows engage in aerial combat with a golden eagle. The crows stay above the eagle and dive toward it. The eagle flaps one wing in irritation but does not leave the sky above the canyon. The jackrabbits, if they are around, are staying out of sight, probably hoping that the crows will soon prevail and they can safely emerge to nibble at clumps of frost-burdened Indian rice grass that sparkle in this light.

All of these natural events—the light, the fog, the shivering jay, the deer, the crows, the eagle—seem to move in slower motion now. The tempo of things has slowed. That is one of the qualities of winter solstice that make it so appealing. It lends itself to meditation rather than action.

I let my imagination out the window. I think about the mountains to the north and east of here. They are covered with more snow now than in years. Snow lies on ice across the streams and muffles the sound of rushing water. I remember a favorite canyon west of here where I sometimes go at this time of year to find a thin, clear layer of ice on a creek through which red pebbles are visible beneath the water. Here and there, leaves are frozen into the ice. A south-facing cliff dwelling provides refuge from the icy cold of the canyon bottom. I resolve to go there soon.

The peaceful beauty of the winter solstice is but part of its magic. There is also the realization that the days will soon grow longer and today's slow tempo will quicken. Owls, silent now, will again call in the night. There will be more sound in the world. One year's meditation ends, and the next year's renewal begins.

January 5, 1992

I HAVE NEVER PARTICULARLY THOUGHT about where eagles go when it is snowing. Outside my west window the ground falls away quickly toward the canyon floor. One recent afternoon a thick curtain of snow moved up the canyon from the south. It shut out the view of the canyon and the Sleeping Ute beyond. It engulfed the house. I went to the window and watched the snow. It was the sort of storm I find appealing, it shuts out the world. It was then that I saw the eagle, level with the window and fifty feet away. It was motionless above the slope, facing into falling snow. Occasionally a wing tip fluttered softly, and the bird's head moved back and forth scanning the rock below. It stayed there for more than a minute before wheeling and vanishing into the storm over the canyon.

It was dusk before the snow stopped falling. I wondered where the eagle had gone. I could not see it on its usual perch across the canyon. I went outside for a brief walk in the trackless snow. Clouds descended to the canyon rims and the light failed. I would not see the eagle that evening.

The next morning, in the predawn darkness, I heard the call of a single owl. It was the first I'd heard in some time. I went outside to hear it better. The canyon was filled with mist but brilliant stars shone through clearings in the patchy clouds above. The clouds reflected softly the light of the nearby town.

As the morning light came, I could see rabbit, mouse, and small bird tracks in the new snow. I went outside with my dog, and we added our own tracks to those of the dawn creatures. The snow-laden trees and sage muffled all sound. I found the tracks of the small fox; a neighbor tells me it is a regular visitor to his house. The fox must make regular rounds. Its tracks led in both directions along precisely the same path.

It occurred to me that then was the time to discover the fox's living quarters. I could follow its tracks home. They led along broken rims—easy going for a fox but perilous for me. Here and there I could see where the fox had taken a brief rest, sitting on a point of rock suspended above space. The tracks went beneath trees and through patches of sage. I began to feel a little as if I was invading the privacy of another creature. Soon other tracks began joining the fox's trail, deer and rabbit tracks. I lost the fox's track then. I did not find its home.

I wandered back to my house musing about the pattern of animal tracks in newly fallen snow. A single set of tracks merges with another. From one side and the other, more tracks join the trail like small brooks joining a river. Soon there is a beaten path followed by many creatures large and small.

The mist lifted from the canyon. The opposite canyon wall was white but for vertical cliffs of wet, brown sandstone. I looked up for the eagle. It had not yet appeared. I wondered then if eagles suspend themselves above well-traveled paths in newly fallen snow. I knew where to watch.

February 16, 1992

A SQUIRREL HAS JOINED the chickadees, juncos, plain titmice, jays, and occasional magpies that visit the place where I put scraps and birdseed outside my west window. The russet-colored creature, its tail held high, stuffs bits of stale popcorn into its cheeks and scampers back into the broken, rocky rims beyond the deck. In the canyon below my house the stream is free of ice and is tan with clay washed into it by melting snow. Along the stream the willows have taken on the bright burnt orange hue that signals their awakening from winter dormancy. Mallards have reappeared, using the void between the canyon rims as a flyway to travel north in the morning and south at dusk. Penstemon leaves, purple and green, are appearing from beneath melting patches of snow. Buds of new growth are appearing on the tips of the piñon pine.

At winter solstice, the sun set into the midsection of Sleeping Ute Mountain. Now it slides down the north face of Ute Mountain itself, the landform local legend says is the folded arms of a sleeping god. It will not be long before the sun sets into the face of the silhouette and then moves north farther yet, leaving the mountain behind until late autumn. The light has lost its slanting solstice dimness and shines more directly upon the stone.

I watch this shift of seasons and tell myself I would be a better person if I spent more time looking at my TV screen instead of out my window. I should be watching the human drama in that black box rather than the natural drama outside my door. Looking out my window tells me nothing about presidential campaigns, an inexplicable economy, and the corrupting effects of celebrity on politicians and athletes. Looking out my window accords me some peace of mind in a time when peace of mind is probably an inexcusable luxury.

I used to think that if one looked at, walked through, nature for long enough that one would learn something which could be taken back to civilization and applied to the betterment of the human condition. That may be true, but I've yet to stumble upon such "natural truths." It is true that, on one level, nature and the human condition are part of the same whole. On another level, nature and the human condition seem to have taken separate paths leading them farther and farther apart. Maybe humanity is on the high road, a path which leads beyond, transcends, nature. As long as I don't turn on my television set, I can cling to that bit of optimism.

What Ralph Waldo Emerson said more than one hundred fifty years ago about the value of nature to humanity may still hold. Emerson wrote:

> . . . The solitary places do not seem quite lonely. At the gates of the forest, the surprised man of the world is forced to leave his city estimates of great and small, wise and foolish. The knapsack of custom falls off his back with the first step he makes into these precincts. Here is sanctity which shames our religions, and reality which discredits our heroes. . . . Here no history, or church, or state, is interpolated on the divine sky and the immortal year.

I like that sentence, "The solitary places do not seem quite lonely." Solitary places may, in fact, be the least lonely places of all. They contain nothing to remind us of ourselves. If we are unaware of ourselves then, when in nature, we can temporarily do as Emerson says and "quit our life of solemn trifles."

March 15, 1992

LAST WEEK I SPENT a pleasant and thought-provoking morning with my uncle John Zink in his home by the waterfall in the Animas Valley. The conversation quickly turned to gardening. John and Ruby Zink have spent more than half a century coaxing sustenance from the red soil of the Waterfall Ranch and, as a youth, John spent a great deal of time working in the Zink greenhouses at

Hermosa. When he talks about gardening, John is talking about more than a small plot in the backyard containing a few straight rows of vegetables and flowers. Gardening to my uncle is a visionary concept embracing a whole host of natural and social issues, a framework within which the people, plants, soil, and weather of the Four Corners Country can come together to make this a better place to live.

Successful gardening in the Four Corners Country means matching the right plant, native or imported, to the right conditions to create either a useful harvest or beauty or, ideally, both. It means acknowledging the scarcity of such plant-producing resources as water. It means understanding that the Four Corners Country environment contains an almost limitless diversity of microclimates, each of which imposes its own constraints upon any given species of plant. It means going beyond merely learning how to successfully grow a plant to learning all the uses of any given plant, wild or cultivated, from food value to medicinal value to aesthetic value.

In addressing the issues contained within gardening, John sees a problem. More significantly, he envisions a solution. The problem is that successful gardening in the relatively harsh environment of the Four Corners Country is more than an exacting science that can be learned from books and in classrooms. Gardening here is an art that can only be learned from experience here. Four Corners Country gardening could well be a vanishing art soon to become a lost art. The best and most practiced gardeners here are old-timers who grew up in a time when the garden was an important, immediate source of sustenance. A failed garden had a direct result; there was less food on the table in the ensuing months and less beauty in the dooryard in a harsh land. As an art, gardening has not been passed on to more prosperous younger generations nor to newcomers.

John, along with others in the Animas Valley and Durango, has been working on a project to restore the art of gardening in the Four Corners Country. It would bring old-time gardeners together with young people and newcomers. It would create a volunteer network of experienced gardeners who could provide specific and vital information to learning gardeners. It would introduce many

Four Corners residents to the joy of producing food for their own tables, enhancing the beauty of this place, and appreciating the natural environment which shapes the successful garden.

As I drove home, west from the Animas Valley, I recalled the gardens I like the best. They are grown north and west of Cortez alongside farmhouses set in vast dryland fields. Corn, beans, squash, additional vegetables, fruit trees, and a multitude of flowers flourish without a drop of water other than what falls from the sky at the whim of nature. The secret lies in knowing the right plants, the rhythm of the seasons, and the ways of tending the soil. Those gardens are grown by old-timers. Only those old-timers could teach others the secrets of those gardens.

I appreciate John Zink's use of the term gardening. For one thing, unlike farming or agriculture, gardening is within reach of anyone who wants to learn the art. For another thing, gardening extends beyond the cultivated places into wildness itself. To learn gardening, one must step out of the immediate present into a tradition . . . a tradition that respects the peoples, places, and seasons that shape the Four Corners Country.

March 22, 1992

AT FIRST LIGHT I WALKED up a knoll from the stony place where I'd camped for the night. Not far away the caprock ended and the mesa's edge plunged a thousand feet into the canyon where I had camped and hiked the previous two days. There in the dawn I could turn around slowly and see mountain ranges in four states: the La Platas, Ute Mountain, the Chuskas, Black Mesa, Navajo Mountain, the Henrys, and the Abajos. Between me and Navajo Mountain I could glimpse a short segment of the San Juan River deep in its gorge that seemed only a stone's throw away. The snowy Henrys, beyond the Colorado River, floated on a brilliant, fiery, harshly eroded, early Triassic landscape in the middle distance. The spires of Monument Valley caught the first rays of sunlight against the backdrop of Black Mesa.

There was no dawn breeze and the air was warm. Only the melodious song of an occasional canyon wren broke the silence. Thin golden clouds caught the color of the earth below. The sky above seemed more solid than the rock below. I was glad to be alone with a whole day ahead of me during which I could wander home along any backroads that came to mind. At that moment I wasn't given to sweeping thoughts about the insignificance of self in a timeless land. Instead, I recalled recent explorations there.

I looked beyond the San Juan gorge at a long mesa stretching across the landscape between me and Navajo Mountain. I remembered three days there last spring when, carrying the appropriate permits from the Navajo Nation, I'd visited remote archaeological sites around Navajo Mountain with friends Mark Varien and Jim Martin. By midway in that journey we'd lapsed into uncharacteristic silence, overwhelmed by the enormity, complexity, color, and beauty of the plunging, soaring landscape and sky embracing us. Not long after that visit to Navajo Mountain, I spent a week with Stanton Englehart and others, moving slowly through most of the vast sweep of country that surrounded me on that knoll. We were silent much of the time.

I left the knoll and spent the day wandering back across the Great Sage Plain, skirting the McElmo Dome, and arriving home in late light. Less than forty-eight hours later I was in the Fine Arts Gallery at Fort Lewis College with, among others, Mark Varien, Jim Martin, and Stanton Englehart. The occasion was the opening of a two-man show of paintings by Stanton and ceramics by Mike Englehart.

As I stood in the center of the gallery and turned slowly around, I felt as if I were back on the knoll. With each passing year Stanton's paintings go further beyond what is seen by the rational eye to reveal the true inseparability of—the unified structure and energy of—stone and sky in this place we call home. I felt fortunate that I can go into this country with friends and I can go into it alone but, when alone, accompanied always by the memories of friends' perceptions of a place that no single mind alone could ever comprehend.

April 26, 1992

THE MINIATURE PHLOX and Indian paintbrush are blooming on the slopes outside my window, and serviceberry bushes are mounds of white blossoms. These signs of spring here greeted me on my return from a recent business trip to Los Angeles. Never has the scene outside my house seemed so welcome.

I drove to Los Angeles.

Beyond the Colorado River, the Mojave Desert was awash with color. The air was filled with butterflies, thousands of butterflies, all flying in a northeasterly direction a few feet above the ground. The butterflies flew against a backdrop of thickening haze on the western horizon. My little pickup sort of buzzes at 65 miles per hour. There wasn't much choice but to keep it at buzzing speed. I had the distinct feeling that the sixteen wheelers behind me—when I look out the rearview mirror of my vehicle I'm looking at their undersides—weren't going to slow down for my mini-Tonka Toy. I was collecting butterflies, mustard colored splotches on the windshield and hood.

I topped Cajon Pass and glanced down in shock. The valley below was hidden beneath a solid layer of smog shimmering in the hot desert sun. I descended into a dimmed landscape where open space is a forgotten concept. An hour later, deeper into the smog, I sped down the exit into the suburb where I was to spend the night and finally found my motel. It was located in an upscale retail center where signs are restricted to the size of postage stamps. Graffiti had recently been sandblasted from the outside door to my room. Later, I walked among the trendy shops. At 3 P.M. they were deserted but for bored clerks.

The next morning I got back on the freeway in the midst of rush hour traffic. Fog had joined the smog. I had forgotten how many freeway junctions there are when traveling through the heart of Los Angeles. I sped down another exit and found myself on a narrow road that snaked over a ridge and down into Beverly Hills. Curve signs said 15 miles per hour. A string of Jaguars, all forest green, were pushing me up the hill at 40 miles per hour. For the winding descent toward Sunset Boulevard, the pushy Jaguars upped the speed to 50 miles per hour. It is not for nothing that this particular street stars in every chase scene ever filmed.

In Beverly Hills the street signs are tastefully illegible. I was looking for Sunset Boulevard. I sped across Sunset Boulevard and into the mansion-lined streets. I didn't yet know that I was lost. The realization dawned slowly. Does one, I wondered, walk up to a mansion, ring the door bell, and ask for directions to a place called the Hamburger Hamlet? Probably not. I parked in front of a house the size of a college dormitory, took out a street map, and began walking back toward Sunset Boulevard, hoping all the while that my little pickup would not be consumed by a street sweeper in my absence.

The Hamburger Hamlet was not the fast food place I'd anticipated. The red leather upholstery was real. No drive-up window, no salad bar, no kiddy playground. Lunch there lasted two-and-a-half hours. That is the longest I've ever spent eating a mediocre hamburger . . . or any hamburger. My lunch companion spoke Hollywood with a Manhattan accent. I lived to tell about it.

Driving home I watched for the butterflies in the Mojave Desert. They were not there. Near Kayenta I encountered the butterflies. They had traveled far in three days. Now they float along the canyon rims outside my house. I'm glad they're here. I'm glad I'm here, too.

June 7, 1992

THE WEST SLOPE OF THE LA PLATAS is at the height of mountain spring. The aspen and Gambel oak on the lower slopes are leafing out, and the higher meadows are emerald green beneath solid yellow patches of dandelions. The music of rushing water is everywhere. Main roads through the aspen groves are passable, but once they reach the towering stands of shadowing fir above, they are blocked by snow. I walk to the edge of the snowbanks and look through the dark trees at the wall of peaks ahead. It is still winter there. From the snowbanks I can turn and look west across a vista that reaches from Mesa Verde in the south to the LaSals in the north. The centerpiece in that vast sweep is the canyon-gouged Great Sage Plain stretching from the La Platas in the east to the Abajos in the west. I do not know who first named it the Great Sage Plain. Escalante refers to it as that in his account of the Dominguez–Escalante party's search for a route across the region in 1776. Whether earlier Spanish explorers called it that, or whether it was known by that name by earlier Ute, Navajo, and Puebloan peoples in the region may never be known.

Escalante first saw it when he crossed the low ridge between the Mancos and McElmo drainages where the entrance to Mesa Verde National Park is now located. That is one viewpoint from which the term "plain" seems to make sense. The land sweeps, seemingly unbroken, toward the distant Abajos. What the earliest Europeans here saw differed some from what can be seen today. Then it would have been forested by piñon and juniper or blanketed by sage. Today much of that region is plowed red earth or green fields. The view is deceptive. The "plain" is in fact a series of southwestward-running mesas separated by yawning chasms. One can't cut across the "plain" from Mesa Verde by any means but on foot. Equestrians and motorists can skirt the "plain" along the northeastern heads of the canyons or the southwestward mouths of the canyons.

From the edge of the snowbanks high in the La Platas, the true topography of the Great Sage Plain is a bit more apparent, but not much. From there the sandstone rims of the canyons are light colored streaks running southwestward. The route taken by the earliest Europeans was the upper one, between the canyonheads and the nearby gorge of the Dolores River. It is not a route which they would have logically chosen for themselves but one which was pointed out to them by Indian guides.

I stood at the edge of snowbanks, at the edge of the prevailing winter in the mountains, and looked across the Great Sage Plain where summer this year has come early. Black thunderheads laced with lightning rolled across that place from the west. Curtains of rain blocked the view. I left the mountains and descended into the storm.

June 28, 1992

For a few weeks beginning in late May, I experienced the limbo of being between writing projects. I had made great plans for filling this gap in a rational, directed manner—straighten out bookshelves, catch up on correspondence, take long, purposeful hikes, etc. That was not to be. Instead, the usual moody, directionless, post-project letdown took control of my life. I have experienced these post-project blues, and read about them in the lives of other writers, enough to know that I should just accept them and ride them out. Guilt inspired by the work ethic, however, can't just be swept under the rug. I couldn't stop asking myself, as darkness fell, what I had accomplished during a particular day. Nothing.

During these periods I'm not particularly inclined to seek out friends, because friendship requires explaining one's life at the moment. How do you explain "nothing"? Friends, too, are unlikely to be accepting of unhappiness. Not only is happiness seen as the most basic American right, but expressions of unhappiness are viewed as downright unpatriotic, the ultimate nonconformity in a conformist society. I've started another writing project now, one I'm particularly enthusiastic about, so I can reflect upon the last few weeks and perhaps even laugh at my own gloomy responses to social and personal expectations.

What I did physically during this slow period was wander among the canyons and mesas west of here, visiting this ruin or that, without much sense of gaining a greater understanding of what I was seeing or of appreciating the beauty around me. I saw myself as killing time. I usually went wandering alone but, occasionally, with others. During one of these journeys, a friend remarked in great frustration that he was experiencing writer's block. My first silent thought was that, for me, the comment could not have come at a worse time. Hours later, alone again, I was grateful for the remark. It allowed me to remind myself, once more, that these apparently nonproductive downtimes are, in fact, the most productive phases of a writer's work. It is then that new and original patterns form in the chaos. One emerges from these low periods with a sense of beginning, middle, and end to the writing about to commence. The hardest work has, in fact, just been completed.

My new writing project focuses on an ancient Puebloan community located in the center of the Great Sage Plain northwest of my home, precisely the ruins and the places among which I have wandered for the last few weeks. The recent images I have gained of these places are now surprisingly vivid and fresh in my mind. When I return to them, it will be with specific questions in mind. I will also have specific questions of the research literature I am reading and of the archaeologists I will be interviewing. Those questions provide an intellectual framework—a beginning, middle, and end—that was not obvious to me a few weeks ago. I will discover that many of my questions cannot be answered, but such questions are as important as answers when writing nonfiction essays. They give definition and shape to knowledge, to the surfaces where the known stops and the unknown begins.

In reflecting on the last few weeks, it occurs to me that I was not wandering aimlessly and I was not killing time. On one level I knew that all along. I've been through it before. But I don't always listen to what I know, I listen to what I've been told. Sometimes they aren't the same.

July 5, 1992

A NEW WRITING PROJECT has me thinking every waking hour, and probably in my sleep, about the ancient communities of the Four Corners Country. This is a topic I thought I'd understood long ago. Now that earlier understanding seems more like a mere beginning. I have no idea where this new thought process will lead me, what changes in my thinking will occur in the next few months.

I will be writing about particular pre-European Puebloan communities not far west of my home in Cortez. Archaeologists have been scrutinizing those and similar communities for a century, so I have plenty of completed research material to absorb and to use in my text. The difficulty is not in summarizing completed research. The real challenge will be to incorporate new, ongoing, community-oriented archaeological research into my text.

Since the late nineteenth century, the Puebloans of the Four Corners Country have drawn the attention of some of the world's best archaeologists, and research methods and theories developed in this region are now applied throughout the world. That process continues. Much of the archaeological research throughout the last century has focused on the material culture—the architecture, ceramics, tools, diets—found in specific sites. Much progress has been made in ordering changes in material culture over time. Research into material culture continues and finer-tuned sequences of change will continue to emerge.

In the last quarter of a century, a great deal of research has focused on the interrelationship between prehistoric peoples here and their environment. This research has led archaeologists to question earlier conclusions about why the Puebloans left their long-established communities in the San Juan River Basin and moved to Puebloan communities just outside the rims of this basin. Forty years ago the explanation was that they were forced out by drought. Recent research indicates that no drought alone was severe enough to cause widespread emigration. Personally, I'm less fascinated with why they left than with how they managed to stay put for a thousand years. When they moved, they didn't move far.

Now new research questions are being pursued. These questions are centered on the social organization of the Puebloan communities that occupied the San Juan River Basin. They examine the meaning, extent, content, and dynamic of community in itself. These are the questions, I suspect, of greatest interest to most non-archaeologists, since all of us are a part of community and identify ourselves in relation to community. These questions demand the creation of new research methods and theory. That creative process is under way now by progressive, innovative archaeologists. This new research depends upon all past material and environmental research, but it goes beyond that in its attempts to locate geographical boundaries of specific communities and to examine community changes over time within those boundaries as opposed to changes in early Puebloan culture in general.

As this new knowledge accumulates, it will, I suspect, result in a much greater sense of affinity between the Puebloans and those of us who occupy the San Juan River Basin now. Knowledge of material culture tends to emphasize differences in the way people live. Knowledge of community will ultimately reveal the very human traits all of us share.

July 26, 1992

Not far from here is a deep, narrow red rock canyon with a clear, cool stream running through it shaded by ancient box elders and Ponderosa pine. I go there this time of year because it is cool in the shade and the sound of running water makes one forget the heat on the mesa tops above. From the canyon rim, the cliffs stair-step down through Cretaceous, Jurassic, and Triassic time. The bottom set of cliffs are of stone with a pink interior that weathers to deep red on the surface. The blocky, rectangular shapes that form the cliff are laced with pale green lichens on the red.

In the afternoon thunderheads build in the narrow slot of sky above the cliffs, and hawks and eagles ride the thermals. Sometimes showers wet the stone and thunder echoes through the canyon. Wind whips through the firs that cling to the terraces between the higher cliffs. The roar of the wind fills the spaces between claps of thunder.

Because I live in a place of sweeping vistas, distant horizons, and an enormous sky—an exposed place—part of the appeal of this particular canyon may be that it is so completely enclosing. I cannot see a mile in any direction in the bottom of the winding canyon. The longest view is to the canyon rim, nearly half a mile above. This forces my perspective from the general to the particular, from the landscape as a whole to details of leaf, pebble, and pool.

Recently I returned to a place in the canyon that had caught my attention a year ago or so. When I was there a year ago, a fire had swept through a few acres of Gambel oak. The warmth of fire was still apparent, and the air was filled with the sharp smell of burning oak. My first response was dismay at the destruction caused by the flames. As I looked, however, I was struck by the beauty of the black trunks rising from the powdery ash on the canyon floor.

Now there is no powdery ash but a lush green carpet of new growth beneath the dead, blackened trunks and a few sprouts of green from a few of the trunks indicate that life survived here and there in the oaks themselves.

On my most recent visit there, the afternoon thunder and gale came with a brief cooling rain. I thought of something I had just read in Frank Hamilton Cushing's *Zuni Breadstuff* written a hundred years ago:

> The drum sounded till it shook the cavern; the music shrieked and pealed in softly surging unison, as the wind does in a wooded canyon after the storm is distant . . .

I left the canyon then, ascending into the vastness once more where there are distant purple mountains beyond golden fields of winter wheat. I feel no regret when I leave that canyon, because it will not be long until I return.

August 23, 1992

THERE IS A CONTRADICTION between what the sign says and the scene behind the sign. The sign reads:

McPhee Park
Established 1925 through cooperation of New Mexico Lumber Co. and U.S. Department of Agriculture Forest Service to preserve a sample area of virgin ponderosa pine timber.

My son Jonathan and I walked around the sign and inspected the area behind it. In an area the size of an acre or so were a dozen pine trees that obviously predated 1925. Many more did not. There were sawed off stumps behind the sign. How, we wondered, could this be a "sample area of virgin ponderosa"? Some of the stumps were more than four feet in diameter, much larger than the largest of the standing trees.

We had spent the last hour driving east from the Dolores River through thousands of acres of Ponderosa pine broken here and there by wide, grassy glades ringed by aspen. Mountains towered on the eastern horizon, from north to south—Lone Cone, the Dolores Peaks, Mount Wilson, El Diente, the La Platas. The air was clear, and every cirque and crevice looked near enough to touch. Thunderheads billowed above the peaks.

As we left McPhee Park and that "sample area of virgin ponderosa pine timber," I thought back on where we'd been. At some point, decades ago, those thousands of acres of rolling plateau must have presented a scene of awful clear-cut devastation. Even now there is a certain monotony to the new pine forest, as there is in any managed community where all the organisms are the same age and size, lacking diversity. Whose idea was it, I wondered, to leave a few trees standing on an acre of land? There is something about McPhee Park that mocks its own intentions. Those enormous sawed off stumps say it all.

I recalled century-old photographs I have seen of virgin Ponderosa forest near Mancos Hill. The great trees stand yards apart. There is no Gambel oak beneath the high forest canopy, only tall grass. Today the oak dominates—the great pines are gone. The new forest floor around McPhee Park is covered with Gambel oak, though prescribed burns in recent years have reduced the oak. The new trees often grow a few feet apart in thickets unlike the spacious original forests of giant pines. I know nothing about harvestable timber, but I do wonder how many years it will be before the forest around McPhee Park will be cut again. It probably won't be soon—the best trees were all taken.

Forest management practices have changed and clear-cutting is a thing of the past. McPhee Park is more a monument to greed and misdirected management than it is to the grandeur of a forest that once was.

September 13, 1992

I HAVE BEEN SPENDING a lot of time in Hovenweep National Monument working on a writing project for the Mesa Verde Museum Association. From my home I can drive either to Pleasant View, Colorado, and down the top of Cajon Mesa to the canyonhead ruins or down McElmo Canyon into Utah, approaching Hovenweep from that direction. Either route provides a lot of scenery, and each winds through a wealth of pre-European archaeology. I usually try to go one way and return the other, traveling in a loop.

When driving down Cajon Mesa, the vistas are of Black Mesa, Monument Valley, Navajo Mountain, Cedar Mesa, the Bear's Ears, Elk Ridge, and the Abajos. Driving up Cajon Mesa, the eastern horizon is ragged with mountain peaks. The McElmo Canyon route winds through colorful Jurassic and Cretaceous formations occasionally framing sere mesas in the west or the lavender La Platas in the east.

Shrub-covered rubble mounds, hand and footholds, crumbled towers, small cliff dwellings, petroglyphs, ancient reservoirs, and even a segment or two of pre-European roadway—all visible here and there from modern roads to Hovenweep—are a silent legacy to the San Juan Puebloans who flourished here for so long before moving south to join other Puebloans already living in the Rio Grande and Little Colorado river basins. In many places the visible archaeological record is overlaid by modern farms in Colorado and neat Navajo hamlets set among the Aneth oil wells in Utah.

As I drive through the modern economic landscape picking out the material remnants of the pre-European communities, a single topic nags relentlessly. Where were the Puebloan farms? How did they farm? Recent research has indicated that in an average year of agricultural production, four acres per capita of mesa top farmland would have been required to support a healthy population. Several thousand people lived in this area in the mid-thirteenth century. Most of the arable canyon and mesa land must have been in production. Yet, there is little trace of those farms. What can be seen today are check dams in the bottoms of small drainages and garden terraces on the slopes. If one totaled the acreage of known terraces and of silt-filled areas behind known check dams, the total acreage would not feed many people at four acres per capita.

In the middle Rio Grande Valley, archaeologists are finding pre-European fields, rimmed by stones, covering hundreds of acres. In the Salt River Valley, canal systems once irrigated countless acres where Phoenix now sits. There is nothing like those fields and canals here that can be seen by the naked eye.

Stretching out from the canyonhead communities of Hovenweep are thousands of acres of mesa top soils. What is now a sage-covered plateau must have once been fields of maize. For the time being, however, that remains a matter for speculation.

September 20, 1992

I FIND MYSELF THINKING about friendship a great deal lately. This line of thought is mostly the result of the departure from Cortez recently of a good friend. Since I have a number of good friends here, I've been somewhat surprised at my reaction to his departure. In general, I only saw him a couple of times a month and then not for long. There is nothing past tense about this friendship; I can pick up the phone and talk to him or write a letter. What's changed?

I've slowly come to the realization that this particular friend was the one whom I always called and told when I was taking off for a few days backpacking alone. I told him where I was going and when I'd be back. I knew that if I broke an ankle or my pickup didn't start fifty miles from the nearest pavement, I could stay put and he'd show up when I didn't get home on schedule. That particular part of the friendship is easily replaced. There are other people I can tell and now do. The difference is that most people in my life knew who to call if I had to be reached while I was backpacking alone. That element of a friendship, having others know who your friend is, is more significant to a person living alone and working at home, as I do, than for most of humanity.

Friendship was on my mind, too, as I drove west into the canyon country recently. I was on my way to meet three men whom I first met fifteen years ago. One of them I had not seen or talked to in the subsequent fifteen years, one of them I had not seen for ten years, and one of them I saw very briefly six years ago. We live hundreds of miles apart. One of them called a couple of months ago and suggested that the four of us meet for a few days of hiking, camping, and conversation . . . mostly conversation. I agreed, hoping that my mixed feelings weren't evident in my voice. I envisioned hours in camp talking about our lives in the intervening fifteen years. I wondered if long-ago friendships would survive the harsh reality of a face-to-face meeting when so much had changed.

So I was amazed, as we set up the first night's camp, at how quickly we seemed to resume the very conversation we'd begun fifteen years before. The next day we didn't so much hike as stroll along a canyon rim, talking about politics, music, literature, religion, and life in general. Three of us are fathers and talked some about our sons. If anything had changed, it seemed to be that we found even more to laugh about now than we had fifteen years ago. We take life less seriously now. We stopped often to look at things we encountered along the way: a ruin, a rock, a bird, an animal track, or an ancient tree. Sometimes we didn't talk at all, we just looked. Probably the characteristic we all share is a fascination with light, substance, and color. That led to our meeting in the first place.

What we didn't talk much about was our lives for the last fifteen years. Because we have such similar interests, we have a lot of common friends and acquaintances who have kept us up on the major events in one another's lives. There wasn't much to say about ourselves that the others didn't already know. The man I hadn't seen in fifteen years I knew least about. He has led the most unpredictable life of all of us. My frozen image of him was of a fearless technical climber and river runner and a not particularly social being. He talked openly about fear he'd felt and the effect it had on his life. He's had reason to think about it. He wrote his doctoral dissertation on the psychological and emotional benefits of rock climbing. He's probably become the most attentive observer and listener of us all, though all of our livelihoods depend almost solely on our powers of observation and expression. He seems least constrained by the apparent demands of daily life. He was the one who I thought would most easily stay behind on a canyon rim, seeing beneath the surface of things, as we parted and headed home.

Our time together in the canyons renewed our friendship. I won't wait another fifteen years before seeing any of these men again. The older I get, the more friends matter . . . even if I can't articulate the definition of friendship.

October 4, 1992

OUT MY WEST WINDOW all that remained of day was a deep red glow at the bottom of the sky across the canyon. A thin slice of moon and Venus raced one another toward the black silhouette of Sleeping Ute Mountain. The moon won. The breeze died. Night came silently. I stared out the window until all I could see was my own reflection, lit by a dim light somewhere else in the house. I went outside and looked at the stars. It had been a warm day, but the early night air was already too chill for comfort.

I awakened the next morning to the sound of a robin calling in the first light. By sunrise there were many more robins in the somewhat unlikely area surrounding my house. I think of robins as being creatures of green lawns and leafy trees, not of the rock-ribbed earth and sage in which my house sits. I went outside and watched, thinking I would see the robins suddenly fly south in the new light. I thought maybe they had just paused here a night in their autumnal migration. They stayed. They're still here mingling with the piñon jays. The cottonwoods in the canyon below my house are green as summer. The first snow has already frosted the higher peaks and subsequently vanished. It may be that the robins took flight with that first snow, looked back and saw it gone, and settled in here until snow reappears on the peaks.

Autumn does seem to be a season when the mountains and the canyons exert an equal pull. In the October light, the lavender, green, and gold mountains look as translucent as stained glass.

Spruce and fir branches are covered with the golden fallen leaves of aspens. Brooks are crystal clear and fringed with tawny grasses. Fern patches are yellow beneath the scarlet berries of mountain ash. Hawks and ravens play in the updrafts above glacial gorges. The birds of summer have left the mountains. Winter seems at hand.

In the canyons, September rains renewed the streams. Cougar, deer, and coyote tracks are pressed into the shining red mud around pools. Squirrels scold from ancient pines. Streaks of orange are appearing in oak leaves. Clumps of maple near shaded seeps are beginning to turn crimson against weathered stone. There are more birds than ever. Nights are warm and filled with sleepy birdsong. Winter seems seasons away.

Around my house are dense clusters of purple asters and yellow flowering rabbitbrush. The hot, midday air is filled with bees buzzing around the rabbitbrush. I know it is autumn the minute the sun vanishes behind the far rim of the canyon. The bees depart and the air turns cold. Darkness comes quickly. The scratchy sound of lizards scurrying in the depths of the woodpile ends abruptly. A few crickets begin their song. A robin chirps softly nearby. I wonder how long I will have robins for neighbors.

November 1, 1992

ONCE IN THE NARROW, descending bottom of the side canyon, we found it choked with house-sized boulders, small pouroffs, and pools ringed with slippery silt. It was slow going. At last the boulders ended, the canyon floor leveled, and shining water trickled over expanses of white slickrock. It was still early morning. Sunlight had not yet reached the eight hundred foot depths of the canyon. We walked in cool shadow filled with birdsong beneath a narrow ribbon of deep blue sky.

With me was Boyce McClung, an avid amateur photographer from Flagstaff. His long, concentrated pauses to make photographs were welcome; they left me plenty of time to look around. There was too much beauty to absorb hurriedly. Sunlight glanced off from high on one sheer pink cliff and into the shadow below. The reflected light cast subtle diffused shadows of its own and deepened the brilliant colors of autumn leaves and grasses. Towering trees glowed against the opposing cliff which remained so darkly shadowed as to appear black in contrast.

We reached the main canyon. For once I ignored the ancient dwellings tucked into overhangs high above us. There was a transitory quality to each shift of light and shadow. A deep, narrow canyon in autumn is an illuminated reminder that the earth spins beneath the sun at more than a thousand miles an hour and what is seen now will be gone in a single blink of the eye. The ruins, I thought, will be there another day. I didn't want to miss a minute of what would never be seen again, that changing light on those leaves trembling in that breeze.

Hours later we began the ascent up another side canyon. Dark, towering fir trees replaced the juniper and piñon. Thin clouds moved beneath the sun. The sun dipped beneath the canyon rim. The clouds thickened, diffusing a shadowless, wintry evening light in the canyon. We neared the head of the canyon and entered a scattered grove of aspen. Golden leaves spun down from the trees and floated on the pools.

It rained throughout much of the moonless night. The next morning, during a brief break in the storm, we walked through a dripping mesa top forest to a cliff edge where we could see another nearby canyon. A curtain of rain dimmed its walls and the free-standing pinnacles of stone that rose to its rims. The rain moved toward us. A small patch of sunlight broke through the clouds and spotlighted the rain-washed cliffs and pinnacles. They mirrored the shining light. The rain poured down on us, but we stared transfixed. Minutes later the sunlight faded, and the pewter light prevailed. We walked slowly along the canyon rim and back onto the mesa top. Neither of us said much. There were no words for what we'd seen.

November 8, 1992

Al was a great teacher and there are scores and scores of Southwestern archaeologists who learned from him. He was the best reader of stratigraphy and dirt I have ever met and he had a remarkable memory. He remembered everything he'd seen over the years so he was a tremendous source of information. He could tell you what you were looking at when no one else could. He taught me much of what I know. Bob Lister always felt the same about him. I owe Al a great debt.

Alden C. Hayes
November 1, 1992

THE RECENT DEATH of James Allen Lancaster in Cortez at age ninety-eight ended an era in Southwestern archaeology. Al Lancaster was the last of the great archaeologists of this century to learn his profession outside the classroom, off the college campus. What he knew about Southwestern field archaeology, which was more than any one person will ever know again, he learned from the ruins themselves. Others before him made significant contributions to archaeology without formal academic training in the subject, but Al Lancaster will be the last to do so and the greatest.

It is a tribute to Al Lancaster that he was revered by the leading scholarly and field archaeologists of the middle and late twentieth century and was constantly sought out by them for his advice and counsel. It is a tribute to him, too, that he continued to offer his knowledge to the profession well into the last year of his life—standing alongside Fort Lewis College students and professor James Judge at a site being excavated by them last summer on the family farm near Pleasant View, a few hundred yards from the site where he began his career. His knowledge was the sort that doesn't become obsolete, out of date, or out of fashion. His knowledge was based on experience, on reality. He was respected for his uncanny ability to stand on an unexcavated archaeological site and know what was hidden beneath the surface of the ground. That was the product of his highly disciplined powers of observation and concentration and of his ability to continually transform his thinking based on what he'd seen and experienced.

Al Lancaster was associated with many of the major archaeological research projects of the twentieth century—Lowry, Alkali Ridge, Awatovi, Snaketown, Wetherill Mesa, and Dolores, to name only a few. He worked alongside the leading archaeological scholars of the century—Paul Martin, Earl Morris, J.O. Brew, Emil Haury, and Alden C. Hayes, to name only a few. David Breternitz's simple tribute was read at the funeral, "He was my mentor." Dave spoke for hundreds of dedicated archaeologists at work in the field, in laboratories, and in college anthropology departments today.

Millions of people from around the world have been touched by Al Lancaster's work, most of them without ever knowing it. He pioneered modern methods of ruin stabilization at Mesa Verde, Chaco Canyon, Aztec, and Hovenweep. His stabilization methods and techniques are applied now far beyond the Southwest. The many awards and honors he received for his contributions to archaeology include some of the highest in the nation.

His funeral was a moving tribute to the man, a celebration of a life well lived. It brought together his fellow farm families and his fellow archaeologists. He symbolized the best of both, and the fact that he integrated the two so well may, in time, be seen as one of his greatest achievements. His wife of seventy years, Alice Lancaster, was no mere supporter of his career, she was an active partner in his work. As such, she and her six children, including Mary Murphy and Judy Crow of Durango, will continue to be sought out for insights into what they have witnessed: a remarkable career in archaeology spanning much of this century.

December 6, 1992

WHILE THE WOMAN finished typing the permit, I stared out the barred windows of the adobe building into the long shadows of afternoon falling across the desert. She smiled as she handed me the document and requested that I read it carefully before signing it. Her words were spoken with the same gentle friendliness I'd encountered among all the Tohona O'odham I'd talked with that day. I scanned the document quickly, expecting the standard waiver of responsibility for injury or death. I came to one sentence, stopped, and read it twice more. It said, "Baboquivari District is not responsible for any physical attack, death, injury or emotional trauma, from the result of a sighting of a lion."

I signed the permit and then asked her if there was a problem with mountain lions. She said the area had been closed for a while because lions were coming into people's camps. She added that some people got very upset when a lion came into their camp. Good, I thought, we'll have the place to ourselves.

The rough, dusty road from the ranger station ascends slowly through the mesquite toward the canyon that was our destination. Above the canyon, a peak—more a blunt, sheer spire of naked rock—towers into the Arizona sky. Most of the few outsiders drawn to the area are mountain climbers headed for the peak. My son Geoff and I were there to look at plants in the canyon. At the mouth of the canyon the arid basin-floor plant zone ends, and we entered a lush, shaded oasis of hackberry, willow, and live oak. Campsites are scattered through the trees at the end of the road. There were a few other vehicles there when we arrived, but as night fell, helmeted climbers returned from the peak and drove away. We did have the place to ourselves.

The next morning we were joined by Tucsonians Karen and Rex Adams. Karen is director of environmental research for the Crow Canyon Archaeological Center and studies arid floral zones around the Mediterranean and in Mexico, as well. Rex is a scientist at the National Laboratory for Tree-Ring Research in Tucson and is knowledgeable about the plants of the region. Geoff, who brought along a weighty tome, *The Flora of Arizona,* spends much of his spare time looking at plants in the deserts and mountains surrounding Tucson, where he works for a landscaping company. I was along to listen and learn.

The canyon flows west from the peak and climbs rapidly above its mouth. The south-facing wall of the canyon is a steep talus slope topped by orange cliffs hundreds of feet high. The talus there is blanketed by mesquite, saguaro, and agave. The north-facing wall of the canyon gets no sunlight this time of the year. The lower slopes are thickly forested with oak. Golden-leaved native walnuts grow in the steep side drainages. The upper cliffs are covered with green lichens. The streambed in the bottom of the canyon gets less than an hour of sunlight now. It is shaded by walnut trees, ancient oaks, alligator juniper, and native ash. Native grapevines climb high into the trees. Cotton, beans, chile, coral beans, ferns, columbines, and mulberry are among the scores of native plants growing beneath the riparian forest canopy. We climbed a couple of thousand vertical feet. The plant zones in the canyon bottom and on each canyon wall seemed to change with each hundred feet of ascent. Karen, Rex, and Geoff shouted with delight at each new plant sighting.

I silently assumed responsibility for watching out for lions. My first encounter was a bleached, polished lion skull lodged into the streambed boulders. The teeth were awesome. Hours later we decided to follow a different route down the mountain. We shouldn't have. We were soon in dense thickets of shrubs armed with needle-sharp thorns up to three inches long. Blood dripped down the backs of my hands. Blood stained the sleeves and front of my new cotton shirt. Thorns broke off in my Levis and kept on scratching with each hesitant step. Blood ran down my face into the corner of my mouth. Fleet-footed lions, I concluded, probably smelled me from ten miles away. We detoured. In a small opening we found part of a javelina skull—the bloody upper jaw, forehead, one staring eye, and a bit of bristly ear. The hapless creature had been dead for a few short hours. I didn't dwell upon its fate. I only hoped the lion had gotten its fill for the day.

December 27, 1992

THE DAYS ARE GETTING LONGER now, and each evening the sun sets farther to the north on the Sleeping Ute. Outside my window it looks like winter should look at year's end. Clumps of snow cling to the north sides of piñons and junipers and weigh down the spindly grey tops of sage. Last year's tawny rice grass bends beneath burdens of frost. In the cold nights, frost crystallizes on top of the snow and on the trees. At sunrise each crystal surface catches the light and the world glitters.

The birds coming to eat the seeds I put out are mostly juncos, finches, and piñon jays. From the corner of my eye, while writing, I see them ceaselessly arriving and departing. Sometimes there are a dozen or more at the feeder next to a densely branched juniper. Now and then, startled, the birds flutter deep into the tree. Seconds later a hawk, pale grey and white, glides down the slope just feet above the ground. With slight twists of its body, the hawk curves gracefully around the trees and vanishes below the canyon rims. It is several minutes after the hawk's passage before the first hungry jay ventures out of the juniper to resume its meal.

Deer find their way out of the canyon at dusk. They walk slowly, taking a step and then pausing before taking the next. The deer merge with motionless shapes—boulders and trees—in the dying light. The deer do not look up at a noisy wedge of Canada geese making their way south, guided by the canyon rims. They do not look up at the first planets and stars appearing in the cold, red sky.

It is not because I am separated from these winter scenes by the double panes of my west window that I feel like an observer rather than a participant in life along this canyon rim. It is more that I am pondering human events or listening to the news while staring out the window. I do occasionally see violence outside that window—the quick death of a little bird in the talons and beak of a larger bird, or blood-splattered snow marking the spot where a cottontail's heartbeat ended. That violence differs from the human violence which dominates the news. Violent death along this canyon rim is just as certain but is not the same as dying on L.A. street corners or in Bosnian breadlines. Death along this canyon does not occur at the hands of drive-by gang assassins or religion-crazed militiamen.

As this year ends, what happens outside my window remains much the same as what happened a year ago. But there is that world I cannot see from my window and can glimpse only on the evening news—the human world, my world. I think of lines from a poem, "The Second Coming," written by William Butler Yeats a century ago:

> Mere anarchy is loosed up the world,
> The blood-dimmed tide is loosed, and everywhere
> The ceremony of innocence is drowned;
> The best lack all conviction, while the worst
> Are full of passionate intensity.

Outside my window the ceremony of innocence is not yet drowned.

January 24, 1993

FROM MY HOUSE I CAN LOOK NORTH and see a small wooded knoll on the horizon ten miles away. The knoll sits squarely on the divide between the Dolores River Basin and the San Juan River Basin. The north side of the knoll drains into the Dolores and the south side drains toward the San Juan. On top of the knoll are the walls of a ruined building constructed more than eight hundred fifty years ago. From the ruin it is possible to see the Abajo Mountains and the Bear's Ears in Utah, the fourteen-thousand-foot peaks of the

Wilson Mountains at the headwaters of the Dolores River in Colorado, the La Plata Mountains in the east, and Mesa Verde and Sleeping Ute Mountain in the south. Through a gap between Mesa Verde and Sleeping Ute Mountain, the Chuska Mountains can be seen across the San Juan River along the Arizona–New Mexico border. The western slopes of the Chaco River drainage are visible in New Mexico.

At first glance it is a vast expanse. But there is nothing in that vista which cannot be reached on foot in two days of walking at a steady, comfortable pace. That fact makes the vastness a little less imposing, and it has implications for understanding the significance of the ruin itself.

The building was constructed at the time when the massive pueblos of Chaco Canyon—Chaco Canyon is not visible from the knoll—were in use. The building on the knoll, though smaller, bears some resemblance to those at Chaco—both the architectural formality and the masonry construction technique are similar to those found in Chaco Canyon. Designs painted on some of the ceramics found on the knoll are the same as those which prevailed at Chaco in the first half of the twelfth century. These similarities have led some archaeologists to conclude that the ruin on the knoll is a Chacoan outlier, the product of some sort of system, political perhaps, that was centered in Chaco Canyon at the time.

These so-called Chacoan outliers are found in every direction from Chaco Canyon, and a few of them are even linked to Chaco Canyon by "roads." Thus, the conclusion that these far-flung structures are a part of a Chaco-centered system. The function of the outliers may have been as collection points for local goods to be transported to Chaco Canyon just two or three days' walk away. Some proponents of this Chaco-centered theory argue that the outliers were constructed by residents of Chaco Canyon itself, teams of Chacoans sent out to gather goods from local populations in order to sustain a center grown too large and hungry to support itself on the resources available within its own immediate vicinity.

Other archaeologists, not coincidentally those working some distance from Chaco Canyon, argue that the buildings assumed to be outliers were built by local populations and had little to do with what was going on at Chaco Canyon at the time. The first half of the twelfth century was, in fact, a time of widespread exchange of goods among the communities of the San Juan River Basin and beyond. The resulting intercommunity contact would have allowed trendy architectural styles to spread rapidly over vast expanses. Some archaeologists propose that Chaco Canyon was subject to, not the center of, widespread stylistic fashion among autonomous communities. By the end of the twelfth century, exchange of goods was waning and architectural styles became more diverse among thirteenth-century communities here.

Did that new stylistic diversity mark the collapse of a Chacoan system, or did it indicate renewed economic self-sufficiency and isolationism on the part of long established, politically autonomous, local communities? Someday that question will be answered. Meanwhile I'll go sit on that knoll and take in the view.

January 31, 1993

THE SNOW IS GONE from south-facing slopes here, and it is possible once more to wander from country roads onto slickrock wherever the two, roads and slickrock, intersect. With that expanded walking room comes a tremendous sense of release from the imprisoning snow and mud which have prevailed since early December. Weather events, I think, are the natural phenomena most difficult to recall with any clarity after they pass. It's hard to remember what the weather was like this time last week much less to compare what this winter is like compared to past winters. But the long spell of clouds and storm extending from early December through mid-January is not likely to be forgotten soon.

At first I thought that my listless gloominess during the grey weather was my own response to leaden skies and that others were probably cheerfully pursuing their usual lives. Conversations with acquaintances and friends, however, convinced me that no one was immune to the blues. I began to wonder if Four Corners residents are more vulnerable to weather-induced moods than are residents of wetter climes. We're accustomed to long periods of clear skies and sunlight. We're accustomed to roaming freely about the countryside in any season. If we can't walk at home, we can head for the canyons and walk there. But even the canyons were deep in snow and mud for a month. It may have been the combination of wet, dim days with the impossibility of walking which led to the general malaise accompanying the New Year here.

Now I look back on those stormy weeks and remember the moments of beauty. When the sandstone cliffs here become saturated with rain and melting snow, their color deepens. That subdued brilliance is even more apparent in dim light than beneath a blazing sun. There were the moments when approaching snowstorms obscured Sleeping Ute Mountain and then moved up this canyon until my house seemed isolated from all existence but falling snow. There was the rainy day when, desperately trying to shake off cabin fever, I drove around Sleeping Ute Mountain. The expanses of low buttes and sweeping grasslands in the San Juan Valley shone in the late light. Bands of clay beneath the caprock were a rainbow of deep pinks, yellows, and greens.

After a few days of clear skies and warm sun, I am able to explore the canyon rim where I live. A solid blanket of snow is dissolving into patches on the north sides of trees. Along the south side of my house, the first annuals of the year are sprouting, forming carpets of green seedlings on the drying soil. Native perennials, low rosettes of leaves alongside snowbanks, are emerging from dormancy. Buds are swelling slightly on one cottonwood outside my door.

It is seven weeks until the first official day of spring. To my surprise, I find myself hoping that spring waits seven weeks before arriving. The worst of winter is behind us; the best of winter here always comes in February and March. Spring can wait awhile.

February 21, 1993

SEVERAL TIMES LAST WEEK I looked down from my west window at a golden eagle gliding along the rimrock below my house. The eagle circles and returns. I think it is the same bird I have watched in seasons before, but it has grown. Its back is a shimmering mosaic of dark browns and burnished gold. The eagle's flight, from my perspective, seems so effortless as to be motionless. The earth beneath the eagle is now bare but for a few white patches on the north sides of trees. Beneath the trees are brilliant emerald cushions of moss. New grass is quickly mown down by rabbits and deer. Light green sprigs of flax are springing up from the moist soil, and there is green in last year's tawny clumps of rice grass. Lichens are turquoise and copper on exposed stone. Everything—juniper, sage, and stone—is washed clean by rain and melting snow. On the higher elevations of the Great Sage Plain, which rises to the north and west of my house, the snow is still deep on the fields. Its crusted surface is strong enough to walk across, and it shines with blinding intensity beneath the sun. When I look into that shimmering expanse, I cannot see the subtle landmarks by which I orient myself in that place and sometimes feel lost on a crystalline sea. South of my house, the snow lies deep on the northern face of Mesa Verde and on all of Sleeping Ute Mountain. In the gap between Mesa Verde and the Sleeping Ute, I can see the Carrizos and the Chuskas shining in the distance across the San Juan River.

The sun now sets an hour later than it did two months ago, sliding down the north slope of Ute Peak into the face of the sleeping giant. Soon it will be north of the Sleeping Ute and setting into McElmo Canyon. Because there are fast-moving clouds every evening, sunset is a light show. Patches of light move across the slopes and valleys of the snowy mountains lighting the cloud shadows from beneath.

I can only wonder now what spring will look like when it arrives here. Last spring, after a dry winter but with March and April rains, blossomed brilliantly through May and June. May this spring do the same.

February 28, 1993

LONE CONE PEAK, which I can see from my house, is a smooth, unruffled mound of white on the northern horizon. No rock outcropping nor stand of trees punctuates the whiteness on its steep southern slope. I don't see it often. Most of the time it is hidden by the clouds and storms which continue to sweep across this place.

When it is visible, I go outside and scan its slopes to see if an avalanche has scoured any spot down to stone. If so, the snows have buried the avalanche path and the whiteness continues to reign.

Avalanches are the winter equivalent in the Four Corners Country of the flash floods that thunder down dry washes in summer. They are often described as killers or as deadly. But that's only if someone gets in their way. Otherwise they are awesome natural phenomena. They were doing their part in shaping this rugged country long before anyone was around to be killed. One reason I look for avalanches on Lone Cone Peak is that no one is there to get in the way.

According to news reports, eleven people, mostly skiers having fun, have been killed by avalanches in Colorado so far this winter. That is being described as a record number of deaths. Not quite. According to a history of avalanches in San Juan County, written in 1976 by Betsy Armstrong, eighteen men died during a single storm in that county alone in 1906. Twelve of the men were in the Shenandoah Mine boarding house in Cunningham Gulch, and the remaining six were traveling in the county—probably on their way to Saint Patrick's Day celebrations in Silverton.

The death and destruction wrought by that storm alone moved *The Silverton Standard* to suggest in its April 7, 1906, edition:

> The Standard has a suggestion to offer which it believes will be of great practical good to every mining camp in Colorado . . . briefly it is to have a state law enacted by which mining counties may appoint inspectors, or a commission, clothed with the power of protecting, as far as possible, lives and property from snowslides . . . Upon such a commission should the power be bestowed to decide whether sites for such buildings are safe or unsafe, and their licenses issued accordingly . . .

The Silverton Standard's call for avalanche zoning went unheeded. The boarding house was rebuilt and reoccupied. Another building in San Juan County, the Iowa-Tiger Mill in Arrastra Gulch, was destroyed twice by avalanches and damaged another six times. If there were ever a testament to human optimism, it is the fact that the Iowa-Tiger Mill was not relocated but was rebuilt or repaired seven times in twenty-three years.

At the turn of the century the mountains around Silverton were filled with operating mines, mills, and flourishing mining camps. Winter travel was unavoidable. In the century from 1875 to 1975, ninety-five people died in avalanches in San Juan County. Today there are no mines operating in the county. Avalanche deaths are now rare because the people of Silverton are better educated about avalanche hazards and conditions than anyone else in the world. They don't get in the way.

There are a few people who have no choice but to get in the way. They are the highway crews responsible for keeping Highway 550 open from Cascade Village to Ouray. They deserve a lot of credit for sheer bravery. The rest of us ought to just stay out of the way.

March 28, 1993

THE PART OF MONTEZUMA COUNTY that is inhabited today is something of a central plateau between the mountains in the east and the canyons in the west. Paved highways link the towns of Cortez, Dolores, and Mancos. Most community life is now centered in those towns. The high schools, banks, supermarkets, and most of the churches are all found in those towns. The life of rural residents is oriented to those towns.

A half century ago, that was not the case. Rural communities had a much greater sense of their own identity centered on one-room schools, Granges, community churches, post offices, and general stores. People knew where one community began and another ended simply by knowing where each farm family went to church, school, and Grange. Today many of the Granges no longer function, the elementary schools are consolidated into larger systems, the churches are in town, the general stores are closed, and Rural Free Delivery has replaced the daily trip to the post office. A person from here has to be a half-century old to say, "I'm from Sylvan . . . " Or Ackmen, or Beulah, or Mildred, or Lebanon. The listener has to be a half-century old to know where those communities are in the vast sweep of farms and fields occupying central Montezuma County.

This transformation from rural communities to town-centered

communities was brought home to me recently when I read an oral history of Dolores and the surrounding areas. *Our Past—Portals To The Future* was published by the Dolores Public Library. Most of the interviews were conducted by my sister, Shirley Dennison, who has lived in Dolores for nearly forty years. The individuals interviewed are not Montezuma County pioneers. They are the next generation, the children of pioneers. Many of them grew up in the rural communities surrounding Dolores rather than in the town itself.

They speak of an era before television and satellite dishes, all-weather rural roads, rural water systems, center pivot irrigation systems, and mountain ski resorts. The economies were more localized—the apple orchards of Lewis, Lebanon, and Summit Ridge, the mines in Rico, the sawmill at McPhee, the ranches at Ground Hog . . . Tourism, energy, and service industries—connected to the larger world as a whole—had little impact on these local communities.

These children of pioneers speak in voices that might, on one level, now seem quaint. A neighbor's death, a mine closing, a sawmill fire, a Grange dance, a pet bear, a foreclosure, a hint of scandal, a Depression hardship . . . all these seem to take on equal significance when recalled from the distant past. The quaintness derives from the fact that we can now experience all of these things, times ten and neatly packaged, in a single evening of television viewing. In the end, though, these local voices are not quaint. They are talking about selves and neighbors, real people in real communities. They are talking about a time before the line between reality and fantasy became so blurred that the two are no longer distinguishable. Entertainment Tonight, Prime Time Live, and tabloid shows pale in comparison to these oral histories, but they are what people talk about today.

A second volume of Dolores oral history is in preparation. I'm looking forward to reading it.

April 11, 1993

AT KAYENTA THE WIND drove the rain with stinging force as I ran from the restaurant to my pickup. I drove south then toward Tuba City. The red rocks slanting up from Laguna Creek shone silver in the light of the storm. The paved highway was covered with a slick layer of mud where pickups turned onto it from unpaved side roads. At Tuba City the rain stopped. I headed east toward the Hopi villages and the first in a series of meetings I was to have with leaders in Indian communities in Arizona and New Mexico. The evening sun broke through the clouds and lit a landscape of golden clay and stone. A south wind prevailed with such strength that sheets of damp soil were torn from that land and became an opaque film on my windshield.

By the time I neared Hotevilla, the wind had died and the late sky was a leaden grey. The villages of Hotevilla and Kykotsmovi were surrounded by patches of newly turned soil awaiting planting, and ancient apricot trees were in bloom against outcrops of cream-colored stone. The rain began in the night, and I awakened several times to the sound of it pounding on the roof of my room. In the morning I walked through juniper, sage, and mud toward fingers of mist reaching down to touch Black Mesa in the north. It was hours before my first meeting in Kykotsmovi, so I took my time in the silent dawn.

That afternoon, at Ganado, snow began to fall, and soon I could not see the pine forests along the highway. At St. Michael's the snow became rain, and in Window Rock the rain became fog that obscured the rock formations surrounding the town. By the time my meeting there was over, sunlight was visible through the fog, and later in Gallup, the stars shone in a cold poststorm night.

The next morning I arrived early in Zuni and walked along the lake in Black Rock. The still waters reflected the pink dawn, and thousands of ducks floated in the mirrored light. At noon I went east toward Acoma through the Malpais lava flows. There the wind tore patches of snow from the hardened black stone and hurled them across the frozen earth. Banners of snow and mist boiled and whipped around the summit of Mount Taylor. Near Acoma, willows were flattened against the ground by the gale.

In Santa Fe I walked along Guadalupe Street with my son Jonathan through wet snow that was not falling but speeding horizontally through the streets and alleys carried by a wind so cold that it cut to the bone. Days later I left Santa Fe in a blizzard, drove through sunlight in Española, and re-entered the storm once more in Abiquiu. Around Coyote the layered cliffs of red and gold stone, washed by melting snow, caught moving patches of sunlight that lit the storm. North of Cuba the great expanses of sage were turquoise beneath the mist.

I arrived home in Cortez beneath a clearing evening sky. Sleeping Ute Mountain was white beneath newly fallen snow and puddles in my yard were evidence of recent rain. For ten days I had traveled through storms listening as men and women spoke in heartfelt phrases about the meaning this living land has for them. As I watched the sun set across the canyon, suddenly what I saw had more meaning for me.

April 18, 1993

THE ROADSIDES through Monument Valley are blanketed by lavender lupine, and yellow composites are blooming across patches of red earth near Mexican Hat. The San Juan River is a thick red soup fed by rushing streams in all of its lower tributaries. Cottonwoods are leafing out in the canyons. Rising above this red land and spring color are distant white mountain ranges still buried beneath winter snow. A lot more water will flow down the rivers before summer.

I have spent several recent weeks driving alone to communities throughout the Four Corners Country, so I quickly accepted when a friend said she would drive me to meetings one day last week in Kayenta and at a remote spot in southeastern Utah, a round-trip of more than three hundred miles. My pickup deserved a day of rest, and I could lean back and look at the countryside. As we traveled, my friend talked about what the land meant to her. She spends every nonworking minute hiking and camping, usually alone, in the canyon country in every season, regardless of weather conditions.

For her, she said, the slickrock country is a spiritual place. She is a knowledgeable student, not a practitioner, of world religions and doesn't use the word "spiritual" loosely.

The meeting in Kayenta was with a man from Hopi who spoke fervently about the place of this land in Hopi religion. Hopi religion virtually defines his relationship to the land: the mountains, mesas, canyons, and rivers. Ancestral villages and burials scattered across this land anchor the past and present to the future in Hopi religion. Hopis don't "manage" these natural and cultural resources, he said. They honor and respect them.

The meeting in southeastern Utah started out at the mouth of a canyon filled with the sound of rushing water and required walking up a steep, narrow side canyon where pools of clear water reflected the afternoon sky. The walk ended at a small, smoke-blackened cave. Vandals and looters have stolen and damaged much of the cave's contents over the last century. Recent archaeological research about the cave indicates that it was first used as a shelter by humans nearly eight thousand years ago. Two thousand years or so ago it was being used as a burial place by local residents of the time. Beginning a century ago it became a place to pillage.

As we traveled home through the evening light, I tried to figure out whether I view the land and archaeological sites as spiritual places. I didn't come to any conclusion. My mind kept going back to the small, desecrated cave in the watery canyon. The descendants of the people buried there would view it with religious respect. The archaeologists now conducting research there treat it with humanistic and scientific respect. The vandals who destroyed so much of what was there treated it with no respect. Spiritual or not, the place—cave and canyon together in a larger, mountain-rimmed land—continue to evoke a sense of the profoundness of human existence.

> *April 25, 1993*
>
> Something will have gone out of us as a people if we let the remaining wilderness be destroyed; if we permit the last virgin forest to be turned into comic books and plastic cigarette cases; if we drive the few remaining wild species into zoos or to extinction; if we pollute the last clear air and the last clean streams and push our paved roads through the last of the silence, so that never again will Americans be free in their own country from the noise, the exhausts, the stinks of human and automotive waste. And so that never again can we have the chance to see ourselves single, separate, vertical and individual in the world, part of the environment of the trees and rocks and soil, brother to the other animals, part of the natural world and competent to belong in it.
>
> Wallace Stegner
> *The Wilderness Idea*—1961

With the recent death of Wallace Stegner, the American West lost an eloquent champion. Stegner was among the first writers to examine the popular history of our region and to proclaim it more myth than reality. He saw that the mythical "winning" of the West that poised the brave pioneer against the wilderness had, in fact, become an ideological tool justifying the damming of the last wild rivers, the cutting of the last virgin forests, the polluting of the last clean air, the grazing of the last grasslands, the strip-mining of the last plateaus, and the paving of the last footpaths through the wilds. He became an effective advocate for the preservation of our rapidly vanishing wildlands. His writing helped bring about the passage of the Wilderness Act and the subsequent setting aside of Wilderness Areas throughout the West. His writing will continue to inform and inspire wilderness advocates for generations into the future.

Stegner was effective because he avoided the tactics of some environmentalists. He was less interested in merely winning than he was in assuring the preservation of wilderness in perpetuity. He didn't run around in a white hat looking for black hats, evil corporations, and self-serving government agencies. Stegner looked further than that and into the heart of the problem. The heart of the problem, in Stegner's eyes, is us, all of us.

Stegner was effective because his writing did not serve to polarize Americans, it eloquently described the reality of something called wilderness. According to Stegner, we do not have to physically go into wilderness ourselves in order to experience it, treasure it, and benefit from its continuing preservation. Just knowing it is there is adequate justification for the preservation of wilderness.

> Without any remaining wilderness we are committed wholly, without chance for even momentary reflection and rest, to a headlong drive into our technological termite-life, the Brave New World of a completely man-controlled environment . . . It is good for us when we are young, because of the incomparable sanity it can bring briefly . . . into our insane lives. It is important to us when we are old because it is there—important, that is, simply as an idea.
>
> Wallace Stegner
> (1909–1993)

May 30, 1993

I SPENT A LOT OF TIME on the road this spring traveling to Native American communities and other destinations as part of a project I'm working on for the Four Corners Heritage Council. The purpose of the proposed project is to introduce American Indian perspectives into interpretation of heritage sites in the Four Corners Country. The response to the concept has been positive, but the meetings have also touched on other issues, some of which are of serious concern to Native Americans in this region.

A number of American Indian communities are faced with a dilemma. They appreciate the positive benefits of tourism. The numbers of tourists, however, are becoming unmanageable. These communities are reluctant to do anything that will increase the numbers of tourists. Some communities are closing ceremonial and social events that once were open to the public in order to assure that their own people can attend the events. At Hopi, for instance, where the population of the twelve villages is now nearly ten thousand, a major ceremonial event may be attended by several thousand Hopis. The events occur in plazas the size of basketball courts. The plazas cannot accommodate the thousands of tourists who also want to attend. The main spectator areas are on surrounding rooftops. The roofs cannot bear the weight of the masses of spectators. One building recently collapsed with several resulting injuries. Other communities are experiencing the same problems with public events. The events themselves cannot be moved because the plaza location itself is of great religious significance.

A second problem confronting these communities is the destruction or desecration of shrines, many of which are located on public lands outside the reservation boundaries. Offerings left at the shrines are stolen. Worse yet in the eyes of many Native Americans, unwanted offerings are being left at or buried beneath the shrines by practitioners of New Age religions. This is viewed as a form of desecration and deepens the Native American determination to keep the location of the shrines secret. Ironically, in order to keep shrines on public lands from being destroyed by modern development, Native Americans are forced to disclose their location and significance. That only results in other forms of desecration or destruction. The commitment to secrecy is so great that some pueblos will choose secrecy rather than stop development. These pueblos want the laws changed so that shrines and other sensitive areas can be protected from development without disclosing secret information. They argue that the burden of proof should be shifted from Native Americans to those who want to destroy shrines in the process of development.

A third area of concern is the use of religious symbols—particularly representations of certain petroglyphs—on everything from T-shirts to coffee mugs. This only heightens the Native American perception that their cultures and religions are for sale for profit by everyone but themselves. Native American artists and artisans living in their own communities are aware of what is appropriately sold to the public and what is not. Outsiders lack this knowledge and often openly, if unintentionally, insult the people whose religious symbols they are incorporating into their own work. No one would wear a T-shirt decorated with a dying Christ into the Vatican. The equivalent happens all the time in Indian communities.

The Native Americans of the Four Corners Country are beginning to form their own tourism organizations. Their highest priority is not to increase tourism but to manage tourism. If they do not succeed, then many Indian communities will simply lock the gate and keep all outsiders out. We'll all be the losers.

June 20, 1993

THE DUSTY ROAD followed the section lines on a flattopped mesa bounded by deep canyons. We traveled through expanses of alfalfa, winter wheat, and fallow red earth before reaching the sage and junipers that blanket the central areas of the mesa. On the distant horizon ahead of us were Monument Valley, Navajo Mountain, and Black Mesa. To the north were the snow-streaked peaks of the LaSals and Abajos and to the south was Sleeping Ute Mountain. With me were archaeologists Mark Varien, John Stein, and Heidi Reed and archaeobotanist Dr. Karen Adams. Our guide was Ruth Slickman, an avid amateur archaeologist.

We stopped first at two pueblos on the mesa top well back from the canyon rims. They dated to the late twelfth or early thirteenth century. The first was a single square of rooms surrounding a large central kiva. Chacoan specialists Stein and Reed thought it resembled the great houses associated with the Chacoan influence throughout the San Juan River Basin. The second was a series of smaller buildings, each with at least one kiva, clustered along the crest of a low ridge. The pattern of architectural relationships in this community was similar to that of several pueblos of the time throughout the Great Sage Plain.

Next we visited five pueblos dating to the late thirteenth century. They were on the canyon rims and on the talus below the rims. This movement from the mesa tops to stony canyon rims in the thirteenth century is typical of much of the Great Sage Plain. On Mesa Verde, settlements moved from the mesa tops into the cliff dwellings.

We made camp at sunset on an expanse of flat rimrock overlooking the junction of two canyons. A breeze dispersed the gnats and cooled the hot stone. A lone butte rose above the point where the mesa ended and the canyons joined. Ruins could be seen along one side of the butte's caprock and along its base high above the surrounding landscape. We speculated about the choice of the site. Was it a fortified pueblo intended as a refuge against real or imagined enemies? Was conflict and violence as much a part of the thirteenth-century Puebloan world here as it is throughout all the world today?

The next morning we traveled to another site on another butte above the junction of two canyons. Though it was only a few miles from our campsite as the crow flies, it took us nearly two hours driving time to get there. That is the effect of canyons on modern modes of travel here. This site was much older than the sites we'd visited the previous day. It included a large circle of stones more than seventy-five feet across. In the seventh century the circle probably served as a dance plaza. People living on the surrounding landscape would have gathered there for ceremonial and social events which renewed community ties. Once more we found ourselves speculating on the origins of the circular plaza. Who planned and directed its construction? Was it someone seeking to extend personal influence over the larger surrounding community? Smaller structures were scattered across the top of the butte around the circle. Had they been built before, during, or after the construction of the circle?

We turned homeward with more questions than answers. Archaeologists will continue to do research in pursuit of answers to these questions. I will continue to eavesdrop as they talk among themselves.

July 4, 1993

I WENT WALKING with an archaeologist friend one recent evening. We began by exploring an ancient pueblo built around a spring on the edge of a canyon. We weren't looking for anything in particular. We talked about the pursuit of archaeology in general. Should archaeological research strictly confine itself to what can be proven scientifically and empirically? Can the present be used to interpret the past? Is much of the current archaeological interpretation of the past nothing more than storytelling? Is there any good reason to conduct archaeological research? Should archaeological sites be disturbed for any reason, including for archaeological research? Can just anyone study and accurately interpret the prehistoric past, or is that something only trained archaeologists can and should do? These questions are being debated within the archaeological profession itself.

We wandered among the ruins. The clouds thickened and the light dimmed. The flight of two baby owls, so young they could only flap wildly from tree to nearby tree, interrupted our conversation. We looked for kivas in thick stands of oak. We followed low stone walls surrounding the pueblo linking one structure to the next within the complex. We searched for ancient dams on an expanse of exposed slickrock. We walked up a drainage that opened onto the slickrock. We followed what might be an ancient footpath linking a nearby cluster of buildings to a water source. The sun set and the sky turned crimson. Curtains of rain became cascades of embers falling across distant mountains, embers dying before they touched earth. Tall grass blazed green in the last light.

It struck me then that discussions such as ours should be held only in ancient places. In classrooms the questions we were examining could only lead to even more questions until one finally questioned the existence of the past whatsoever. In that ancient pueblo, surrounded by a natural landscape so old that it made the pueblo look new, the past was undeniable, not subject to question. My friend observed that archaeology may be on the brink of splitting into two disciplines, one absolutely scientific and one not, and that the two would lose communication with one another. I'm sure he's right. It's already happening. In the beginning of knowledge there was only general knowledge of all things physical and metaphysical. Within early knowledge, all things were connected and inseparable. Knowledge grew and divided into more than one body of knowledge. Now there are many bodies of knowledge, each with no knowledge of the other. What we call archaeology is a young body of knowledge. It is growing. It will follow the path of all knowledge and split into two, then three, then four. Conservatives within the discipline will be dismayed by this fragmentation. Radicals will be cheered by it because they can gravitate to the body of archaeological inquiry and knowledge most closely reflecting their own intellectual inclinations, a luxury they couldn't enjoy when all archaeological knowledge was shared by all archaeologists.

Absolute science or not, the disciplines now called archaeology are not like other disciplines. Archaeological research is driven by the desire of all human beings to know the human past from the dawn of humanity. That is a universal desire so intrinsic that it is almost an instinct. We cannot know the future so we cannot measure ourselves, define ourselves, against it. We can only turn to the past in order to define our present selves and societies. We hunger for that definition, to know who we are in the context of all human time up to this moment. What the archaeologists divide into parts in order to focus on particular past moments using particular methods of inquiry, the rest of us will put together again to our own satisfaction.

July 31, 1993

A FEW MONTHS AGO the drought was declared over. No one needed to ask which drought. For five years precipitation was below normal throughout the Four Corners Country and the greater Southwest. Then, last winter, near record rainfall and snowfall in the region had some people remembering the drought fondly. The drought was over. But, wandering through the landscape around my house, I'm beginning to doubt the end of the drought. Only a few isolated raindrops have fallen here since early May. If there is any evidence of heavier winter precipitation, it is the dense thickets of annual plants, including cheat grass, that took advantage of the springtime moisture to make up for the effects of the dry years. Those plants are now tinder dry. Walking through them stirs up clouds of dust.

Even during the drought years of the late 1980s and early 1990s, summer thunderstorms were rolling across the evening sky by early July. Now, at the end of July, there is not a thunderhead to be seen. A few lesser clouds sail through the sunsets.

I thought about water and drought recently while hiking with my son Geoff. We walked along a narrow strip of mesa between two deep canyons. The pink canyon walls were stained with blue and white streaks where mineral-laden water has seeped down from springs under the rims for centuries. The springs and stains are now waterless and parched. Even the perennials and manzanita on the mesa top are wilting. A few stagnant pools could be seen in the canyon bottoms. We took along a gallon of drinking water, but by the time we'd reached our destination we and the dog Chaco had drunk most of it.

We walked around the end of a side canyon and stared down into it from the opposite side. We could see a cliff dwelling beneath an overhang above the canyon bottom. The structures were beautifully preserved. Even the roofs were intact though the buildings have been empty for seven centuries. Geoff looked for a way down but found none that were easy enough to overcome my acrophobia.

The head of the side canyon was shaded by a grove of towering fir and pine above a sheer pouroff. The pouroff was wet. We climbed down the rim and slid on slick pine needles toward the pouroff until we found a place where water dripped from exposed roots then vanished back into the soil. Chaco rolled gratefully in the cool mud. I thought it would take hours to fill our water bottles from the drip. To my surprise, it took minutes. I imagined the people of the cliff dwelling bringing their huge ollas to the seep for domestic water and water for their gardens.

We followed a low ridge of red soil back down the narrow mesa top between the canyons. The ridge was scattered with the remains of Basketmaker homes that were lived in fifteen hundred years ago or more. We found an occasional later pueblo that was occupied between seven and eight centuries ago, the same time as the cliff dwelling. There was little evidence of mesa top occupation in the centuries-long interim between the Basketmakers and the later pueblos. The gentle slopes down from the ridge contained stone features which may have been check dams and farm terraces dating to one or both occupations.

The Puebloan farmers who had once lived on the narrow mesa

top would have preserved every drop of precious moisture to grow their crops. But in the summer of 1993, even their ingenuity would have failed them.

August 22, 1993

WE SAT IN OUR CAMPSITE in a mountain meadow near Taos and scanned the night sky. The lights of town lit the lower end of the valley. The Sangre de Cristos were black against the stars on the opposite horizon. Perseid meteors flashed along the Milky Way. Not far away, in the trees, was a thirteenth-century pueblo, much of which was built around a large, enclosed plaza. Across the valley each meteor was greeted with a chorus of shouts from Southern Methodist University students who had gathered in a compound of Fort Burgwin to watch the falling stars. I wondered if similar shouts from the plaza in the pueblo had greeted the meteors on a summer's night seven hundred years ago.

Earlier that evening we had visited the pueblo with archaeologist Mike Adler of SMU who is now overseeing excavation there. Research in the ancient village has been under way since the 1950s by a succession of prominent Southwestern archaeologists including Durangoan Jim Judge. The pueblo is considered to be ancestral to the modern communities of Taos Pueblo and Picuris.

The next morning I went alone to Picuris, which had celebrated its feast day earlier in the week with a pole dance that may have originated long before the pueblo at Fort Burgwin was built. This year's pole, several stories high, was still standing in the plaza at Picuris. There was a hint of coming autumn in the chill morning air. Not far from Picuris I walked a few miles through an aspen and fir forest to a point where El Camino Real passes through a notch in a high ridge. The road was used for more than a thousand years, ultimately extending from Taos Pueblo to Mexico City. Walking along El Camino Real makes the long, varied history of the Four Corners Country seem almost tangible. Indians, Spaniards, French trappers, Mexican traders, and U.S. soldiers followed the trail before it was closed by Kit Carson in the middle of the nineteenth century and replaced with his El Camino Militar up the Rio

Grande Canyon to Taos.

The following day I went early to Taos Pueblo and wandered through the empty plaza before sitting down on a footbridge across crystal clear Red Willow Creek, which separates the north and south halves of the village. The thousand-year-old community slowly awakened around me. I went from there to the reconstructed Martinez Hacienda, originally built in the early eighteenth century by an influential Spanish family. The two fortified placitas within the hacienda served as a refuge for surrounding Hispanic settlers when Plains Indians raided their farms. Next I visited the Blumenshein Studio near the plaza in the town of Taos. The home and studio served as a social and intellectual center for the Taos art colony early in the twentieth century.

We arrived at our last campsite, on the banks of the Rio Grande next to Kit Carson's El Camino Militar, after dark and in the rain. At dawn the rain stopped and clouds above the towering lava cliffs caught the pink and golden light of dawn. That light and the cliffs were reflected in the shimmering river . . . a painting by Blumenshein. We departed reluctantly and traveled homeward slowly, stopping in the Jicarilla Apache town of Dulce and at the Aztec Ruins along the way.

I entered my silent house just as rain began to fall. I winced when I saw the red message light on my answering machine blinking more times than I could count. I wasn't ready to shake off the past and face present reality. A blinding flash of lightning surrounded the house. The red light stopped blinking. The machine died instantly and permanently. I will never know whose disembodied voices were erased in that millisecond. They'll call back. The voices of the past cannot.

August 29, 1993

THE TRAIL PLUNGED PRECIPITOUSLY hundreds of feet down the steep canyon wall toward a narrow sage flat. Along the edge of the flat, a clear brook, fringed by thick stands of cattail, provided a watering place for the deer and elk whose fresh tracks followed the trail. Beyond the brook, the trail climbed toward a rocky promontory overlooking the junction of two canyons. That was our destination. With me were Linda Martin, a naturalist and committed hiker who has been exploring this area for more than eighteen years, and archaeologist Mark Varien. We were looking for a great kiva and a cluster of ancient Puebloan houses on the talus slope beneath the promontory. Linda described the surrounding geology, botany, and bird life as we walked through the piñon and juniper forest. Linda's long experience as an interpreter for the National Park Service makes her a particularly welcome and valuable hiking companion no matter where she is in the Four Corners Country.

We looked at the great kiva, a circular structure with an interior circumference of more than twenty-five feet, now shaded by large trees growing from the fill above its floor. The enclosing wall had been constructed of stone masonry. Near the great kiva were the stone foundations of small houses. No stone had been used in the walls of the houses. The lack of stone walls in aboveground structures is often an indication that they predate those in which shaped stone is used in the walls, though earthen architecture continued to be used long after the first stonemasonry appeared. Ceramics around the small houses, however, indicated that they were occupied somewhere around a thousand years ago, before shaped stone was used in wall construction.

Mark's current research is seeking, among several things, to determine the function served by great kivas in the Puebloan communities which once covered the Great Sage Plain. Did they serve as activity centers where members of the surrounding houses gathered to renew their sense of community? Did the great kivas continue in use even when the original cluster of nearby houses was abandoned? I have visited numerous deserted Puebloan settlements with Mark, some with great kivas and some without. As a result, I find it nearly impossible to avoid these questions even when I'm wandering among the ruins alone. As Mark and Linda examined the small houses, I pondered the great kiva. Did the stone in its walls mean that it was built after the small houses were abandoned? Or had there been an earlier great kiva there when the small houses were occupied, a great kiva subsequently remodeled by later residents of the same vicinity?

I lack the training, the experience, and the analytical skills to answer these questions on my own. Architectural styles and ceramic styles changed over time and experienced Southwestern archaeologists can assign approximate dates to individual sites by examining the ceramics and architecture visible on the surface. However, the rate at which styles changed was often relatively slow in comparison to the rate at which houses were built, occupied, and abandoned. Therefore, a succession of several house clusters could display the same architectural and ceramic characteristics even though they were not simultaneously occupied. Mark is currently trying to devise a method of determining just how many years a particular house was occupied. If he succeeds, it will allow archaeologists to do much more refined analysis of changes in communities over time.

Meanwhile, I will simply keep wandering among the ruins compiling an ever longer list of questions.

September 5, 1993

As I drove through the brilliant landscape of southeastern Utah, I thought ahead to my destination. It is a place I have long visited at least once a year. But this year's visit will probably be my last. From a high pine- and aspen-covered plateau there, one can look down upon a network of deep canyons slashing through a mesa. Just below the rim of the plateau is a spring enclosed in an old fence of aspen logs. Not far away is a deep, clear pool of water fed by another spring and surrounded by waist-high grass.

From dawn to dusk the air is filled with birdsong and the musical wing beat of the hundreds of doves that come to the place to drink. Deer and a few determined summer cattle have always been welcome company when I visited the springs and pool in the past. It is a perfect place for quiet contemplation, looking across the clear pool at the deep canyons far below.

Access to the springs and pool is difficult. They are rimmed on two sides by a low cliff overlooking a steep, brushy slope. On the other two sides they are surrounded by a tangle of fallen aspen trees that are an effective barrier to two- and four-legged intruders.

Running between the fenced spring and the deep pool are the

barely visible ruts of an old wagon road that is now closed on both sides of the place by fallen aspen. The pool must have been a watering spot for wagoneers and teams of horses a century ago before the newer motor vehicle route was built on top of the plateau. The fence around the spring would have protected it from horses and cattle drives. That little bit of history only made it a more interesting place to visit. The lush vegetation inside the fence now is a relic of what must have grown on the slope before cattle grazing began there a century ago, though grazing has had little impact on the nearly inaccessible spot.

I reached the top of the plateau and crept along a dusty road through the aspen and pine. The effect of the drought was immediately apparent. The usually green forest floor was a parched brown, nearly denuded by grazing. I looked forward to reaching the tranquil oasis around the deep pool. I parked and slid my way down the slope below the rim, then turned and stumbled through the fallen aspen toward the pool.

I was beyond the tangle of windfall when I first noticed that something was different. The earth was grey dust so covered with cow manure that it was impossible to walk without stepping in it. The air was filled with flies and an unpleasant stench. There was no tall grass, and the leaves had been stripped from thickets of mountain shrubs, leaving them nothing more than broken, dying twigs.

I reached the old log-fenced spring. The fence had literally been crushed. The relic vegetation inside it was gone, replaced by a small expanse of cow-churned mud. I walked up to the pool. It was a shallow black puddle of dirt and manure soup, more urine than spring water, surrounded by a ring of deep cow tracks. The silence was deafening. Where there had always been birdsong, now there was none. One of the most beautiful spots I had ever seen was now one of the ugliest. A living place had been killed. There wasn't even enough left to interest a cow; there wasn't one in sight.

I turned to leave, prepared to negotiate the expanse of fallen aspen. I didn't need to. A new trail, where there had been none, came straight down the steep slope from the cliff above. I climbed up it, slipping in manure all the way. A deep notch had recently been dynamited or ripped by a backhoe through the cliff, giving cattle immediate access to the spring and pool below.

The cattle owner had apparently decided that the spring and pool were expendable in the pursuit of his or her profits. The place is on public land well within a National Forest, and Forest Service employees are frequently in the vicinity. It is highly doubtful that ripping the access, and the subsequent destruction of the place below, could have occurred without Forest Service knowledge, if not assistance. The new access is probably permanent.

The place that was destroyed does not belong to the cattle owner. It does not belong to the Forest Service. I am not making any generalizations. There are responsible cattle owners using our public lands. But I believe that the beauty of our American heritage should be documented. And when it is destroyed by a greedy individual, that should be documented as well.

September 12, 1993

I WAS FOUR YEARS OLD when I first met Edith Rhodes. She had known my grandfather and was a friend of my grandmother and my mother. All I remember about that first meeting is that I felt intimidated by Edith. In the ensuing half century, I never quite got over being intimidated. She was an imposing figure. I remember her best in her fur-lined winter coat and high boots, her black hair pulled back into a bun, working in the snow on her Bondad farm.

When my mother and Edith visited, they talked about the past they had shared and the people they had known on Sunnyside Mesa and in Bondad. I came to think of Edith as a keeper of the past. When my mother talked about Edith, outside her presence, it was with admiration for her courage. Adversities that would have made most people resign themselves to fate, Edith tackled without a wince.

That part of her past she never dwelled upon.

I last saw Edith in her adobe farmhouse about a year ago when I took an archaeologist, Richard Wilshusen, to meet her. Richard was working west of Bondad and wanted information about the deserted, early twentieth-century homesteads he was finding while doing an archaeological survey. The only remaining traces of the houses were barely discernible rectangles in the grey soil. There was no clue as to how they had been constructed. Though she was in a wheelchair and nearly blind, Edith graciously invited us into her living room. She said the houses had been built of jacal, upright posts set into the ground and plastered over with mud. She remembered the location of each house and the names of the families who had lived in them. She knew where the descendants of those families lived now.

Edith said there was still a jacal structure standing in La Posta, a small hamlet upriver from Bondad, and from there, the discussion turned to La Posta. Her recollections were filled with the names of the Ute, Hispanic, and Anglo families who had lived there in the 1920s. Life in La Posta then had not been easy. What emerged as Edith spoke was a portrait of a place and time when three still distinct cultures had not only coexisted, they had, of necessity, cooperated. There was a strong sense of immediacy in the way she talked of the Hispanic woman whose skill with traditional medicinal herbs was sought out when there was sickness in any house or of the horse races on Buckskin Charlie's personal racetrack.

I realized for the first time as I listened to Edith talk about La Posta that there was a rare quality to her memories. I understood that she truly respected the differences between cultures and that the history of the Animas River Valley south of Durango is multicultural, a mosaic of Ute, Hispanic, Anglo, and turn-of-the-century immigrant cultures.

Edith's rare quality was that she did not edit cultures other than her own out of her histories—including her books and her columns in this newspaper. She was, in fact, acutely aware of the hurt caused by ethnic prejudices and made reference to that in her conversation a year ago.

A year ago Edith could still read using an enormous illuminated magnifying glass on a stand on her desk. She knew her typewriter keyboard from memory. As we stood to leave, she asked me to hand her a sheaf of paper from a nearby table that she could not see. It was a partially completed manuscript. I turned and looked back as I left the house. Edith was already at work.

October 10, 1993

When I was a kid it was called "taking the Circle trip." There was absolutely nothing practical about taking the Circle trip; one ended up where one started. The favored time for the journey is the last weekend in September or the last weekend in May. In May, snowmelt creates a thousand waterfalls, and in late September, the aspens are a dazzling gold. Now the Circle trip is called the San Juan Skyway. Last weekend my son Geoff and I left early to drive the San Juan Skyway. We were joined by thousands of other motorists out to look at the autumn colors. There wasn't much traffic along the Dolores River as we headed toward Rico. By the time we got to Ophir, however, every possible pullout was a parking lot filled with cars and people armed with video cameras. Everyone seemed to be having a very good time. Fleeting friendships were struck up among perfect strangers at every scenic overlook.

My great-grandparents, grandparents, and parents lived along the San Juan Skyway. I've lived within a few minutes' drive of the San Juan Skyway most of my life. I found it hard last weekend not to contemplate the changes that have occurred along the scenic loop. As recently as thirty years ago the towns along the Skyway remained rooted in the economies that had sustained them since their founding. Rico, Telluride, Ouray, and Silverton were still mountain mining towns. Cortez, Dolores, Ridgway, and Mancos were still agricultural towns. Durango still had the feel of a regional center serving the mining and agricultural populations of the smaller communities.

The main streets of the farming towns included hardware stores, elevators, feed stores, and farm equipment dealers. The mountain towns were surrounded by mines and mills that operated twenty-four hours a day. Today those enterprises are gone. Along the mountain segments of the Skyway most of the historic old mining structures have vanished, victims of natural forces and vandalism. It is difficult to even find traces of the railroad, the Rio Grande Southern, that once linked Durango to most of the towns along the Skyway. Unless steps are taken to preserve them, the few reminders of the historic economies of the Skyway will soon vanish completely.

Despite the decline of the old economies, the communities along the Skyway have the feel of boomtowns. The streets are crowded. New houses are going up in the towns and in the open spaces between them. There are nearly as many real estate for sale signs as there are aspens.

In the past when a basic Skyway economy experienced hard times, whether it was mining or agriculture, there was always a sense of confidence that the decline was only temporary and that better times were just around the corner. Now mining seems to have vanished for good, and mining claims are becoming residential lots. Single, large ranches are becoming many small ranchettes. The private and public infrastructure supporting mining and agriculture along the Skyway has either vanished or is vanishing. It is hard to imagine that mining or agricultural profits will ever soar to the point that either can return to their former dominance of the local economies along the Skyway; it would cost far too much to put the necessary pieces back together again.

There is no benefit in mourning the vanishing traditional economies along the San Juan Skyway. What can be mourned is the loss of historic landmarks on the Skyway and, with them, any sense of local history whatsoever.

October 24, 1993

THE COTTONWOODS in the Montezuma Valley are a blazing golden, and the apple and pear orchards are muted shades of red and burgundy. It has snowed on the Sleeping Ute. In the afternoon, dark, patchy, low clouds cast moving shadows on the vast fields to the west. These are the perfect conditions for autumn lightshows when isolated rays of sunshine spotlight a single tree or patch of rimrock. It is a time to drive slowly along country roads here. I did that recently with my son Geoff.

We parked at the end of one road and walked through a light rain to a canyon rim. A ruined thirteenth-century pueblo stretches along the top of the cliff and sprawls down the talus below. The structures on top of the cliff are D-shaped stone towers enclosed by a low stone wall. Natural depressions in the rimrock were filled with rainwater reflecting the grey sky. At the foot of the talus, the rubble of fallen towers is scattered across the tops of large boulders. Beyond the boulders a small, clear stream winds through the sage-covered canyon bottom.

The opposite canyon wall is thickly forested with piñon and juniper punctuated now by golden clumps of oak and scarlet serviceberry. Usually the canyon is filled with birdsong, but in the quiet rain there was no sound. It was not difficult in the chill afternoon air to imagine the place in winter. In the shortest days the sun would not reach the canyon bottom. But the pueblo, built on a steep, south-facing slope, would be warm on the clearest, coldest days.

We arrived home beneath a clearing sky. The wind went from chill to freezing. Geoff quickly potted the two geraniums, which have grown outdoors alongside a juniper since Memorial Day. The red flowers are a bright contrast to the citrus trees sitting near a south window. That's about all that needed to be done around my house to get the "yard" ready for winter. With the exception of a few marigolds and a single, lonely cosmos, the plant life around my house takes care of itself.

The clouds returned and the Sleeping Ute vanished behind curtains of falling snow. At sunset a thin slice of clear sky appeared above McElmo Canyon. The sun descended into the canyon. The snow curtains blazed a brilliant bronze touched with pink. Darkness came quickly. Night had the feel of winter.

November 28, 1993

AT THIS TIME OF YEAR I live in just one room of my two-room house. Heating one big room is much more energy efficient—and cheaper—than heating two big rooms. After a day or two I find it rather pleasant to live, work, and sleep in just one room. The room contains a kitchen, my writing space with computer, and the couch where I sleep. The walls are white, broken only by a few bookshelves and two Stanton Englehart paintings that bear a strong resemblance to the vistas visible from the windows.

In one corner of the room is a sturdy Kentucky pine stand designed and built by Herb Folsom of Mancos to hold a three volume set of the compact edition of *The Oxford English Dictionary* given me by friends. The volumes include more than fifty-five hundred pages of definitions in type so small that the dictionary comes with a magnifying glass. In another corner of the room is a television set that was last switched on the week that Yeltsin dissolved parliament and stormed Moscow's White House. Since I only turn on the TV in perilous times, I hope it stays off a good deal longer. Flipping through the pages of the OED is more fun than channel surfing.

The room I abandon in winter was a windowless attached garage when I moved into the house. I had much of the south wall removed and replaced with double-paned glass. The sun heats the room by day but, having been a garage, the room is not well insulated. On sunless days and cold nights the room resembles an ice box. The houseplants thrive in the "garage" in winter. I thrive there in summer.

Outside the west windows of the room I occupy in winter are a canyon, a mountain, and a vast expanse of sky. The south window looks out on the junipers that crowd against the house, and a small north window provides a view of farms sloping up toward the forests beyond the Dolores River. Lone Cone is a snowy pyramid on the northern horizon. My computer sits against the west wall of the room so that I can glance away from it and into the canyon.

As I write this column, the canyon is filled with rain, falling snow, and low clouds. The mountain is obscured by the winter storm. The dog and cat—Chaco and Solstice—are asleep on the couch, and there is no sound but the hum of the computer and water dripping from the eaves.

Living and working in a single room has its drawbacks. The computer is always just an arm's length away, and a sinkful of dirty dishes can't be ignored for days. But there is something about the routine of a one-room life that enhances the sense of solitude that comes with living alone. It's a simpler life.

January 2, 1994

Beneath a juniper tree just outside my house are some pieces of broken pottery. They were there when I bought the house. I asked the couple who built this house about the sherds. They said they'd gathered them up from the property on which the house stands. I find it impossible to look at the bits of broken pottery without wondering about the people who made them, the people who lived here long before I came along. I occasionally show the sherds to archaeologists who respond by naming the pottery types represented in the pile and telling me when they were made. Most of the sherds are more than a thousand years old.

I thought of the sherds recently when I read a paper by George Cowgill, an archaeologist on the faculty of Arizona State University. Cowgill writes:

> Archaeologists tend to underconceptualize the past. Our mental images of past things tend to be impoverished. It is useful to think of four levels of underconceptualization. . . . On the lowest level, the mental images are of pots and other artifacts occupying particular locations in space and time; people are just invisible.

I've taken that quote out of a very complex, well-argued context, but Cowgill's observations triggered some musings of my own. Cowgill is well aware of the problems encountered when attempting to do more than record the locations of artifacts in space and time. It's too easy to slip into storytelling about the people who made the pots—or houses or kivas—with little more to go on than the empty pots, houses, or kivas themselves.

Cowgill, an archaeologist, was talking about archaeologists when he said, "Our mental images of past things tend to be impoverished." But the same could be said for all of us who are not archaeologists. We all tend to think of past cultures—particularly ancient Native cultures—as less complex, less sophisticated, and generally less capable than our own. We may even still cling to the notion that those past cultures were less civilized than our own. An hour in front of a TV set watching the evening news should cure us of that last misconception, but it doesn't.

Cowgill goes on to say that archaeologists whose mental images of the past do include humans see them as "faceless blobs" or, on the next level, as capable of nothing more than rational choices. An example of rational choice might be, "they exhausted the environment here, so rationally chose to move there." Finally, Cowgill says, ancient communities are shoved into inadequate sociocultural pigeon holes, such being characterized by egalitarian or hierarchical social organization. None of these levels of impoverishing the past, Cowgill continues, conveys any real sense of humanity upon ancient peoples.

Cowgill argues that nonrational—in contrast to irrational—choices, such as choosing to create works of art, are as important as rational choices and sociocultural theory to understanding ancient peoples. There's not enough left of the pile of sherds by my house to draw any conclusions beyond their types and dates. But there is in the archaeological record in the Four Corners Country a substantial amount of art.

The ancient Puebloan art that survives here is mostly in certain architectural forms and in ceramic form and design. Those forms and designs, executed with careful, time-consuming attention to detail, can be highly abstracted. They do represent nonrational choices made by the ancient Puebloans. They also indicate that rational choice and art were not as separated from one another in ancient Puebloan cultures as they are in our own.

January 9, 1994

THE LITTLE GREY FOX is half body and half tail. In the dark, when it is standing still, it is hard to tell which end is which. When it walks away, I assume it is the tail that is in the rear. It is a nocturnal creature, appearing outside my window an hour after sunset and returning from time to time until the first light of dawn streaks across the sky from the east. The fox comes for the scraps of food I leave outside the window in the evening. When I get up in the morning I turn on the deck light and sit watching the fox searching for any bits of food it may have missed earlier in the night. Occasionally it glances up at the window as if aware of my presence. Its eyes, golden sparks in that light, seem alert and intelligent. The fox's den is in a crack beneath the rimrock not fifty yards from my house. Unlike the skunks, deer, cottontails, and jays that appear outside my window and act almost tame, the fox seems to be a very wild creature that brings the wilderness with it when it visits.

I thought of the nearness of wilderness recently when Leo Black took my sons and me to look at some petroglyphs in a network of canyons less than a mile from my home. Large mountain lions had broken a trail past petroglyph panels in two separate canyons. Their tracks were nearly as fresh as our own. Where Leo had put a plank across a stream making a footbridge only inches wide, the lions crossed the plank and followed the trail up the opposite bank out of the willows and into the junipers. I wondered how close the lions venture to my house which overlooks one of the canyons where we found their tracks.

Leo is not an archaeologist, but he and his family have lived on a ranch in that small maze of canyons for nearly a quarter century. He's an astute observer of the archaeological record there. He reads the latest research writings on petroglyphs and has had one of the foremost experts on Southwestern petroglyphs, Sally Cole, examine the panels twice. He has fenced one of the more accessible panels, and blocked access to others, to keep his own cattle from damaging the ancient symbols pecked into the rock.

Leo has concluded that one of the panels was used as a shrine for unknown centuries by a succession of passing cultures. As he points to the evidence supporting that conclusion, he makes the silent past come alive. As I listened to him speak, I found myself envisioning the ancient ceremonies encoded within the symbols in the stone. I also envisioned the only night visitors to those places now, the lions and the foxes.

January 16, 1994

As part of a current writing project, I am reading stacks of books about historic communities in the San Juan Country of southwestern Colorado. The product of this effort will be a small book that, I hope, describes the regional patterns of human settlement rather than treating each community in isolation. Because most local history books concentrate on a particular community, that search for a shared history reaching beyond the town limits is more difficult than I first thought it would be. This difficulty is compounded by the fact that many local histories are written by a citizen of the community who wishes to avoid offending his or her fellow citizens. Often these histories become little more than unquestioning praise for prominent pioneers—mining investors or main street merchants—intermixed with town boosterism and a few personal reminiscences of how much better life was then than now.

There are notable exceptions to this sort of local history. Duane Smith's histories of San Juan communities explore their common threads. Mallory Hope Ferrell's history of the Rio Grande Southern Railroad touches on the regional and national economic trends that shaped life along that railroad's spectacular route. Ira Freeman's much disputed history of Montezuma County bounces back and forth between rosy optimism and outright criticism of mindless local land use practices that laid waste to forests, streams, fields, and grasslands. David P. Smith's biography of Chief Ouray of the Utes—particularly of the symbiotic relationship between Ouray and the most prominent San Juan pioneer of all, Otto Mears—leaves one questioning whether the two were heroes or scoundrels.

There is one local history, written by a citizen of Silverton, that transcends all of the limitations, self-imposed and otherwise, which usually shape and restrict our local view of our local past. That is Allen Nossaman's work in progress, *Many More Mountains*. Thus far, two volumes have been printed. Together Volume One, *Silverton's Roots,* and Volume Two, *Ruts Into Silverton,* total more than seven hundred pages of text and photographs. Volume Two ends before the Denver & Rio Grande Railroad reached Silverton 112 years ago. Nossaman has many more volumes to go before *Many More Mountains* is completed.

Nossaman grew up in the San Juan Country and arrived in Silverton in 1963, the new editor and publisher of the town's historic newspaper, *The Silverton Standard*. He immediately immersed himself in local history. In 1965, along with several equally dedicated volunteers, he was a founder of the San Juan County Historical Society. It was at a time when local history was made to conform to the Hollywood wild, wild west rather than to the facts. Even Silverton had to have its "gunfight at the OK Corral." Allen did nothing to conceal his impatience with such local myth-making. He became the disciplinarian of Silverton's past.

It was at a time, as well, when many historic structures were being purchased by newcomers attracted by the growing tourism industry. Some newcomers shared Allen's attitudes, some did not. The latter loaded cartons of yellowing papers from attics into pickups and hauled them to the town dump. I never caught Allen in the act, but I think he went to the dump every night with a flashlight and hauled every scrap of paper with ink on it back to his house at the end of Greene Street. That was the beginning of the incomparable Historical Society archives now being moved into a new state-of-the-art curation and research facility nearing completion next to the San Juan County Historical Society Museum.

Many More Mountains probes the past of the San Juan Country. The prominent pioneers are there, but so are the usually faceless men and women who did the backbreaking work. Nossaman continues to deflate the myths, sometimes with careful, painstaking detective work. There is the myth that the Utes deliberately set the Lime Creek Burn. That piece of local color has gone unchallenged for more than a century, despite the bigotry and racism it was intended to inspire and justify. Nossaman demonstrates that it would have been nearly impossible for the Utes to have set the blaze, and then he goes on to identify a more probable suspect.

That tendency both to set the record straight and to complete the record is what distinguishes *Many More Mountains.* With only two volumes completed, it is already an epic work . . . and it reads like an epic novel. I'm looking forward to Volume Three.

January 23, 1994

AFTER A YEAR OF FLOODS, brush fires, earthquakes, and cold snaps in other parts of the country, people here tend to be a little smug about our good fortune in living where such natural disasters don't upset our lives. But in looking at the calamities besetting other parts of the nation, they seem to be as much man-made disasters as natural disasters. Building in floodplains, atop fault zones, and in forests—where floods, quakes, and fires are an inevitability—is the prime ingredient of the disasters we've been witnessing this year.

Probably the greatest "natural" disaster ever to occur in the Four Corners Country was the flood of October 10, 1911. Roads, bridges, train tracks, dams, farms, power lines, phone lines, and homes were wiped out in a few hours. The steep topography of the Four Corners Country creates deadlier floods than those in the Mississippi Valley. No flood here since then has ever approached the destructive force of the flood of 1911. That flood has been forgotten. Homes, businesses, farms, and highways now occupy the floodplains that were scoured bare in a few hours in 1911. It rained steadily for several days before that historic flood. The earth was saturated. Mudslides, laced with boulders, blocked rising streams. Usually dry tributary canyons spewed more mud and boulders into major streams and onto roads and train tracks. Today much of the sloping black clay and shale most likely to slide into the valley bottoms when saturated is covered with new homes or slashed by roadcuts and buried utility lines.

In southern California the "big one" will be the inevitable earthquake measuring 8+ on the Richter scale. In the Four Corners Country, the "big one" will be the inevitable repeat of the flood of 1911. Unlike earthquakes, floods such as the one eight decades ago give plenty of warning. They are not isolated flash floods triggered by cloudbursts. They are several rainy days in the making. Most of the major floods here in the last century have occurred in September or October when monsoon rains can last for days. Few floods are the result of spring snowmelt. The Labor Day flood of 1970, after several days of rain, turned the Animas Valley into a lake, stretching from near Trimble Lane to the Durango city limits, and wiped out miles of train track in the Animas Canyon. Roads, bridges, and homes were damaged throughout the region. The 1970 flood was minor in comparison to the flood of 1911.

My favorite reminder of the 1911 flood is the bleached skeleton of a huge cottonwood lying on a rock shelf thirty feet above the San Juan River in the narrow canyon near Bluff, Utah. It's a mute testament to the power of nature doing its own thing.

No conceivable flood control engineering could lessen the force of such a flood. There are many surviving photographs of the flood of 1911. The best way of preventing the recurrence of the damage caused by that flood would be to require every town and county planner in the Four Corners Country to study those photos. Floodplains should be left to nature and cow pastures. Steep clay hillsides should be left alone entirely.

February 20, 1994

It was a tense drive west from Durango on a recent Friday evening. The snow came down faster than either the snowplows or my windshield wipers could keep up with. West of Hesperus a fierce north wind whipped opaque sheets of snow across the highway. The storm ended suddenly as I crossed the low divide between the Mancos River and McElmo Creek at the entrance to Mesa Verde National Park. The evening sun broke through black clouds and cast brilliant shafts of light across the Great Sage Plain between Sleeping Ute Mountain and the Abajo Mountains. I tuned in to "All Things Considered," accelerated a bit on the wet road, and relaxed. I'd sleep in my own bed that night after all.

Minutes later a towering, moving white wall blotted out the western horizon and engulfed the Sleeping Ute. The Great Sage Plain vanished beneath it, and the sunlit Abajos blinked out. I pulled to the side of the road and tried to comprehend the sight. The top of the wall raced toward me faster than did the bottom. Avalanches of whiteness fell down the face of the wall, obliterating all traces of the Montezuma Valley. I thought it might be fog. Arcs of pink lightning lit the wall from within. I resumed driving slowly toward Cortez and into the wall. The sun was still up, but suddenly the light was late dusk. Street lights flickered on. Traffic slowed to a crawl. Wet, grainy snow plastered my pickup and slid off the hood beneath its own weight. The tall orange barrels that are a perpetual part of the Cortez street scene these days—one never knows what the route from here to there will be at any given time—were barely visible and turning white. As I wove my way through the barrels—on a horizontal slalom course of sorts—I realized that I was enjoying myself. This was some kind of storm.

The blizzard broke briefly as I walked into my house. Scores of birds descended on the birdseed outside the window, gobbling it down as if preparing for the worst. The storm resumed and the birds vanished into the sheltering junipers.

The next day dawned clear, cold, and blindingly white. A variety of birds began arriving outside the window—juncos, virtual clouds of jays, pine siskins, house finches, and a plain titmouse. A pair of phoebes appeared on the snag they've claimed north of the house. The siskins were the smallest birds in the crowd but made up for that by being the most aggressive. The titmouse was the shyest. An osprey flew slowly down the canyon keeping a close eye on the icy stream below. Two red-tailed hawks floated on the dawn breeze. Seven mallards, flying north in a straight row, veered westward at the sight of the hawks.

That night a thin sliver of a moon slid down the chill sky at dusk and into the arms of the Sleeping Ute. There were no clouds. I wondered briefly if I'd only imagined the white wall that had engulfed this place the evening before. I'm fairly sure it had actually come out of the west and taken this familiar world away, briefly erasing the landmarks that anchor this life.

May 8, 1994

THE SERVICEBERRY BUSHES are mounds of white blossoms on the slopes below my house, and four o'clocks are coming up beneath the junipers. Phlox and Indian paintbrush are blooming beneath the sage, and buds are swelling on the prickly pair and claret cup cactus growing from cracks in the stone. Yellow Utah thelypody bends in the dawn breeze. Cottonwoods are leafing out along the rising creeks. Ravens engage eagles in aerial combat over the canyon, and noisy flocks of piñon jays gather in the trees on the canyon's rim. The snow is gone from the north face of Mesa Verde and almost gone from Sleeping Ute Mountain.

There is always something fleeting about this season that swings unpredictably between March and June, March one day and June the next. It is a time when I resolve in the mellowness of evening to go fishing at dawn and rise to hear a cold north wind whipping around the eaves. I put off fishing yet another day. This postponement is never a disappointment. I no longer fish for fish and have yet to decide what it is that I do fish for. I think it may be for the sight of the sparkling river flowing clear against red cliffs. It may be to hear water ouzels calling from their nests in the rock above the whispering water or the plaintive poorwills talking themselves to sleep as darkness falls.

There is a place I go to fish where a river forms still pools several hundred yards long between burnt red cliffs of Wingate Sandstone topped by pink Navajo Sandstone. I can stand high above the pools and see schools of four-foot-long catfish moving slowly in the blue-green water. I have fished there for years. I do so with a slight sense of apprehension, wondering what would happen if I ever caught one of the monster denizens of the pools. Who would have caught whom? So far that question has gone unanswered. I waver between wanting the question answered and not really wanting to know. If I ever do catch one of those fish, it will go right back into the water, and I may never want to go there again.

Fishing for catfish, if that's what I'm fishing for, is about as effortless an endeavor as can be imagined. It requires nothing more than baiting a hook, a single cast, and sitting down to watch the tip of the pole. In these particular pools, the tip of the pole always begins bobbing before I sit down. I have gotten so that I just let it bob until it stops, which it usually does in about ten minutes. I then re-bait the hook, cast again, and sit down to watch the tip of the pole until it stops bobbing. Once again, I repeat the entire process. I'm not fishing for catfish, I'm feeding the crayfish that swarm across the stony bottom of the pool toward the baited hook. Sometimes I just leave the hook out of the sequence and put the bait at the edge of the water. The crayfish approach cautiously, then hastily retreat with the food.

I suspect that I go fishing for some new philosophical insight, some new metaphysical tidbit that will make the world make more sense. Sitting idly and watching the tip of a pole then becomes a form of meditation. But I have found that watching crayfish is not conducive to philosophizing.

June 12, 1994

ONE STRETCH OF THE NARROW DIRT ROAD is carved into a nearly vertical slope that plunges into a river hundreds of feet below. The road twists and turns around sharp bends and sometimes pitches upward at steep, tire-spinning angles. There is no place to turn around. It is impossible to see what one will encounter next. The road is no longer maintained. To enter that stretch of road is to make a commitment to follow it to its end. I recently drove to the end of the road for the last time. I'll never do it again.

I've driven that stretch of road many times in the last twenty years but, until this most recent trip, had not been there for nearly two years. I drove past the last spot wide enough to turn around in my usual manner, with the steering wheel tightly clutched in both sweaty hands. The usual silent question came to mind, "Why am I doing this?" Because, at the end of the road, is one of the most isolated and beautiful fishing holes I've ever seen.

I rounded a bend and knew that I'd finally pushed my luck too far. A boulder larger than my pickup blocked most of the road, leaving only a thin shelf at the edge of the drop into the river far below. While my son Geoff walked ahead to survey the situation, I wondered if I could ever back down the hill. He signaled reassuringly. I inched the pickup around the boulder. I drove around another bend only to see another big boulder, higher than the hood of my little pickup, blocking the entire road. Dirt had slid down the hillside and buried one end of the rock blockade. Geoff went ahead and looked. He told me that the dirt formed a ramp and I could drive over the boulder. I inched the pickup over it.

The road makes a hairpin turn and drops steeply back down to the river. We were soon at our campsite. Within minutes I was sitting at a bend in the river watching my pole. I was certain that no one else would be foolish enough to drive that last stretch of road and we would be undisturbed. My satisfaction was slightly diminished by the knowledge that I would have to drive back over that stretch of road the next day. But it is hard to worry in that place. The river was running high and fast. I could only see a short stretch of water from where I sat, but it reflected the color of the pink and white cliffs rising hundreds of feet above the canyon floor. Birdsong filled the air. A trio of common mergansers rounded the bend and floated by my fishing line. They ignored me. I fished until dark, until bats filled the sky beneath flashing stars.

I got up before dawn and resumed fishing. Beavers greeted me by loudly slapping their tails on the water. I tried to pretend that it was the sound of giant catfish jumping. The sky lightened and the day birds began singing. I caught several submerged branches and boulders. Perfect.

I thought I heard human voices but knew that couldn't be. I heard them again. They came from no definable direction. Happy shouts and laughter filled the air. Soon a group of kayakers rounded the bend. I wondered what they would think when they spotted a middle-aged man sitting in a lawn chair staring at the river. When the first one saw me, he paddled to a stop on my fishing line. "How did you get here?" he asked. "Life is good," I answered. He laughed, "I can see that." "Have you caught any fish?" "No, that's not the point." He laughed again and went on his way.

Hundreds of kayakers and rafters passed us that morning. Almost every one of them asked the same two questions. I felt no resentment toward these human intruders. It was like watching a parade. And besides, I told myself, if I can't get my pickup out of here I'll hitch a ride down the river to the nearest civilization.

I got my pickup out of the canyon, though it now has some new scratches where I hugged the boulder too tightly on the way past. I won't drive that stretch of road again. Next time I'll walk it. When I was past the boulder, I felt glad it was there. Walking that stretch of what was once a road will be a much more peaceful and satisfying experience than driving it ever was.

July 24, 1994

It was more a sprinkle than a shower, and it was laced with crackling lightning. But those few drops cooled the evening and filled the air with the nearly forgotten fragrance of rain. Chaco, the dog, perked up noticeably, and we walked to a knoll where we could see dark curtains of rain falling on the northwestern horizon. Within minutes birds began singing in the canyon. I realized then that, with the exception of a few talkative jays, there is little birdsong here in the heat of the day. The musical voices of kingbirds and mockingbirds fill the dim light of dawn but fall silent as the sun rises.

As the rain obscured the northwest, I thought back to a recent visit I'd made to an ancient pueblo there. It was my first visit and Ruth Slickman, who'd been there before, was my guide. We bumped along many miles of unpaved road through vast dryland fields of winter wheat and pinto beans. Combines trailing dust harvested the wheat. Somewhere along the way we crossed the state boundary and entered Utah. There was no visible line across the hot, shimmering, dusty fields to tell us where that might have been.

The vague sense of guilt I was feeling about having fled this computer vanished when we reached our destination. First there was the welcome, if unlikely, sight of a large pond in a ravine. It was ringed with cattails. Mallards rose and circled above the rippling water. The pueblo itself stretched along both sides of the ravine. We did not have much time to inspect it, and it was overgrown with sage, cheat grass, and some tamarisk. I came away with only a vague notion of what I'd seen.

One building on the west side stretched along the ravine for more than a hundred yards. It contained several rows of rooms and kivas. Much of the building had probably once been two or three stories high. There was at least one smaller building to the north of the large building. Across the ravine was another large structure or tight cluster of structures.

Stretching west from the largest structure for fifty yards is a linear earthen berm at least ten feet high in places. I couldn't tell if it was ancient or modern, but it crossed a wide, shallow drainage, and even in that drought-stricken landscape, the grass growing along its upper side was lush and green. The berm may be a dam that catches runoff. Farther up the drainage, at the foot of a sloping expanse of slickrock, is another earthen dam. That one is covered with potsherds and is definitely ancient. On the mesa top to the west of the thirteenth-century pueblo are two more large mounds. Those pueblos may have been occupied in the late twelfth and early thirteenth centuries and abandoned when the pueblo on the ravine was constructed. Both have been badly damaged by looters in recent years.

The morning after visiting the pueblo I had breakfast with archaeologist Bill Lipe. He and a group of participants and interns from the Crow Canyon Archaeological Center had recently spent a day counting kivas in the pueblo along the ravine. They had identified seventy-eight possible kivas. Based on the visible architecture and ceramics, Bill believes construction of the pueblo began about A.D. 1240 and that it was occupied until the time of the final Puebloan migration from this region late in that century. I know of one pueblo of that time with ninety-seven kivas and another with seventy-eight kivas. The pueblo on the ravine may be one of the three largest mid-thirteenth-century villages on the Great Sage Plain. There are others nearly as large.

If there are ghosts, those pueblos are now occupied only by ghosts. As I sat on the knoll near my house watching the rain in the northwest, I thought that even ghosts would find that rain as welcome as I did.

August 21, 1994

WE SAT AT THE EDGE of the water looking west, watching the tips of our fishing poles from the corners of our eyes. It doesn't work to stare directly, expectantly, at a fishing pole leaned on a twig, line dangling, for the same reason that a watched pot never boils. The evening cumulus turned bronze and then pink. The still water mirrored the setting sun. With me was my son Geoff and his friend Bart. They planned to stay there all night catching monster catfish. I drove home beneath a darkening sky along country roads winding through fields of new-mown hay.

Once home I found the spot near my house where I can see the most stars at one time and settled back to watch the sky. I planned to look for meteors for a while and go to bed. The meteors became visible, falling toward earth and trailing long green tails. I watched until the sleepy calls of poorwills floated up from the dark canyon.

I kept watching until the first owls called from across the canyon. Squeaking bats zigzagged beneath the stars. The Big Dipper did most of a quarter turn around the North Star before I gave up and went to bed. I thought I'd get up to morning darkness and watch more meteors before first light. But when I opened my eyes the sky was too light to see meteors. I'll have to wait a year before I see another meteor shower of that intensity.

Watching the setting sun, the falling meteors, and the circling stars the night before made me more aware of light in the brightening dawn. The light comes later now. The rising sun no longer shines into my north window. The afternoon sun has begun shining into the south windows. Darkness comes earlier. Though the days are shorter, summer's heat continues unabated. I've never been one to regret the end of August and the onset of the cooler days of September.

Early peaches are ripe in McElmo Canyon and the pickups at the farmers market in the courthouse parking lot on Saturday mornings are loaded with produce from throughout the county. Last year the market continued through October, until only pumpkins and winter squash were left in country gardens. A visit to the farmers market is as much a local social activity as it is an opportunity to take home garden-ripened fruits and vegetables.

The annual passage from August into autumn brings with it more than just the promise of cooler days. It is a time when the light shifts, shining at a greater and greater slant on this landscape. The color of sky, stone, and soil deepen in that less direct light. It becomes possible then to imagine winter.

September 18, 1994

I DROVE EAST ON A COUNTRY ROAD at dawn. The valley floor ahead of me was hidden by mist upon which the peaks of the La Plata Mountains looked like a giant sailing ship becalmed against the brightening sky. Not long after the sun rose, I headed west on the same country road watching new clouds pouring down the slopes of Ute Mountain. Throughout the day as I traveled from place to place on the Great Sage Plain, I watched mountains—the

La Platas, the Wilsons, the Dolores Peaks, Lone Cone, the LaSals, Navajo Mountain, the Chuskas, and the Sleeping Ute—vanish behind cloudbanks and then reappear in the ever-changing light looking nothing like they'd looked before. I've repeated these journeys across the Great Sage Plain several times in the last three weeks as part of a project I'm working on for the Crow Canyon Archaeological Center.

During a two-day break from these journeys I sat at this computer glancing out the west window more often than I should. Late the first afternoon, clouds moved across the sun and the hot air cooled. In less than five minutes my sleeping bag was in my pickup and I was headed west. Half an hour later I parked at the edge of a cliff where the land plunges toward the San Juan River. Beyond the river Monument Valley was silhouetted against the low sun. Walls of dark clouds boiled above Black Mesa south of Kayenta. The lightning-laced storm spread across the western horizon from the Lukachukais in the south to the Abajos in the north. Ravens rode the evening thermals above the cliff. Curtains of backlit rain advanced toward where I sat on the rimrock. A chill, damp wind rose suddenly and roared through nearby junipers. It was an hour until sunset, but the place became as dark as late dusk. The first raindrops struck me with stinging force. A nearby lightning strike was all it took to send me into retreat. I sat out the fast-moving storm in my pickup. Later, beneath a clearing sky, I walked along the wet and shining canyon rim toward the setting sun. Pools in the rimrock mirrored golden clouds.

I awakened the next morning beneath a bowl of flashing stars. The first light came quickly. I walked along the cliff to a large boulder covered with the remnants of an ancient stone tower. From there, in that new light, the north rim of Black Mesa was a thin dark line on the horizon. The modern Hopi villages are on the south rim of Black Mesa. It would take only a few days to walk from the ancient tower where I stood to those villages. At least one of those villages, Oraibi, was occupied at the same time as the tower.

I drove home slowly toward the rising sun through dryland fields where windrows of ripe pinto beans lay across damp red soil. New clouds formed around the La Platas and the light dimmed.

A chill breeze greeted my arrival home. The rabbitbrush around my house had, it seemed, bloomed overnight and the serviceberry leaves taken on a coppery hue. Soon there will be snow on the peaks and the angle of light across this place will be lower even than now. In that light the mountains change with every blink of the eye.

September 25, 1994

THE HARVEST MOON rose last week through the gap between the La Plata Mountains and Mesa Verde. Its deep golden hue brightened quickly to silver before it vanished behind thick black clouds. Pink lightning flashed on every horizon in the falling darkness. I awakened late in the night to the sound of rain against the west windows. These predawn rains, while not substantial, come more frequently now, cleansing the junipers, settling the dust, and leaving the fragrant sage dripping with flashing crystal raindrops. In the wake of these rains, the sky fills with fast-moving clouds that catch the first rays of the rising sun before gathering once more around distant peaks. Those peaks are often covered by a silvery dusting of new snow that rarely lasts until noon.

Birds that spent the summer elsewhere, blue birds and flickers among others, perch briefly on juniper snags near my house before flying into the canyon to spend the day. In a nearby, new-mown field hundreds of Canada geese stay the night, eat a leisurely breakfast, and ascend to form wedges plying the morning sky. Across the road from that field of geese, clouds of red-winged blackbirds spiral nervously above a pond, then vanish into thick stands of cattails. A black-headed Oregon junco comes alone to the bird feeder, but he will soon be joined by many more of his kind coming down from the mountains to spend the winter in town. Now his meals are interrupted by crowds of noisy, aggressive, hungry jays who pick through the millet looking for sunflower seeds.

The first color can be seen in the Gambel oak on the north face of Mesa Verde and in the aspen groves on Ute Mountain. Purple asters blend with yellow sunflowers along the edges of dryland fields on the Great Sage Plain. Each blooming, drooping clump of golden rabbitbrush at every canyon seep hums to the wing beat of a thousand honey bees, and countless hummingbirds hover above the fading scarlet gilia and crimson paintbrush in the canyon bottoms.

This is a season when I like to go alone in the evening, after a day of writing, to the rims of nearby canyons. I'm not sure why this season affects me in this way, makes me want to find solitude in wild but familiar places so close to home. It may be that I am now old enough to know for certain that, beneath the busy, brightly-hued surface of this season, nature is irrevocably slowing down and I'm ready to slow down with it. By evening I find myself not wanting to shape my thoughts into written or spoken words, nor to hear words spoken no matter how softly.

Solitude is more than the presence or absence of words. There is a unique rhythm to wild places which cannot be felt in the company of another human being, no matter how silent or removed that human companion may choose to remain. There is, for instance, a certain elegant eloquence to the beat of a raven's wing—an inimitable, airy music—that cannot be heard except when alone. That is because that music is as much felt as heard and that feeling is original and impossible to share. There is a rhythm to the way the dusk wind rises, sings in the branches and broken stone, then dies away. That must sometimes be experienced alone. It may be that, unlike the sound of words, the sounds of a raven's wings or of windsong enter the heart, not the mind.

October 2, 1994

THE ANCIENT PUEBLO is built around and on top of two small buttes overlooking a cottonwood-shaded stream flowing from nearby mountains. When we arrived there, my son Geoff set out in one direction and I in another to explore the fallen houses. Before long I was sitting in the shade looking across the pueblo at the mountains beyond.

I thought then about a project I'm working on for the Crow Canyon Archaeological Center. The project invites Pueblo Indians to provide their views of the archaeology of this region, which was occupied by their ancestors until seven hundred years ago. The project was conceived of by Richard Wilshusen, director of research at Crow Canyon, and the final written material will be used by the Bureau of Land Management in interpreting a thirteenth-century pueblo west of here. The project is being funded by a grant from the Colorado Historical Society. Each visiting group is here for two days and is accompanied by Crow Canyon archaeologist Bruce Bradley and myself. We spend time at Crow Canyon and at several archaeological sites on the Great Sage Plain. My role is to write down the interpretations provided by the American Indian visitors. Thus far people have come from Hopi, Zuni, Zia, Santa Clara, San Juan, and Taos. People have been invited from additional Pueblo communities and from the Ute Mountain Ute Tribe.

There has been much talk within the archaeological profession in recent years about inviting American Indians to provide their interpretation of the silent material record left by their ancestors . . . and very little action. Crow Canyon is one of a small handful of archaeological research institutions which is actually involving American Indians in its work. While Crow Canyon is already at the leading edge of disciplined scientific archaeological research in America, its involvement of American Indians in this and similar projects will give its interpretation of the archaeological record a unique dimension. When visiting an archaeological site, Indians and archaeologists speak in distinctly different, though not opposing, ways. Indians speak passionately. Archaeologists—except when they're disagreeing with one another—speak dispassionately. By providing a forum for American Indians to speak about their own past in their own terms, Crow Canyon will have allowed passion to join science in interpreting the human past of this region and the world. This does not mean that Crow Canyon's interpretation of the archaeological record will become less scientific. It does mean that that interpretation will become broader and more human in scope.

While I sat in the shade looking across the ancient pueblo at the nearby mountains, I tried to understand what the Pueblo people I've accompanied in the last few weeks are telling me about these places where their ancestors lived. It is going to take time for me to gain that understanding, perhaps a lot of time. For Pueblo people these places are not abandoned. They are still occupied by the people who lived in them. Every one of the Pueblo visitors here has emphasized the connection, the very real communication, they feel between themselves and the people who lived here centuries ago. As I witness this universal, deeply-felt Pueblo Indian response to these places, I find it difficult to maintain my usual skepticism. I am seeing very familiar places through different eyes. But seeing and understanding are not the same thing.

October 9, 1994

THICK GREY CLOUDS swirled around the snow-covered peaks towering above us. Gusts of chill, wintry wind sent golden aspen leaves soaring across a russet meadow against thick backdrops of swaying blue spruce. An occasional ray of sunshine broke through the clouds, lending a brilliance but no warmth to the scene before us. We stood by the highway and looked across the meadow at two men, their horses standing nearby and sheep dogs circling, rushing to load the last of a small herd of sheep into a large trailer truck. Occasionally the bleat of a protesting ewe could be heard over the roar of the wind. Between us and the corrals was the railbed of the Rio Grande Southern where it crosses the summit of Lizard Head Pass and where no train has been seen since 1951. We could only imagine the day when sheep were loaded onto narrow-gauge steam trains there rather than onto trucks.

With me were Dick and Merrill Varien of San Angelo, Texas. Dick is a retired sheep buyer, and he quietly reminisced about the days when he traveled in autumn into the mountains where Vail Resort is now located to buy sheep from Basque herders and of the camp meals they shared with him along the way. He talked with respect about the Colorado and Utah ranchers who once ran thousands of sheep across the highest reaches of the San Juans. The scene we watched at the summit of Lizard Head Pass suddenly seemed a mere relic of a bygone era. The men finished their task and began breaking camp.

We traveled the few miles to Ophir and stood by the highway

looking down at Ames, which is located at the foot of a series of waterfalls where the south fork of the San Miguel River plunges more than a thousand feet into the canyon below. Ames is where L. L. Nunn completed construction of the world's first commercial alternating current hydroelectric plant in 1891. Nunn, owner of the Gold King Mine and Mill 2.6 miles above Ames, had been paying $2,500 a month for coal hauled by mules to the steam-powered mill. When he replaced the mules with copper lines, the cost of powering the mill dropped to $500 a month. Nunn went on to construct more power plants in the high San Juans before leaving Colorado to build the enormous hydroelectric plant at Niagara Falls.

While Nunn was building the Ames plant, hundreds of railroad laborers were concentrated there working on another engineering challenge. Their job was to get the route of Otto Mears's Rio Grande Southern Railroad up out of the canyon and on to the waiting mines of Rico beyond the summit of Lizard Head Pass. The Ophir Loop, a series of trestles and switchbacks suspended over dizzying drops, was the result. The aspens were golden and the peaks dusted with new snow when the tracks reached Rico on September 30, 1891. Rico boomed. The mines and mills operated twenty-four hours a day. After the entire Rio Grande Southern route was completed in December of 1892, four passenger trains left Rico every day, two bound for Durango at the railroad's southern terminus and two for Ridgway at the northern end. Ore trains ran almost every hour of the day and night. Mears celebrated by handing out solid silver and gold railroad passes to his friends. Less than a year later the Sherman Silver Purchasing Act was repealed, and the price of silver plummeted out of sight. The mines fell silent and thousands of Ricoans rode the Rio Grande Southern on a one-way journey out of town. Rico and the Rio Grande Southern never recovered.

We turned back and stopped at the Rico Hotel in that now quiet hamlet for homemade apple pie. The sun came out, the wind died, and the aspens on the healing slopes blazed in the late light. It was hard to believe that it had not always been thus.

October 16, 1994

IN THE FOUR CORNERS COUNTRY the phrase "fall colors" usually brings to mind mountainsides covered with golden stands of aspen. Motorists flock to the high country to see the short-lived show. By the end of the first week in October the brilliant groves are nearly bare and the white bark of the aspens a reminder of the winter snows to come. But here in the low country, in the Montezuma Valley surrounding Cortez, the autumn colors are just appearing, and they will continue into November. From my north window I can see a long, gentle slope that tilts upward several miles to end at the rim of the Dolores River Valley. The slope is a mosaic of color. Pastures are still emerald green. Apple orchards are a deep burgundy. Long, winding lines of yellow cottonwoods follow the bottoms of draws toward the floor of the valley. Far beyond the Dolores River, Lone Cone is a lavender pyramid on the northern horizon.

Sometimes in the late afternoon light, I get in my pickup and follow country roads onto that slope through rural communities named Mildred and Lebanon, and beyond them to the communities northwest of here, places with names like Beulah, Arriola, and Lewis. My route takes me past country churches, one-room schoolhouses converted into homes, rural cemeteries, and at least one Grange hall. This is an area of small farms that have been irrigated for a century. Together they form a pastoral landscape dotted with ponds connected by cottonwood-shaded ditches following the ridge tops. There is a vastness to the sky here and a vastness to the vistas beneath that landscape. Red-tailed hawks fly up from fence posts, linking earth to sky.

The low light and the vastness together remind me that these brief, spontaneous afternoon drives are solitary exercises. I then contemplate the meaning of solitary acts. The thesaurus lodged somewhere in this computer describes "solitary" as being the opposite of "accessible" and "accompanied." Driving alone along country roads in my pickup certainly makes me inaccessible. I'm not at all sure that that means I'm unaccompanied. My mind remains filled with the images of friends' faces and the sounds of their voices. The slant of late light on this expanse of earth and stone evokes the voice of an artist friend who frequently creates images of this place on paper and canvas. The sight of an ancient pueblo evokes the voice of an archaeologist friend who frequently visits these ancient pueblos with me. If I pass the home of friends, I hear bits of dinner conversations that have taken place there. If I glance at a house where I once lived—there are three of them in those small communities—my mind projects the home movies of times in those houses that are stored in my head.

I have come to believe that after a certain age it is still possible to choose to be temporarily inaccessible but no longer possible to be unaccompanied . . . at least not within a half day's drive of home. I have gone alone to many places within that radius, but very few remain that I've been to only once. At other times I've gone to those places with a friend or friends. This power of familiar landscapes to evoke familiar voices may be what is meant by "a sense of place." It may also be that as one grows older the single voice that begins to fade and speak less frequently at these places is one's own.

October 23, 1994

I KNEW WHEN IT STRUCK that the gust of wind was the first blast of winter. We were wandering through the remnants of a twelfth-century pueblo on a bench overlooking a river at an elevation of forty-five hundred feet. Low clouds hugged the cliff tops above us. It had stopped raining and the air, for the moment, was still. Then the first cold, cutting gust of wind seemed to come from everywhere at once. We didn't tarry long and were soon headed homeward along a circuitous route which avoided dirt roads made impassable by the storm. As we climbed from the river valley, the rain resumed. When we reached an elevation of six thousand feet the rain turned to snow. At seventy-five hundred feet the falling snow reduced visibility to about one hundred feet, and the highway was covered with slush. The road then descended onto the Great Sage Plain, and the snow turned into rain.

By the time I was home the sky was clearing and the setting sun was painting the fleeing clouds crimson. The wind was cold and rising. The first snow was visible on Ute Mountain and the northern slopes of Mesa Verde. The next morning a thick layer of frost glistened on the sage outside my house. To the north the golden cottonwoods stretched for miles up to the rim of the Dolores Valley which was white with the night's snow. For the next three days the sun broke through the clouds only occasionally to spotlight the autumn landscape. There was more rain, but snow has yet to fall on the canyon rims where I live.

My dog Chaco likes this passage into winter. In hot weather her sleek black coat absorbs heat, and she spends the days indoors, going outside now and then to roll in the dust, then returning to the suffering couch to resume her panting nap. When she does take a walk in that heat, her tail points at the ground, and she moves slowly as if bearing the weight of the world on her shoulders. Now, the colder it gets the livelier Chaco gets. There is a spring to her step, and her tail points straight up at the clouds. When snow does begin to fall here, she will ask to go out at dawn so she can follow cottontail tracks, her nose pressed into the fresh snow, to the edges of the saltbush thickets below the house. Chaco seems to have no desire to catch the rabbits. She may only want to know where they are spending the day.

Perhaps the surest sign that the season is changing is the return of a grey fox to this neighborhood. The fox comes at night to take the apple I put out for it at dusk. I occasionally catch a glimpse of it during the day when it bounds through the trees on the canyon rim, its tail held straight back, looking neither right nor left, moving with great determination. I can only guess at the nature of the fox's daytime missions. That fox and another spent last winter here, coming every night for apples. One March dawn the apples were still there and stayed for days until eaten by the jays. I put out more apples. They were eventually consumed by the birds. I don't know where these creatures spend the summer. I do know that it's good to have them back.

October 30, 1994

THE ANCIENT ROAD ARCS from the mouth of one deep canyon to the mouth of the next. On ridges above it are the remnants of great kivas and small pueblos. Pottery sherds, painted and plain, are scattered across the red soil. Beyond the road a small stream flows over red pebbles and pink sand beneath golden cottonwoods. Five of us, including Durangoans Louise Teal and Bill Karls, wandered slowly across the place looking at the sherds. The design on one of them indicated that the pot had originally been brought there from hundreds of miles away.

I departed for home then thinking back on the day spent in the canyons with another friend, a Pueblo Indian. Looking out from the walls of the canyons were small cliff dwellings containing rectangular rooms and round granaries or rooms. There are hundreds of them in the canyons that slash through that mesa west of my home. We have names for those canyons and many of those ancient dwellings. They appear on our maps of the area.

When I'm walking in those canyons, I often ponder the unknowable. What were the names the people who built those dwellings gave to their buildings and to the canyons we know by our own names? A Pueblo Indian friend recently told me that in his pueblo there is an annual ceremony in which the names of the places at which his people stopped and lived on the way to the place they live now are recited. It takes a full three hours to recite those ancient place names stretching back into time immemorial. It is only in the last five minutes of that oration that my friend recognizes any of the place names being recited or the locations to which they refer. Perhaps somewhere halfway through that recitation are the names of the canyons we visited last weekend.

On the rim of one of those canyons is the circular foundation of a house which predates the nearby cliff dwellings by more than a thousand years. I ponder more unknowables. Is the ancient name of the place where that foundation is located mentioned early in the three hour oration? Did the people who built and lived in the cliff dwellings also have a ceremony of remembrance, a recitation of the places they'd stopped on the way to the canyons? If so, was the place on the rim of the canyon named in their ceremony?

The house on the rim of the canyon is one of several forming a small hamlet. The hamlet is the location of some of the earliest known corn found in the entire San Juan River Basin. By the time of the cliff dwellings, domestic corn was an important part of Puebloan life here, as witnessed by the countless corn cobs strewn through the ruins and the depictions of corn plants found here and there on the canyon walls. Today corn remains the essence of modern Puebloan life in Arizona and New Mexico.

I drove home slowly pondering not only these unknowables but the knowable as well. I had spent the weekend visiting the ancestral homes of a people who have resided in the Four Corners Country for more than two thousand years, a people who are still here today.

December 11, 1994

A FEW DAYS AGO I was working at this computer and listening to public radio at the same time, which meant I wasn't paying full attention to either endeavor. I heard a man on the radio talking about ethics in the twenty-first century. He said something to the effect that we need to become more ethically fit, to be better prepared to confront ethical issues when they arise. Ethical choices, he said, must be made at unexpected moments, they do not occur at predictable times. That is about all my divided brain recorded and retained of what was being said. Incomplete and fragmented as my recollection of the interview is, it has kept me pondering the subject of ethics ever since.

The Oxford English Dictionary defines "ethic" as "pertaining to morals" and "ethics" as "the science of morals, the department of study concerned with the principles of human duty." "Science of morals" really doesn't offer a great deal of food for thought and neither does "principles of human duty." Oddly, *The Oxford English Dictionary* contains no definition of the word "morals," and it seems at something of a loss when defining the word "moral." Its first definition refers to the titles of works by St. Gregory the

Great, Plutarch, Seneca, etc., though the definitions go on for half a page in type so small that a magnifying glass comes with the dictionary.

At one point, while pondering the issue of ethics, I was staring out the window at the bird feeder about fifteen feet away. It's a makeshift bird feeder, an old-fashioned metal TV table heaped with birdseed. It is near a juniper intertwined with a serviceberry bush. Jays swoop down from the juniper onto the table top sending seed flying in every direction. Juncos and cottontail rabbits hop around on the ground below eating the spilled seed. When I was staring at the bird feeder, it was surrounded by birds. Suddenly they took startled flight. A sharp-shinned hawk settled into the serviceberry bush. The hawk is a frequent visitor to that bush, always hunkering down to make itself as small as possible and holding perfectly still. Sharp-shinned hawks dine on small birds, and it is almost possible to hear that hawk hoping to go unnoticed while the hapless juncos return. It amazes me how much a hawk can look like a serviceberry branch when it really wants to do so.

A junco lit in the bush just above the hawk. The hawk remained motionless. The junco fluttered onto the table. The hawk slowly lifted one foot. There it was, the unexpected ethical crisis. I immediately thumped the windowpane with my finger, proving my ethical fitness. The hawk soared away down the slope toward the canyon. The ungrateful junco never stopped eating, never once glanced gratefully in my direction. His companions soon rejoined him.

My self-righteousness at having made the proper ethical choice at an unexpected moment began to fade. The hawk, of course, would return, and I can't spend the *whole* day looking out the window. Was I, by putting out birdseed, enticing innocent juncos into a bloody death trap? Hawks have to eat, too, I assured myself, and this hawk would certainly dine on juncos elsewhere if not at my table.

The bird feeder poses other dilemmas. Every afternoon I put an apple by the bird feeder for the grey fox to pick up at night. Every evening now, at dusk, several deer—sleek, fat, well-nourished deer—come to the bird feeder to consume what little birdseed is left at day's end. That's fine. What is not so fine is that one of them inevitably goes for the fox's apple. The first few times this happened, I saved the apple for the fox by thumping on the window. The deer fled hastily. Then they began ignoring my thump. So I resorted to opening the window and shouting at the deer standing a few feet away. They now ignore my shouts, glancing up at me with barely concealed contempt.

Ethically speaking, I'd probably be going too far if I started throwing things at the deer. But, if hawks ate deer it would be perfectly OK with me.

January 1, 1995

ONE OF THE GREAT ADVANTAGES to living alone—in addition to not having to wash the dishes or close the bathroom door when showering—is that it enables one to make truly grandiose New Year's resolutions. No one is around when I don't keep them. With that in mind, I resolve the following:

—I am either going to get my TV set repaired or buy a new one. It's been broken for nearly a year. As it stands now, I don't know what Newt Gingrich looks like. I listen to public radio, so I do know what he sounds like. I constantly wonder if Newt's looks resemble his sounds. For his sake, I hope not. If it weren't for long checkout lines at the supermarket, I wouldn't know what Judge Ito looks like either, but one of my favorite tabloids (I only read the cover) featured a postage-stamp-sized picture of him this week. This same tabloid has recently switched from proclaiming O.J.'s innocence to proclaiming his guilt. If I had the courage to pick up the tabloid and read it until my turn at the cash register came, I would be better informed about how it came to be that tabloids have replaced juries. I could just buy the tabloid, but that would contradict the image I have of myself—an image I want the clerk behind the register to share. I'm already beginning to rationalize my way out of this resolution. Instead of buying a TV set, I'll just wait for Newt's picture to show up on tabloid covers in the supermarket. That should be just about any day now.

—I am going to throw something away this year, preferably old magazines. A friend gives me a yearly subscription to *The New*

Yorker—which never carries photographs of politicians—and I've got stacks of them. I've kept them for so long that I can now go back to the beginning and look at cartoons I'd completely forgotten and laugh at them as if I'd never seen them before. I used to subscribe to weekly news magazines until they started looking and reading like the tabloids . . . there's that snobbish image thing again. I may not know what Newt Gingrich looks like, but if I ever start forgetting what Gerald Ford looked like as President—my memory has started replacing him with Chevy Chase—all I have to do is rummage through the closet, find an old *Time Magazine*, and refresh my memory. I have a fading image of what Bill Clinton looks like, because I watched the election returns at a neighbor's house in 1992. Maybe my neighbors will let me watch Clinton's next State of the Union message on their TV. That will refresh my visual image of Clinton, and I'm sure I'd see plenty of Newt Gingrich at the same time. I've never found myself looking forward to a speech as much as I am the next State of the Union message. Seeing it will probably be even more entertaining than just hearing it. Where is Chevy Chase now that we need him?

In short, I resolve to improve my visual literacy in 1995. It's hard to be a responsible citizen without knowing what my country's leadership looks like. On the other hand, in 1995 I may just go on settling for sunrises, sunsets, and the Milky Way.

January 29, 1995

THIS IS A TIME OF YEAR when it is easier to imagine destinations than it is to actually reach them. The ground here is covered with patches of snow. Where bare earth shows, the soil freezes at night, but by noon there is a thin veneer of mud soup atop the deeper layers of frozen clay. The only time one can walk with ease is at dawn before the morning thaw begins. It is impossible to walk in meditative silence across frozen snow. Each crunching footstep is a reminder of one's own presence, and meditation in nature requires forgetting one's separateness from stone, tree, owl, fox, rabbit, and deer. It is a season when I tend to stare out the window and let my imagination do the walking. I revisit past destinations and plan future journeys.

In early January I went with Ruth Slickman to a thirteenth-century pueblo I had never visited before. The journey was part of a project I've been working on with Crow Canyon archaeologists Mark Varien and Bill Lipe and others for nearly six years. Mark is working both at Crow Canyon and on his doctoral dissertation at Arizona State University. One element of his research is an analysis of twelfth- and thirteenth-century communities in the Mesa Verde archaeological region, which includes the Great Sage Plain north and west of Cortez. His analysis requires that he know where people were living in the Mesa Verde region in the those two centuries. There are thousands of archaeological sites, most of them quite small, in the Mesa Verde region that were occupied at least briefly in the twelfth and thirteenth centuries. The locations of most of these sites is unknown because much of the Great Sage Plain has never been surveyed for sites. Some small, limited areas, however, have been comprehensively surveyed by contract archaeologists and others. Mesa Verde National Park has been surveyed for sites, as well. Federal law makes it illegal to reveal the locations of unprotected archaeological sites on public lands, though such information can be used for legitimate scholarly research—and access to the information requires federal and state research permits.

Because locating all the sites in the Mesa Verde region is a little like locating all the electrons in the universe, Mark decided to concentrate on sites containing fifty rooms and more. Most of the information has come from archaeologists working in specific areas of southwestern Colorado and southeastern Utah. Mark visits the sites in order to verify their size and list other attributes, but it would take months of doing nothing else to see them all. I've visited enough sites with Mark that I've found myself caught up in the process. If, when wandering across the Great Sage Plain, I spot a large site, I check it out to see if it qualifies for Mark's list. That was what Ruth and I were doing one morning earlier this month.

It was beginning to snow when we pulled off the dirt road and walked toward the site about a mile away in a sage flat. All that could be seen was a rubble mound, but it looked promising. What could not be seen was the canyon between us and the site. The ruin was on the far rim of the canyon overlooking springs and a small stream. What had seemed like a beeline walk through the sage became a zigzag traverse across the canyon, arroyos, and running water. A light blanket of snow covered the crumbled pueblo when we reached it. It was not a fifty-room pueblo. What gave the rubble mound its apparent size was its location. The building had once been quite tall and probably resembled Hovenweep Castle. The high walls had tumbled down the canyon slope, covering a large area. I watched the falling snow and heard the running water.

Now I sit looking out the window at snow and mud and think about other pueblos that might qualify for Mark's list. Finding them is the easy part. Finding the ways that they fit into ancient communities will be the challenging part. That's Mark's job. Meanwhile, I'm making a list of my own: more pueblos to visit this spring.

February 5, 1995

It was pitch dark and snowing hard when Ernest House and I left Towaoc for the pueblo of Acoma. Ernest is director of the Ute Mountain Tribal Park and former chairman of the Ute Mountain Ute Tribe. He is a member of the American Indian Cultural Interpretation Steering Committee and of its sponsor, the Four Corners Heritage Council. We were on our way to a meeting of the Steering Committee in the tribal administration building at Acoma. The Committee is designing a project to introduce American Indian perspectives into the interpretation of archaeological sites. I am not a member of the Committee—it is made up entirely of American Indians from throughout the region—but I attend the meetings and make a written record of its proceedings.

We left the snow behind when we crossed the New Mexico border. First light touched the low clouds at Newcomb, and a powerful wind blew down from the Chuskas. East of Gallup, along I-40, the wind grew fiercer yet, rocking vehicles and sending swirling sheets of ice crystals across the highway. Occasional rays of sunlight broke through the clouds and lit the red cliffs lining our route. Mount Taylor was obscured by clouds and snow. When we arrived, the flags above the tribal headquarters at Acoma whipped and snapped in a wind so cold it cut like a knife.

We were greeted by Darwin Vallo, a member of the Steering Committee and chairman of the Acoma tribal council. He talked quietly about the sixty-nine hundred people of Acoma. The reservation, a fraction of the size of the original Acoma domain, boasts few resources. Cattle grazing is the primary source of tribal income. Arts and crafts provide income for some members of the pueblo, but most of them are paid far less for their work than it sells for in retail outlets in Albuquerque. Unemployment on the reservation is an unbelievable seventy-three percent. Darwin and other leaders of Acoma are determined to improve these grim conditions while, at the same time, preserving the language and traditional culture. That requires a real balancing act. As I listened to Darwin, I felt confident those leaders would succeed.

Following the meeting we traveled to the visitor center in the shadow of the mesa where the City in the Sky is located. As we ate a lunch of traditional food, Darwin talked about the significance of the pueblo atop the mesa to his own culture and to other Pueblo people. Hopi elders, among others, make pilgrimages, stopping at shrines along the way to pray for permission to continue their approach to the mesa.

After lunch Darwin took us to the mesa top where we joined a group of visitors about to begin a tour. The wind was harsher and colder there than it was on the valley floor. My face and ears were numb before we got to the first stop, the enormous church built by Acoma slaves in the seventeenth century. The church is unheated and is not used in the winter. Its high, heavy, pink and white wooden doors stood open. Entering its dim interior was like stepping into a freezer. The massive beams stretching across the ceiling nearly sixty feet above us were brought from Mount Taylor, thirty miles away. The huge wooden pillars framing the altar were not allowed to touch the ground throughout that torturous journey.

We left the church, made our way along the mesa's edge, and entered narrow streets lined by stone and adobe buildings up to three stories high. Tree-ring dates from some of the roof beams stretch back to the A.D. 1050s. There is no electricity and no running water on the mesa top and few families live there year-round. One group of people who must live there are the field chiefs who, for the first nine months of their tenure, are not allowed to leave the mesa top for any reason whatsoever. In medical emergencies, doctors are brought to their houses. The field chiefs mark the progress of the rising and setting sun along the rugged horizons and announce upcoming religious events when the sun approaches certain landmarks. They also designate the location of fields on the valley floor. Darwin motioned me to the mesa's edge and pointed to last year's fields hundreds of feet below. I glanced down quickly and stepped back, afraid that a gust of wind might hurl me down into one of those fields. Such a fate might have earned me a place in Acoma legend, right along with the soldiers and priests who were thrown from the mesa by Acomans in a revolt against their European conquerors.

Despite the cutting wind and cold, I felt a sense of regret when it was time to leave the City in the Sky. It is an enduring monument to the fierce determination of a people to preserve a unique and dynamic culture while creating better lives for themselves in twenty-first-century America at large.

April 30, 1995

I HAVE LIVED IN THIS LITTLE HOUSE alongside a narrow, dead-end dirt road for seven years. The road extends beyond the end of a paved street. The pavement ends where the town ends. In order to get to the post office or grocery store, I drive along the paved street to its intersection with a four-lane, divided highway. I cross two lanes of traffic and turn left, or at least that is what I used to do. Now, though the post office and store are where they have always been, I almost always turn right onto the divided highway. That is because the traffic on the highway has increased so much in seven years that it is hazardous to cross two lanes filled with oncoming vehicles and enter the crowded two lanes coming from the other direction. So now I turn right, drive a few hundred yards, make a U-turn, and proceed on to my routine destinations in town.

Even the wait for a break in the traffic in order to turn right is growing longer. Sometimes I sit at the stop sign for five minutes or more. I use this time to ponder the changes that have taken place at the intersection in the past seven years. Not only is there more traffic, but it is moving faster. There are many more enormous semi-trailer trucks and many of them—not all—are whizzing by at speeds much higher than the posted 35-mile-per-hour limit. They run a yield sign giving no clue to oncoming drivers that they intend to yield an inch. When flashing, the yellow school zone light down the highway does little to slow these monsters down. The growing number of passenger vehicles take their example from the big trucks; many of them are keeping pace with the semis. It might be that there is safety in numbers. Where in the past the occasional speeder was an easy target for the police, there are now so many speeders that the police may have just given up.

While sitting at the intersection waiting to turn right, I conduct highly scientific studies. I scan the license plates on the passenger vehicles whizzing by from the left. I would like to report that most of them are California plates. Not so. Most of them are Montezuma County plates. This increase in traffic is an indicator of an increase in population. Not only is it evident in the number of vehicles speeding past that intersection, but it can be seen elsewhere as well. Checkout lines are longer in the vast Cortez City Market, and the nearest empty parking spaces to the post office are often more than a block away. As my son and two roommates recently arrived from Phoenix can attest, rental housing is virtually nonexistent. New houses—some of them mini-mansions by local standards—are popping up overnight along most country roads. Often the traditional, friendly wave to the drivers of oncoming vehicles on country roads is no longer returned. The person barreling down the gravel road is less and less likely to be someone you know.

You may think I'm complaining. I'm not. I know that the people moving into the Montezuma Valley are doing so for the same reason that I intend to stay here. Cortez is a friendly, slow-paced, uncomplicated place to live, and the surrounding landscape is just as friendly. The population here has boomed at least twice in the past—once during the oil and uranium booms of the fifties and again during the simultaneous development of the carbon dioxide fields and the Dolores River Project in the seventies. Those construction booms went bust. This population boom has a different feel to it, like it's here to stay.

On second thought, I do have one complaint. It doesn't have to do with the growing number of vehicles at that intersection. It has to do with the speed at which they are traveling. I've witnessed the same phenomenon in Santa Fe and then in Durango. Many of the ex-urbanites moving into these places bring their big city driving habits with them. And they don't wave back. I thought it couldn't happen here.

May 7, 1995

THE SERVICEBERRY BUSHES along the canyon rim are clouds of white blossoms, four o'clocks are coming up beneath the piñon trees, there are buds on the claret cup cactus growing from cracks in the rock, and the rabbits are eating the mariposa leaves as soon as they sprout. White and pink creeping phlox hug the stone, and a number of purple, yellow, and white flowering plants I can't name bend in the dawn breeze. The space around the bird feeder is aflutter with brilliant lazuli buntings, black-headed grosbeaks, rufous-sided towhees, rose-hued finches, cowbirds, mourning doves, and juncos. Cliquish, noisy piñon jays and loner scrub jays add shades of blue to the kaleidoscope of bird wings beneath my window. A kestrel rockets past, sending the birds fleeing into the shelter of nearby shrubs. Swallows fill the sky beneath low, dark storm clouds at dawn.

The scene outside my window is fleeting. Many of the birds are passing through on their way from the south to mountain and northern destinations. The pastel flowers will soon drop their petals. The towering cumulus clouds that build above the peaks in the afternoon already have the look of summer, and the distant thunder that awakens me in the night has the sound of July. For the moment, though, it is spring in the Four Corners Country.

I'll probably never learn, but because it is spring, I made my annual pilgrimage to the Four Seasons Greenhouse between Dolores and Cortez. I went there vowing that I would just look and not return home with a vehicle full of plants that will only grow in yards filled with hoses and sprinkler systems. My cistern is filled every two weeks from a water truck and holds enough water to provide me with fourteen days of showers and tea water. There is no water left for plants. Seven years of drought have taught me that it is foolish to depend on summer rain to nurture the little plants I set out each spring. Nonetheless, for the past several years I've returned from the Four Seasons Greenhouse with pots full of plants that normally grow in marshes. In springtime, hope springs eternal. I've become the serial killer of the plant world. Aside from all that, nature is a superb gardener in the rocky ground that surrounds my house. Why should I tamper with nature? As I left the house for Four Seasons, I glanced at a large, dead piñon tree next to the carport. It has a stark beauty of its own, silhouetted against ever-changing skies.

While wandering through the perennials at Four Seasons, I noticed large flowers on vines. I took a closer look. They were clematis vines. The flowers were red, white, blue, pink, rose . . . Now, I know that our native clematis grows only along mountain streams. But, I reminded myself, it has been a wet spring. Within an hour after my return home from Four Seasons, my son Geoff and I had the clematis planted and staked beneath the dead piñon tree. Someday, I'm sure, it will look like something out of a tropical rain forest.

The following day a package arrived from my son Jonathan in Santa Fe. It contained packets of seeds—native hollyhocks, climbing milkweed, gourds, squash, and, best of all, *maizillo teosinte,* an ancient relative of corn. These are not fancy hybrids. The seeds come from plants grown by gardeners dedicated to preserving ancient species of ornamental and edible flora and are sold by a company called Seeds of Change in Santa Fe. The plants don't need much water to grow and produce. They should be right at home.

May 14, 1995

WE STOOD FACING EAST at an overlook on the edge of Monument Valley waiting for the sun to rise. It had rained hard in the night and thick, low clouds obscured all but the bases of the monuments. Visibility was about one mile. As it grew lighter the group of people I was with marveled aloud at the beauty of the newly washed, red rock landscape surrounding us. I, on the other hand, could barely conceal my disappointment. I had hoped for a longer view.

The group included management level employees from National Forests in Oregon, Washington, and Alaska as well as resource people from throughout the United States and from Germany, Mexico, Denmark, and the United Kingdom. I was one of the resource people and would spend two days with the group going from Monument Valley to points around Cortez. The Forest Service staff members were participating in a much longer seminar intended to introduce them to concerns and cultures outside the federal government and outside the geographical regions where they worked. The seminar was organized by Dr. Charles DeRidder of Portland, Oregon, and, among other activities, was spending ten days in the Southwest visiting archaeological sites and modern American Indian communities. The Southwest segment of the seminar was led by Jackson Clark, Sr., and it was Jackson who asked me to talk at stops along the way between Monument Valley and Cortez.

The Monument Valley overlook is a place I go when I want to renew my sense of how the Four Corners Country fits together. From there it is possible, on a clear day, to see the La Plata Mountains more than a hundred miles to the east. Before sunrise those peaks are silhouetted against the lightening sky. Landmarks between the La Platas and Monument Valley—Mesa Verde, Sleeping Ute Mountain, the McElmo Dome, McElmo Canyon, Goodman Point, Comb Ridge, the Bear's Ears, and Cedar Mesa—are similarly etched in the dawn brightness. From Monument Valley I wander a zigzag eastward route that takes me from overlook to overlook. Each overlook offers a new perspective of the landforms among which I am traveling until, at last, I am standing near the La Platas looking back at Monument Valley and all the landmarks in between.

This experience—orienting myself to landmarks—makes me set aside two-dimensional road maps and let the landscape itself tell me where I have been, where I am, and where I am going. I have taken people from outside the Four Corners Country along this route before and, for residents of cities or heavily forested landscapes where there are no long distance vistas, the experience is more profound than it is for me. They quickly feel at home in a place, which at the outset was completely alien.

For this particular journey I had prepared and silently rehearsed a mental script tied to the series of overlooks we would visit along the way—some of them at the end of dirt roads now turned to muddy soup. The rain resumed at Monument Valley. I tossed the mental script and silently made a new list of stops along the way to Cortez, stops that were alongside paved or graveled roads. I had no idea of what to say when we got to those places. I'm not good at extemporaneous speaking.

I soon realized that I didn't need to worry about what to say. At each stop I was barraged with questions. Where I saw archaeology, this group saw ancient people in their ecological setting. It was quite apparent that the foresters were not on a junket, rather they were determined to relate this experience to the management of the public lands for which they are responsible. Every discussion of issues being raised by American Indians in the Four Corners Country was discussed in the context of similar issues being raised elsewhere in the nation.

I ended up learning at least as much from the seminar participants as they learned from me.

May 21, 1995

ACCORDING TO THE CALENDAR, summer begins on June 21. In this house summer begins on the first night I leave the windows open to cool the house. Summer began last Sunday night. I awakened at first light on Monday morning to see a full moon low in the western sky. The clear, melodious notes of a kingbird's song came from somewhere outside the open north window. The sky lightened and Canada geese flew in noisy formation above the canyon. In the first rays of the rising sun, a mockingbird emerged from the juniper next to the deck and flew off in search of breakfast. I turned on the computer, and it was after noon before I looked out the window again. Two golden eagles circled above the canyon before heading northwest out of sight. I decided to follow the eagles.

I traveled country roads between vast, greening fields. The snow-covered Lone Cone was a white pyramid floating on a forested horizon. Red-tailed hawks, perched on power poles, kept watch over the nearer landscape. The fields ended and I drove through sage glades ringed by piñon pine and juniper forests. I recalled an Associated Press article I'd read in last Sunday's *Durango Herald* about Michael Rockland, author of *Snowshoeing Through Sewers*. Rockland says, "In the late 20th century, a weed and trash-filled city may be a better place than wilderness to contemplate one's relationship with nature." Though I was about as far from a trash-filled city as I could get, I silently agreed.

The road ended and I walked along a faint trail that descended a forested slope to a thirteenth-century pueblo built above and below a high cliff. Crow Canyon archaeologists Melissa Churchill and Mark Varien were working there when I arrived. Melissa, along with Crow Canyon participants, is excavating small areas on top of the cliff where a low stone wall encloses the crumbling remnants of several buildings. Mark is doing similar small excavations with participants on the talus slope below the cliff. Both archaeologists are interested in the stone walls enclosing all or part of many canyon rim sites that were built and occupied in the thirteenth century. The wall on the flat rimrock atop the cliff is fairly well preserved and quite apparent to the eye. Where these walls were built on the steep talus slopes, they have succumbed to erosion and all but vanished. At this particular pueblo, Mark has located a few surviving remnants of wall that may once have enclosed the lower portion of the site. He pointed them out to me.

Stone enclosing walls were the subject of a recent Master's thesis by archaeologist Susan Kenzle at the University of Calgary. I visited several walled pueblos with her while she was doing her field research and have visited several more since. Susan examined several possible reasons for building the walls, ranging from the symbolic to the concrete. Some archaeologists believe they served to make the pueblos easier to defend against marauders.

I find the walls fascinating because, to my eye, they so clearly define the boundary between what archaeologists call the "built environment" and the unbuilt environment. That is, the kivas, towers, and roomblocks are inside the wall and there is very little visible archaeology in the immediate vicinity outside the wall. Many of the walled pueblos exist within relatively blank areas in the archaeological record of the Mesa Verde region. This observation does nothing to prove or disprove any particular hypothesis about any particular function the walls may have served, fortifications or otherwise.

Viewed today, the walls provide as good a place to "contemplate one's relationship with nature" as any "weed and trash-filled city." I like to think they may have served that purpose for the people who built those walls and who lived within them.

May 28, 1995

THERE IS STILL SNOW on the north slopes of Ute Mountain, but the aspen groves on the high ridges are a pale, new green. A blue grosbeak paid a brief visit to my bird feeder on its way elsewhere, and a house wren spends much of the day hopping from branch to branch in a juniper near my deck. I don't know whether the wren is nesting in the tree or feeding on the plentiful supply of spiders that renews itself there every night. I have seen the wren removing small strips of bark from the juniper, so I suspect its nest is somewhere nearby. Lizards have emerged from winter's sleep to sun themselves on the deck rail. Claret cup cactus flowers are brilliant splashes against lichened rock. Deep blue lupine and purple vetch form carpets on the forest floor on the higher reaches of the McElmo Dome and nighthawks are nesting on bare stone along the canyon rims.

After a recent appointment in Bluff—where I was introduced to what is for me the awesome new world of interactive CD-ROM—I went to Sand Island to meet a friend for a picnic lunch. While waiting for her to arrive, I became an observer to a local rite of spring. Sand Island is where rafters push off onto the San Juan River for the ride to Mexican Hat and beyond. Scores of them did so beneath the midday sun. The river was running fast and high, and each group of talkative, happy rafters quickly vanished around the first downstream bend.

Yucca bloomed on the talus along the river beneath the watchful gaze of figures pecked into the cliff. Groups of ancient people and wild animals coexist peacefully in those crowded panels that have been there for centuries. One petroglyph depicts a blooming yucca, and it was right above the real thing. Live lizards scurried across their own likenesses in the stone.

As I drove home from Sand Island, I thought not only about the petroglyphs but about the interactive CD-ROM demonstration I'd seen in Bluff. I'm a consultant in a project—overseen by Anasazi Heritage Center director LouAnn Jacobson—which will create a pilot interactive CD-ROM program interpreting a local eleventh-century pueblo from both an archaeological and a Pueblo Indian point of view. I'd asked the producers, Bluff residents Theresa Breznau and Clay Hamilton, to explain interactive CD-ROM to me. They made a brave attempt. I couldn't visualize what they were telling me. I've seen interactive video, and it's always struck me as nothing more than switching channels. When I hear the word "animation," I think of Donald Duck. When I hear the phrase "three dimensional," a computer monitor is the last thing that comes to mind.

Clay and Theresa explained that the pueblo could be reconstructed in a way that a learner could wander through it at will, choosing his or her own route and whether to view the interior rooms and items from an archaeologist's or a Puebloan's point of view. I couldn't shake the notion that interpreting an ancient pueblo in this multimedia way would be anything but superficial. I came away from Bluff convinced that interactive CD-ROM programs can impart a great deal of knowledge in ways I'd never imagined. In this particular case, supplying part of the knowledge is my job.

I'm a writer who likes best to write in longhand—though I rarely do anymore. What I'd seen in Bluff was more like the blank stone into which the ancient figures at Sand Island are etched. It is the ancient figures, not the stone, that impart profound knowledge through time. They do so without the intervention of the written word. As I begin participating in this CD-ROM project, I may be going back to a time when only images, unaccompanied by written words, imparted knowledge. Whether CD messages can last as long as messages pecked into stone, only time will tell.

June 11, 1995

It is sometimes easier to look ahead and pretend to know where one is going than it is to look back and know where one has been. That thought has occurred to me several times recently as I read through these columns—more than five hundred of them—written since January 1985.

When I began writing the "Four Corners Almanac," I was staying in an isolated farmhouse northwest of Cortez. Friends had lent me the house so I could write undisturbed for a time and ponder the future of my then-disrupted life. I was living in Durango at the time and anticipated returning to my home there in a few weeks. But that was not to be. On one level, the five hundred columns I've written in the last ten years provide little clue as to why I didn't go home to Durango. There is no indication in those tens of thousands of words that I had reached a decision to remain in Montezuma County. There is no indication of a major life event that caused me to stay here. Reviewing the essays has made me recall that I moved from place to place several times in the first three years I was here. So I wasn't exactly attached to this house or that. For several months I even lived out-of-doors. If anything strikes me as I review these essays, it is that I have led an uneventful life for the last ten years.

The seasons and places of the Four Corners Country, though seen through my eyes and in my words, are the major players in these essays. I do notice some changes as the years pass in written form. My sons grow up and make lives of their own. Archaeology plays a greater and greater role in influencing my wandering across the Four Corners Country. I gradually stop naming the places I'm writing about and resort to description alone. World and national events receive less and less mention as time passes. I travel to fewer places outside the region and become more and more tied to a computer in my house. The essays describe the scene outside my window with increasing frequency. There are more mesas and more canyons and fewer mountains, except those peaks seen from a distance. My brief flirtation with a television set in my house is ended by a single lightning bolt.

Some things remain the same. Chaco, the dog, and Solstice, the cat, are there from nearly the beginning and are here today. The seasons pass with a predictable rhythm. There are seasons of drought and seasons of flood. There are seasons of flowers and seasons of snow. There is always the changing light. A certain canyon rim seems to have taken control of my thoughts when they are not focused on events taking place around the bird feeder.

As I reread the essays, I remembered that halfway through the decade I turned fifty. But even that seemed unremarkable. The most adrenaline-inducing event I came across in five hundred essays was an encounter with a skunk. I worry some about the impression left by this decade's worth of words. I'd rather cut a more dashing figure, be a bit more Hemingwayesque in my portrayal of self. I'll work on that in the decade to come.

ABOUT THE AUTHOR—

IAN THOMPSON is a fifth generation Coloradoan who has lived in the Four Corners Country most of his life. His books and essays describe the natural and cultural diversity of a rugged land that has been inhabited by a relatively few people at a time for thousands of years. Thompson was Executive Director of the Crow Canyon Archaeological Center near Cortez, Colorado, for five years and continues to work with research archaeologists at the Center. He is a consultant to several projects seeking to expand interpretation of archaeological sites in the Four Corners Country to include the perspectives of the American Indians in the region. He has served as Editor of *The Silverton Standard* and Associate Editor of *The Durango Herald*. Thompson was a City Councilman and Mayor of Durango and Chairman of the city's Centennial Commission. He now lives in Cortez and writes a column, "Four Corners Almanac," for the Sunday *Durango Herald* based on his continuing experiences in the wilderness and in the diverse communities of the Four Corners Country.

For additional copies of this book,
send completed order form to:

The Durango Herald Small Press Co.
P.O. Box 719
Durango, Colorado 81302

or phone

1-800-530-8318

Sorry no C.O.D.s

ORDER FORM

Please send ___ copies of Ian Thompson's *Houses on Country Roads* at $15.95 plus $4.00 for shipping and handling per book. Colorado residents please add 7% sales tax. Canadian orders require a postal money order in U.S. funds. Allow 4 to 6 weeks for delivery.

☐ Check/Money Order for $_____ enclosed.
   (Make payable to The Durango Herald Small Press Co.)
☐ Charge my ☐ Visa ☐ MC
   Card #_____ Expires_____
   Signature_____

NAME_____
COMPANY_____
ADDRESS_____
CITY/STATE/ZIP_____